THE POINT
OF ITALL

THE POINT
OF ITALL

A Lifetime of Great Loves
and Endeavors

CHARLES
KRAUTHAMMER

Edited by Daniel Krauthammer

CROWN
FORUM

NEW YORK

Grateful acknowledgment is made to *The New Republic* for permission
to reprint:

"Death of a Princess: PBS's Invitation to Suicide" from *The New
Republic*, July 5, 1980 © 1980 New Republic; "When to Intervene:
What's Worth Fighting For" from *The New Republic*, May 6, 1985
© 1985 New Republic. All rights reserved. Used by permission and
protected by the Copyright Laws of the United States. The printing,
copying, redistribution, or retransmission of the Content without
express written permission is prohibited.

Library of Congress Cataloging-in-Publication data is available
upon request.

ISBN 978-1-9848-2548-3
Ebook ISBN 978-1-9848-2549-0

Printed in the United States of America

Jacket design by Christopher Brand
Jacket photograph: Katie Falkenberg/*The New York Times*/Redux

10 9 8 7 6 5 4 3 2

First Edition

To my wife, Robyn

—

With extraordinary intelligence, humor, grace
and lovingkindness, she has co-authored my life,
of which this book is but a reflection.

And to my son, Daniel

—

Whose incisive, brilliant mind has been
an incredible influence and shaper of my own
since he was 10 years old.

CONTENTS

POLITICS, FOREIGN AND DOMESTIC

CHAPTER 15: ON LIBERTY

PART IV

COMPETING VISIONS

America's Role and the Course of World History

CHAPTER 16: RELUCTANT COLOSSUS

CHAPTER 17: THE END OF "THE END OF HISTORY"

INTRODUCTION

By Daniel Krauthammer

I. The Author and the Editor of This Book

Charles Krauthammer was my father. Writing that sentence in the past tense is still a shock to me, and it evokes a sadness far too deep to express in words. My father and I were very close. I feel the pain of his absence every day, as does every son who loved his father. There were a thousand secret private things between him and me that I alone had known and that I alone will miss about the man who was my dad.

But my father belonged not only to me, but to so many more: his friends, his colleagues, his readers, his viewers, the country and indeed the world. He played a large role in the political life of this nation, and though he was far too self-effacing to say so himself, his thinking, his ideas and his convictions shaped generations of political thinkers.

For almost four decades, he wrote a weekly column syndicated in the *Washington Post* and hundreds of other newspapers around the world. He wrote essays for preeminent magazines like *The New Republic*, *Time* and *The Weekly Standard*. He appeared on television to comment on the events of the day throughout his career, culminating with near-nightly appearances on Fox News' *Special Report* for over a decade.

Policymakers and politicians in Washington read him, listened to him and often took their lead from him. But my father did not write solely for the cognoscenti and the power brokers.

He always told me that he wanted to write and speak so that anyone with intelligence and interest could grapple with and benefit from his arguments. He believed in Einstein's (apocryphal) dictum that "if you can't explain it simply, you don't understand it well enough." That, I believe, is the root of his extraordinary popularity. He didn't talk down. He thought that unnecessary complexity and heavy-handed erudition got in the way of true insight and knowledge: "You don't want to talk in highfalutin, ridiculous abstractions that nobody understands," he said. "Just try to make things plain and clear." He wished to express the truths he saw in the most universal, accessible, concise and convincing way that he could.

He felt a responsibility to his readers and viewers and, beyond that, to history itself. As he put it:

> I left psychiatry to start writing . . . because I felt history happening outside the examining-room door. That history was being shaped by a war of ideas and I wanted to be in the arena. Not for its own sake. I enjoy intellectual combat, but I don't live for it. I wanted to be in the arena because some things matter, some things need to be said, some things need to be defended.

My father was not just going through the motions. He cared deeply about everything he said and everything he wrote. He knew it would play a part in the discourses that shaped real policies, affected real people and determined the future of the country he loved. He did not take that responsibility lightly. In a 2013 interview, he described the sense of duty he felt to pursue his vocation with the highest order of integrity: "You're betraying your whole life if you don't say what you think—and you don't say it honestly and bluntly."

He always said what he thought, and he championed the ideas he believed in. That is why he will be missed by everyone who appreciated his arguments and insights. And that is why it was so important to me to complete this book for him, and to complete it well. His thoughts mattered. His arguments mattered. His presence in our national discourse mattered. And I hope, through this book, they will continue to matter for future generations of readers.

II. The Origins of This Book

This book was a long time in the making. Following the success of his lauded collection of columns and essays *Things That Matter*, my father had intended to write several more books. He wished to write an original work on foreign policy, another on domestic policy and a more personal memoir that would trace his family history as well as his own. But in addition to these ambitions for new writing projects, he felt an ever-present desire to publish another collection. There were many more columns and essays of his that he wanted the world to see. Pieces that had not fit with the thematic organization of *Things That Matter*, pieces he had written in the time since and pieces that, frankly, he had felt were too personal to include the first time around. These columns and essays needed a home.

In 2016, my father decided he would move ahead simultaneously toward completion of that new collection and an original work on foreign policy. He put together an initial selection of columns and began organizing them into thematic chapters. Meanwhile, he began writing an extended essay for the work on foreign policy and collecting pieces he planned to draw on in composing the other entries for that book.

It was at this juncture that a health crisis struck my father. In August of 2017, he underwent surgery in Washington, DC, to remove a cancerous tumor from his abdomen. The surgery was thought to have been a success in removing the cancer, but a cascade of secondary complications followed. My father spent many months in the ICU and then many more at a specialized catastrophic care hospital in Atlanta, Georgia. Great progress was made in the following months toward restoring him to health. There were extraordinary difficulties and many setbacks, but the light at the end of the tunnel was clearly visible and we were slowly making our way.

Though his energies were intensely focused on his physical recovery, my father devoted what time and attention he could while he was in the hospital to working on the book. My mother and I were by his side for the entire ten months of that hospital sojourn. During that time I concocted an array of digital and physical displays of all shapes and sizes (with assistance from our favorite hospital staff friends, who helped me rewire our TVs and commandeer the building's wi-fi) to build as practical a workplace for him as we could achieve amongst all the medical gadgets and gizmos. These helter-skelter arrangements worked well enough for my father to get by, and there were times when we were able to talk over his plans and ideas together and I could help him execute some of the details.

However, this progress—with his work and with his health—did not last. In May of 2018, the news was broken to us that my father's recovery would not be successful: The cancer had returned with a vengeance. It moved aggressively and relentlessly. Just four weeks later, my father died.

As the end was approaching, my father handed responsibility for finishing the book to me. The last time we spoke about it, he turned to me and said: "If it's not worthy, don't publish it." I made him an oath, and I have taken it more seriously than any other promise I have ever made in my life. I can only hope that my efforts have done justice to the great legacy of the man I loved.

III. The Organization and Methodology of This Book

This book is, first and foremost, my father's. Every word in it, save this introduction and the final entry—my eulogy for him—is his. Its conception and initial construction were his, as are every thought and argument it conveys. When my father handed the reins to me, he had already chosen the majority of the columns that still constitute this book and set aside many more pieces for further consideration, which in turn constitute the majority of the additions made to his initial composition.

There was still much work to do, however, when I took over the project in full after his passing. I read through every runner-up piece my father had considered, and hundreds more—as many as I possibly could in the time I had to complete the project. I added columns, removed some, replaced others and rearranged their order in many places to make his arguments flow in what I believe he would see as the most natural and logical progression.

In this book, what began as two separate projects became one. The first three sections of the book are essentially the collection he envisioned. Divided into 15 thematic chapters, they cover a wide range of his views on the whole gamut of topics, progressing from the ideas he felt closest to in his soul to his thoughts on society at large and finally to the political questions of the day.

What began as my father's original project on foreign policy and the international order has become Part IV of this book, "Competing Visions: America's Role and the Course of World

History." In it is the long essay that was to form the core of that work, and now anchors this book: "The Authoritarian Temptation." It draws the central themes of the book to a summation point and leaves the reader to ponder what my father believed to be the most important questions and challenges facing the politics of our future. It is the one new piece in this collection, never before seen by the public.

Most of the articles in this collection are columns and short essays. But there are several longer entries on arguments that took more than a column's length to encompass. One is the long essay "When to Intervene," which lays out my father's thinking on American involvement overseas—a set of criteria that remained remarkably consistent over four decades. Two long speeches are included: "Three Pieces of Sage Advice" and "Constitutions, Conservatism and the Genius of the Founders." They explore my father's thoughts on how individuals should approach their lives within society, and how we ought best to structure our politics by the principles of limited government. Several other shorter speeches dealing with more personal aspects of my father's life are featured in the book's final chapter, "A Life without Regrets."

In this book, as in *Things That Matter*, every article is featured in its original published form, with three small exceptions. The first is that some article titles have been changed, either to reflect my father's original wishes (publishers usually choose the titles, and they were not always my father's first choice at the time) or to convey their content more clearly to the reader. The second is that the punctuation has been changed in some articles to make the style uniform across the entire book—continuing, as my father was fond of declaring, his "war on commas." And third, in a very few cases a line or two has been edited for clarity or to remove a historical reference or term that has now become so obscure as to be distracting.

One element new to this book is the presence of speeches. Considerably more editing was done for these than for published articles. Introductory, closing and offhand remarks were removed, as were some passages on subject matter unrelated to the sections of the book in which they were placed. Where my father's written notes for the speech in question were available, some text of the transcript may have been changed to be brought more in line with the initial composition of his message. The titles for all speeches are my own, as my father did not designate any.

To the best of my ability, I have followed the guidelines that my father would have followed himself, had he been able to finish the book. I can only hope it is worthy.

IV. The Ethos of This Book

The final section of this book, "Part V: Speaking in the First Person," is the one section that I know my father would not have included if he were still alive. He did not like to talk about himself, especially in public and in his writing. "I've never wanted to make myself the focus of my career," he said in a 2013 interview. "One of the things I aspire to in all of my columns is I try never to use the word *I* . . . to me every time you use it, it's a failure . . . I'd rather let the words speak for themselves."

In his treatise *On Rhetoric*, Aristotle divided the modes of persuasion into three categories: Pathos—the appeal to the audience's emotions. Ethos—persuasion by the force of the speaker's character, reputation and credibility. And logos—the use of reason, evidence and logical argumentation to convince the other side.

My father was a master of logos. He relied on it almost exclusively. He was methodical, exacting and airtight in the step-by-step progression of his thinking through an argument. He particularly disdained appeals to pathos and pulling the heart-strings of an audience. Indeed, these types of appeals were often the target of his withering criticism. He was a doctor by training, and it trained him, as he often said, to look at the evidence and follow where it led. He had no patience for actions and policies motivated by guilt or compassion or self-righteousness if the practical end result was a bad one. He was a deeply good man possessed of deeply good and noble intentions in his personal life. But he firmly believed that good intention as national policy was at best foolhardy and at worst dangerous.

The mode of argument he rarely engaged with at all was ethos. He wanted his arguments to stand on their own regardless of the speaker. That came from a profound sense of humility, I think—a humility stemming from his own awareness of how little anyone truly knows in the grand scheme of things.

But while he eschewed any privileged place due to his standing, others did not. Sometimes the word of a respected and honest voice matters. And over nearly four decades of working in and writing about politics, he earned a place unique to only a few political commentators in modern history. He was respected by those who agreed with him and those who did not. He was too humble to ever fully embrace it, but he earned the right—as few have—to use ethos in making his arguments. That is why I have included as entries in this book some of the very few occasions, in both articles and speeches, where my father spoke entirely in the first person, imparting his beliefs, his thoughts and his wisdom directly from his own experience to the audience. I know he would never have chosen to highlight these rare moments in a book such as this. But I also know people want to read them. They reveal something of the depth and strength of my father's character, the clarity of his own moral principles and the essence of what he felt truly mattered in life—and, of course, his great sense of humor.

No one will ever again be able to hear new arguments from him based in logos. But they can look to the example of his ethos and find lasting wisdom there for ages to come.

In particular, I have included some entries in this book that deal with my father's physical disability. As many of his readers and viewers know—but many others do not—my father suffered a diving accident when he was 22 years old that severed his spinal cord and left much of his body paralyzed. With a degree of fortitude, strength and dignity that I can scarcely comprehend, he went on to live his life as he intended it and never let his physical limitations alter his path or define his identity. He did not hide his disability, but neither did he highlight it, especially in the public eye. "Everybody has their cross to bear—everybody," he once explained. "All it means is whatever I do is a little bit harder and probably a little bit slower and with a little more effort."

He believed that all individuals should be judged by their character and the worth of their deeds and works in life, not by characteristics given to them by accidents of birth or fate beyond their control. "It's very easy to be characterized by the externalities in your life," he once said. "I dislike people focusing on it. I made a vow when I was injured that it would never be what would characterize my life." He fulfilled that vow and succeeded in defining his own life to an extent I think few of us could ever hope to achieve.

For this reason, I was hesitant and careful about including anything in this book that focused on my father's disability. But I eventually came to the position that the extraordinary power of his example is not something that should be lost to the world. A very few times in his long career, my father wrote columns that touched on the idea that all individuals should be able to define their lives by what *they* choose and what *they* do—not what happens *to* them. Several of these columns are included in this book, spread throughout the chapters without being specially called out, which I know is exactly how he would have wanted it. Their power is such that I overcame my reservations about including them. My fervent hope is that my father would approve of my decision.

When my father was composing his final public statement before his death (included at the end of this book as "A Note to Readers"), I helped him, taking dictation and assisting in the editing.

Reading through a draft, he said to me, "This uses *I* a lot. I don't like using *I*."

"Yes," I told him, "but I think this is the right place to do it."

"Yes," he agreed. "This time is different."

I hope, and I believe, that were he here and able to see the pieces I have selected for this book, he would tell me that I made the right choice. That because he is now gone, "this time is different."

V. The Meaning of This Book

When the time came to choose a title, I began the process by asking myself: What is this book about? I remembered the importance of that question to my father when he published *Things That Matter*. When it was released, I read it cover to cover in just a few sittings. I wrote my father a long letter telling him how incredible and magisterial a work I thought it was, and detailing exactly why I thought so. He wrote back to me the following:

I couldn't wait to tell you how extraordinarily powerful and moving your letter was. And how unbelievably discerning and penetrating. You made me see things I couldn't even see myself.

I've been kicking myself for two days now, because in interview after interview, I have had no idea how to answer the question "What is this book about?" And there you put it in one simple absolutely stunning sentence: "Everything that matters depends ultimately on politics." As soon as I read it, I stopped reading your letter, wrote it down . . . with a few paragraphs of elaboration—and emailed it to myself so I won't lose it.

I thought then, and still think now, that he gave me far too much credit. After all, he had written this same summational sentiment in the book's introduction:

While science, medicine, art, poetry, architecture, chess, space, sports, number theory and all things hard and beautiful promise purity, elegance and sometimes even transcendence, they are fundamentally subordinate. In the end, they must bow to the sovereignty of politics . . . because in the end, everything—high and low and, most especially, high—lives or dies by politics . . . because of its capacity, when benign, to allow all around it to flourish, and its capacity, when malign, to make all around it wither.

Sometimes it takes the fresh eye of someone reading for the first time, looking from the outside in, to point out what was clearly there all along, hidden in plain sight. And so I wondered to myself, if my dad could ask me to lend my fresh eye to *The Point of It All*, what could I point out for him that was clearly there all along?

There is, to begin with, a great deal of concordance and overlap in the core message of the two books, most of all because my father's core beliefs stayed constant and ever-present in his writings throughout his entire career. Seemingly unrelated columns in completely different sections of each book subtly harken back to each other and sow common themes: the preference for quiet dignity over showy self-aggrandizement, for humility in the face of the unknowable over the pretended mastery of human nature, and above all, an appreciation for the supreme importance of getting politics right. He makes you aware, even as you're reading about the beauty of math or the proper appreciation of baseball, that all such higher achievements are dependent on tyrants being kept at bay and free thought kept alive.

How do we keep it alive? In *Things That Matter*, my father's focus fell largely on the threat of politics gone wrong. "The entire 20th century," he wrote, "with its mass political enthusiasms, is a lesson in the supreme power of politics to produce ever-expanding circles of ruin." The ever-present backdrop behind all "things elegant and beautiful" he explores in that book is the specter of totalitarian desolation. The book highlights a century of struggle by liberal democracies against three great ideologies of totalitarian nihilism: Nazism, communism and radical Islamism. "Politics is the moat," he wrote, "the walls, beyond which lie the barbarians. Fail to keep them at bay, and everything burns." He urged us to stand ever watchful on those walls and admonished us never to take them for granted. It is fitting that the great historical figure he chose to celebrate most in that book was Winston Churchill, the man who above all others in the 20th century manned those walls and rallied the free world to their defense in the face of the barbarian hordes.

But what do we do inside those walls? How do we construct our politics to ensure they stay benign and don't turn malign? It is on these questions that my father focused his attention in *The*

Point of It All. The core political focus of this book is on the nature and the future of liberal democracy and limited government, particularly on designing and maintaining government in such a way that it carves out space for individuals to define and pursue for themselves the things that truly matter to them.

My father's political philosophy, he wrote, was one of "restrained, free-market governance that gave more space and place to the individual and to the civil society" and to "the mediating structures that stand between the individual and the state . . . bonds of family, faith, fellowship and conscience." These ideas are explored most fully in Chapter 15, "On Liberty," named after the most famous work of my father's favorite political philosopher, John Stuart Mill. He was a student of Mill, as well as of Tocqueville, Jefferson, Madison and "the sublime texts of the American founding." These political theorists of the 18th and 19th centuries are, fittingly, the most celebrated historical figures in *The Point of It All.* Their ideas, my father believed, laid what is still the "indispensable foundation" upon which our successful politics was built and our civilization has flourished.

In a column that appears in the final chapters of this book, my father wrote:

> Democracy is . . . designed at its core to be spiritually empty. As Isaiah Berlin wrote 30 years ago in his essay "John Stuart Mill and the Ends of Life," the defining proposition of liberal democracy is that it mandates means (elections, parliaments, markets) but not ends. Democracy leaves the goals of life entirely up to the individual. Where the totalitarian state decrees life's purposes . . . democracy leaves the public square naked.

The politics of liberal democracy—"the most free, most humane, most decent political system ever invented by man"—establishes the walls that protect our society from would-be oppressors, tyrants and totalitarians of all varieties. But it does not define what lies inside those walls. Or at least it ought not, my father believed.

Rather, in that open civic space unmolested by government, individuals must define their own meaning and pursue their own happiness by their own free will and in free association with one another. "The glories yielded by . . . successful politics lie outside itself," he wrote. This is the great gift of liberty and the font of all of man's higher loves and endeavors in life.

It is also a great responsibility, one that places the burden on individuals and society to find purpose and direction for life. Such a task is not always easy or natural or attractive. Liberal democracy does not provide ready-made romantic causes or noble callings for its citizens to follow. "Dying for it is far more ennobling than living it," my father wrote.

Our way of life, our liberty and our successful politics are not automatically self-sustaining, my father understood. And they are not the default of the human condition. Quite to the contrary, the allure of "political romanticism" of all kinds is always present, of a "politics of certainty" that offers (and eventually dictates) supposed absolute truths that give meaning to life. My father believed that down the path of such politics—whether of the far right or far left, extreme nationalism or extreme socialism, religious fanaticism or intolerant atheism—lay the ruin of all things beautiful and human, as evidenced most profoundly in the destruction wrought by these political romanticisms in the 20th century. And in the final essay in this book, his original piece "The Authoritarian Temptation," my father identified some of the coming century's great potential threats to liberal democratic society. In an author's note for a column celebrating his favorite contemporary political theorist, Isaiah Berlin—whose great work *Four Essays on Liberty* my father described as "perhaps the finest, and surely the most accessible, 20th-century elaboration of [the classical liberal] tradition"—my father wrote:

> Berlin and his *Four Essays* are indeed needed again. The triumph of limited government has turned out to be far more uncertain and ephemeral than it seemed in the heady "holiday from history" days of the 1990s. Today, a quarter-century after the dissolution of the Soviet Union at the end of 1991, marks the rise of a new appeal to a decidedly illiberal political model. I deal with it in "The Authoritarian Temptation."

My father wished for "the public square" to remain open for individuals to freely chart their own path towards truth. The first article he ever published—for the *McGill Daily* in 1969—was a critique of "monolith[ic]" thinking and "deadening one-dimensionality." It championed pluralism, whose "underlying assumption . . . is that no one has a monopoly on truth."

So what is the point of it all? Of life, of our existence on this planet, of our membership in the vast complexity of humanity? Politics should not say. But, somewhat paradoxically, keeping politics out of it was the point of my father's life's work. He fought for "a vision of limited government that, while providing for the helpless, is committed above all to guaranteeing individual liberty and the pursuit of one's own Millian 'ends of life.'"

In his private life, my father found meaning in what mattered to him: "Lives of the good and the great . . . the elegance of nature, the wonders of space, the perfectly thrown outfield assist" and all the other things that he wrote about within the pages of this book with joy and wit and fascination. He "[did not] claim these things matter to everyone. Nor should they." All individuals, he believed, should choose and pursue what matters to them.

But in his life as a public figure, he appreciated both the

absolute necessity and the essential fragility of politics done right to the very survival of that individual freedom to choose. "The lesson of our history," he wrote, "is that the task of merely maintaining strong and sturdy the structures of a constitutional order is unending, the continuing and ceaseless work of every generation. To which I have devoted much of my life." He found meaning—and his life's calling—in playing his part in that task. And playing that part in the American context.

The United States of America was, to his mind, the greatest and most miraculous endeavor mankind had ever undertaken in its long quest to get politics right. "America," as he described her, is "founded on an idea, and the idea is liberty. That is probably the rarest phenomenon in the political history of the world." And in his heart, my father felt a deep and abiding love for her: "Anybody who, like me . . . is the son of immigrants," he said in a 2015 speech, "you know firsthand in your bones what a blessed place America is, and how proud every son of immigrants—like every American—is of the role we have played . . . in protecting our friends and protecting liberty." He believed that America was, as Lincoln put it, "the last best hope of Earth." And he did what he could in his life to guard her and her noblest ideals.

In his column "The Arrow of History," my father asked the question: "Do you think history is cyclical or directional? Are we condemned to do the same damn thing over and over, generation after generation—or is there hope for some enduring progress in the world order?" His answer: "I don't know—no one knows—if history has an arrow." He was right, of course. No one knows the future or the destiny of mankind. But one thing I do know is that if history does have an arrow toward progress, it is not by random chance. It is because of the great efforts and works and sacrifices of good men and women trying to make the world a little bit better for their children to inherit. My father was such a man.

VI. The Purpose of This Book

As my father's son, I will of course never escape my bias in judging his work. But I do feel I've been on this earth long enough and spent enough of my years with my nose buried in books and newspapers to say with some standing that my father's voice was a uniquely insightful and powerful one in our national discourse. I truly believe that the world will be a better place the longer his voice, and its echoes, are heard and read.

My father's writing, as displayed in this book, is not just thought-provoking but also—and even more impressively—feeling-provoking. Not the feelings of pathos meant to close one's mind to reason and shut down debate. But rather the emotions of awe, reverence, respect and wonder evoked by the intelligent exploration of the majesty, complexity and expanse of human experience and the universe we inhabit. His writing opens the mind, combining passion with intelligence, beauty with concreteness. In the modern world, those two halves of the human self are all too often completely divorced. Art is rendered meaningless by its self-indulgence and disconnectedness, and politics is rendered mundane by its tawdry intrigues and game-playing.

But when my father writes about the majesty of the cosmos or the elegance of a chess move, I can feel the reality and the weight of their beauty. And when he writes about the importance of democratic institutions in the face of tyranny over the mind, I feel a deeper meaning to politics that is all too often lacking in our day-to-day debates. By intertwining art and politics in this way—in both the style and content of his writing—he elevates each of them to a higher level.

One aspect of my father's writing that I've always particularly appreciated is how well he ends his pieces. He often draws his argument to a summation point, but then adroitly leads it into a final parting question or uncertainty that the reader is left to ponder. There is no doubt about the immediate policy stance he's advocating, but he subtly acknowledges that a deeper moral or philosophical question still remains. It is so artful and thoughtful a style, one that has always reminded me of my favorite films, novels and other artworks. They don't tell you exactly how to think; rather, they lead you right to the edge and then, having enlightened you as much as any wise sage can, let you leap off into the unknowable on your own to think about the hard questions that do not—and cannot—have a final answer.

It has always struck me that my father's writing, in both substance and style, reflected his fundamental instinct for and belief in humility: that the most important and profound things are exactly those about which we can never achieve full understanding. In things beautiful and poetic, he describes that beauty as emerging from its incomprehensibility—whether it be the graceful curveball of a rookie pitcher or the love of a parent for a child. He held back from pretending to understand it fully or analyzing it down to the point of losing its majesty. Similarly, in politics, he abhorred ideologies that claimed to fully understand human nature or how entire complex societies should be reorganized to work better—or even worse, "perfectly." It was from this "philosophical skepticism," as he put it, that his political conservatism was born. And it made his brand of conservatism feel uplifting, I think, in a way that conservatism can often lack. It's not just the argument that "it works better," but that there is something good and noble in embracing the Socratic dictum "I know that I know nothing" and organizing man's political life with reverence for those unknowns.

In this book, as in *Things That Matter*, my father applied this worldview to a breathtaking range of subjects: not just foreign

policy, not just domestic, not just social issues, not just issues of art and taste. To everything. And all of it animated by common principles that give it both enlightening reason and moving beauty. His writing broadens one's thinking and stirs the emotions and shows their essential connection. That is why I think his books will last far beyond the immediacy of today's politics. This is the kind of book I imagine a parent would give to a child 10, 20, 30 years from now and say, "Here. This is a book that will make you think. And make you feel. Read it."

That is the ultimate purpose of this book. Yes, it is for all those who heard and read my father and miss him. But even more, it is for those who never had the chance to see him in life. In an interview my father gave in 2013, he spoke about his feeling of purpose in life:

> There's a great line by Tom Stoppard, who said about his own life as a writer and what he tried to do, he said something like, "You know . . . you put words together all your life, and every once in a while, you get them in the right order and you give the world a nudge." So I just hope I get the words in the right order every once in a while and give the world a nudge. . . . It's what I exist to do, really.

He gave the world much more than a nudge in his lifetime. And I believe his words will continue to push the world in a better direction for ages to come.

PART I

WHAT A PIECE OF
WORK IS MAN

CHAPTER I

LIFE WELL LIVED

Reveries of a Newborn Father

Three weeks ago Daniel Pierre Krauthammer, our first, entered the world. It was a noisy and boisterous entry, as befits a 10-pound Krauthammer. It has been just as noisy and boisterous since. I had been warned by friend and foe that life would never be the same. They were right.

Of course, like all exhausted newborn fathers, I am just looking for sympathy. It is my wife, Robyn, whose life has been fully merged with his, in a symbiosis profound and delicate. His sucking, did you know, causes the uterus to contract and helps shrink it back to normal size. Twenty days old, and he is healing her.

What she does for him, of course, would not fit in a month's worth of columns. What do I do? It seems my job is to father, a verb which must count as one of the age's more inventive creations. How exactly to father? I don't really know. The women's movement, to which the idea owes its currency, is right to insist that the father do more.

But more of what? I have been asking myself that lately as I rock him and hold him and speak to him in the gravest of tones. But we both know, we all three know, the truth: Nature has seen to it that anything I can do, she can do better. Mine is literally a holding action.

Of course, the imperative to father is only the last of the social conventions one must bend to on the road to parenting. (I am learning the language.) First, there is Lamaze, the classes that teach you to be natural. Robyn does not fancy oxymorons. And I, as a former psychiatrist, know a placebo when I see one. We said no to Lamaze.

We said yes to the Volvo. In fact, on the Volvo we went all the way. We got the station wagon with roof rack: the ultimate yuppie conveyance. "For safety reasons only," I explain to friends, a protest that meets with knowing smiles.

Finally, there is the supreme modern convention: the now-absolute requirement that father, in surgical gear, attend the birth. Of course, you don't have to if you don't want to. You can, if you wish, wait outside, like Dagwood Bumstead, pacing and smoking and fretting until it's over. You have the perfect right to betray your wife, spurn your child and disgrace your sex. It's a free country.

The transformation of expectant father from nuisance—packed off to boil water, find towels and generally get out of the way—to conscripted co-producer of the birth epic is one of the anthropological wonders of the age. And on the whole, apart from the coercion, a good thing. Father's presence serves two purposes. One is to reduce the anguish of the mother. The other is to increase the anguish of the father. Both seem to me laudable goals. It makes up a bit for the extraordinarily unfair imbalance of suffering that attends childbirth.

Thank God, the new convention does not (yet) command fathers to attend a caesarean delivery. I speak from experience. Robyn needed a caesarean and, hoping I could comfort her, I was with her in the operating room. I was not looking for a Maslovian peak-experience, the kind of epiphany that reputedly accompanies the moment of birth. I was doubtful, not just because of my usual skepticism, but because of my previous career. In medical school, I had assisted at several births, including a couple of caesareans, and always had trouble seeing the poetry for the blood.

There was little poetry this time either. It was an agonizing hour for her, and for me. (Daniel did very well.) The poetry came afterward, in the recovery room, where I found Daniel asleep in Robyn's arms.

It has been poetry and reverie ever since. Having a child, I discovered, makes you dream again and, at the same time, makes the dreams utterly real. Lately I have been dreaming of the future. I find entirely new meaning in what we in Washington call "out-years." Take 1989, the year the budget deficit comes down to $100 billion. A time far, far away . . . until I figured it is the year when we retire Daniel's Pampers. A manageable deficit, only a few thousand nappy changes away.

Stranger years, years of exotic immensity, years that till now had meaning to Arthur C. Clarke only, become utterly mundane. 2001, the year of the mystical obelisk, and Daniel should be getting his learner's permit. 2010, the obelisk returns and Daniel is looking for a job. 2050, a year of unimaginable distance: his first Social Security check.

"Checks? Social Security?" my friend Pepe interrupts. "Where's your imagination, man? They'll all be memories. Think big. 2050: the year he takes a sabbatical on Saturn."

I'm thinking small. I gaze at his body, so perfectly formed, so perfectly innocent. It has yet to be written on. I look at his knee and wonder where will be the little mark that records his first too-hard slide into second base.

The Washington Post, June 28, 1985

Irving Kristol

A Great Good Man

After the plain pine box is lowered into the grave, the mourners are asked to come forward—immediate family first—and shovel dirt onto the casket. Only when it is fully covered, only when all that can be seen is dust, is the ceremony complete.

Such is the Jewish way of burial. Its simplicity, austerity and unsentimentality would have appealed to Irving Kristol, who was buried by friends and family Tuesday. Equally fitting for this most unsentimental of men was the spare funeral service that preceded the burial. It consisted of the recitation of two psalms and the prayer for the dead, and two short addresses: an appreciation by the rabbi, followed by a touching, unadorned remembrance by his son, Bill.

The wonder of Irving was that he combined this lack of sentimentality—he delighted in quietly puncturing all emotional affectations and indulgences—with a genuine generosity of spirit. He was a deeply good man who disdained shows of goodness, deflecting expressions of gratitude or admiration with a disarming charm and an irresistible smile. That's because he possessed what might be called a moral humility. For Irving, doing good—witness the posthumous flood of grateful emails, letters and other testimonies from often young and uncelebrated beneficiaries of that goodness—was as natural and unremarkable as breathing.

Kristol's biography has been rehearsed in a hundred places. He was one of the great public intellectuals of our time, father of a movement, founder of magazines, nurturer of two generations of thinkers—seeding our intellectual and political life for well over half a century.

Having had the undeserved good fortune of knowing him during his 21-year sojourn in Washington, I can testify to something lesser known: his extraordinary equanimity. His temperament was marked by a total lack of rancor. Angst, bitterness and anguish were alien to him. That, of course, made him unusual among the fraternity of conservatives because we believe that the world is going to hell in a handbasket. That makes us cranky. But not Irving. Never Irving. He retained steadiness, serenity and grace that expressed themselves in a courtliness couched in a calm quiet humor.

My theory of Irving is that this amazing equanimity was rooted in a profound sense of modesty. First about himself. At 20, he got a job as a machinist's apprentice at the Brooklyn Navy Yard. He realized his future did not lie in rivets, he would recount with a smile, when the battleship turret he was working on was found to be pointing in the wrong direction. It could only shoot *inward*—directly at the ship's own bridge.

He was equally self-deprecating about his experiences as an infantryman in World War II France. ("Experiences?" he once said to me. "We were *lost* all the time.") His gloriously unheroic view of himself extended to the rest of humanity—its politics, its pretensions, its grandiose plans for the renovation of . . . humanity.

This manifested itself in the work for which he is most celebrated: his penetrating, devastating critique of modern liberalism and of its grand projects for remaking man and society. But his natural skepticism led him often to resist conservative counter-enthusiasms as well. Most recently, the general panic about changing family structures.

Irving had an abiding reverence for tradition and existing norms. But he thought it both futile and anti-human to imagine we could arrest their evolution. He never yelled for history to stop. He acknowledged the necessity of adaptation (most famously, to the New Deal and the welfare state). He was less concerned about the form of emerging family norms, such as France's non-marriage Civil Solidarity Pact, than whether they could in time perform the essential functions of the traditional family—from the generational transmission of values to the socialization of young males.

That spirit of skepticism and intellectual openness was a marvel. One of Irving's triumphs was to have infused that spirit into the *Public Interest*, the most serious and influential social policy journal of our time. Irving cofounded it in 1965, then closed it 40 years later, saying with characteristic equanimity, "No journal is meant to last forever."

A new time, a new journal. On September 8, 2009, the first issue of a new quarterly, *National Affairs*—successor to the *Public Interest*—was published. Irving Kristol died 10 days later, but not before writing a letter to its editor—two generations his junior—offering congratulations and expressing pleasure at its creation.

That small tender shoot, yet another legacy of this great good life, was the last Irving lived to see. We shall see many more.

The Washington Post, September 25, 2009

Ronald Reagan

He Could See for Miles

What made Ronald Reagan the greatest president of the second half of the 20th century? Well, he certainly had the one quality Napoleon always sought in a general: luck. Luck in his looks, luck in his voice, luck in his smile, luck in his choice of mate (although for Reagan the second time was the charm).

And the greatest luck that any president can have: trouble, serious trouble. An acquaintance of Bill Clinton's has said that he felt frustrated that September 11 did not happen on his watch. That is understandable (if characteristically self-centered) because the best chance any president has for greatness is to be in power during war or disaster. Apart from the Founders, the only great president we have had in good times is Theodore Roosevelt. Abraham Lincoln and Franklin Roosevelt were the "luckiest" of them all, having had the opportunity to take the country triumphantly through the two greatest wars in US history.

Reagan's luck was to find a nation in trouble—in post-Vietnam retreat and disorientation. His political genius was to restore its spirit. And his legacy was winning the longest war in American history, the long twilight struggle of the Cold War.

He achieved all that with two qualities: courage and conviction. Conviction led him to initiate economic shock therapy to pull the United States out of the stagflation of the 1970s. Courage allowed him not to flinch when his radical economic policies (and those of a merciless Federal Reserve) initially caused the worst recession since the Great Depression—and during a congressional election year (1982) to boot.

Reagan didn't waver, and by 1984 it was morning in America. The new prosperity gave a lilt to the rest of his presidency. But you don't get called great for lilt. You get called great for victory. And Reagan won the Cold War.

Conviction told him that the proper way to deal with this endless, enervating, anxiety-ridden ordeal was not settling for stability but going for victory. Courage allowed him to weather the incessant, at times almost universal, attacks on him for the radical means he chose to win it: the military buildup; nuclear deployments in Europe; the Reagan doctrine of overt support for anticommunist resistance movements everywhere, including Nicaragua; and the *pièce de résistance*, strategic missile defenses, derisively dubbed Star Wars by scandalized opponents. Within eight years, an overmatched, overwhelmed, overstretched Soviet Union was ready for surrender, the historically breathtaking, total and peaceful surrender of everything—its empire and its state.

Reagan won that war not just with radical policies but also with a radically unashamed ideological challenge, the great 1982 Westminster speech predicting that communism would end up in the "ash heap of history" and the subsequent designation of the Soviet Union as the "evil empire." That won him the derision of Western sophisticates, intellectuals and defeatists of all kinds. It also won him the undying admiration of liberation heroes from Vaclav Havel to Natan Sharansky. Years later, Sharansky testified to the life-giving encouragement that Reagan's unadorned words about Soviet evil and Western determination gave to those buried with him in the Gulag.

Rarely does history render such decisive verdicts: Reagan was right, his critics were wrong. Less than a year after he left office, the Berlin Wall came down.

The ungenerous would say he had a great presidency but was not a great man. That follows the tradition of his opponents who throughout his career consistently underestimated him, disdaining him as a good actor, a *Being There* simpleton who could read scripts written for him by others. In fact, Reagan frustrated his biographers because he was so complex—a free-market egalitarian, an intellectually serious nonintellectual, an ideologue with great tactical flexibility.

With the years, the shallow explanations for Reagan's success—charm, acting, oratory—have fallen away. What remains is Reagan's largeness and deeply enduring significance. Let Edward Kennedy, the dean of Democratic liberalism, render the verdict: "It would be foolish to deny that his success was fundamentally rooted in a command of public ideas. . . . Whether we agreed with him or not, Ronald Reagan was a successful candidate and an effective President above all else because he stood for a set of ideas. He stated them in 1980—and it turned out that he meant them—and he wrote most of them not only into public law but into the national consciousness."

There is no better definition of presidential greatness.

Time, June 14, 2004

Thomas Jefferson

The Sublime Oxymoron

Thomas Jefferson will ever haunt us. The right eyes him suspiciously as a limousine Jacobin so enamored of revolution that he once suggested we should have one every 20 years. The left disdains him as your basic race hypocrite. And in the popular imagination, inflamed by Hollywood, the man is Mr. Sally Hemings.

All these views wildly miss the mark because no one view can begin to comprehend so large a man. In everything—talent, imagination, writing, indeed, curiosity—Jefferson was prodigious, Continental and, hence, supremely American.

The Library of Congress bicentennial exhibit of Jefferson's books and writings offers a splendid display of the vastness and the complexities of the man. The complexity begins, of course, with the central contradiction: prophet of freedom, owner of slaves. You see in his own hand the journal entry deploring the removal from the Declaration of Independence, at the insistence of Georgia and South Carolina, of the clause condemning African slavery. You recall the famous line regarding slavery in his *Notes on the State of Virginia*: "I tremble for my country when I reflect that God is just."

But then there is that most peculiar door at Monticello, the revolving serving door outside the dining room. One side has shelves. The other is flat. Food would be brought up from the basement kitchen and placed on the shelves on the outer side of the door. It would then be swung around. What did Jefferson and his guests see? Dinner, minus the slaves who prepared it.

Jefferson resorted to many devices, architectural and intellectual, to enjoy the bounties of plantation life without having to face its injustices. He was more clear-sighted, however, in facing that other American conundrum, the Native American. Jefferson had great respect for the Indians. He considered them the equal of the white man. And yet he fully understood that America would have to be built at their expense. Hence his remarkable letter to Benjamin Hawkins on August 13, 1786: "The two principles on which our conduct towards the Indians should be founded are justice and fear. . . . After the injuries we have done them, they cannot love us."

Justice and fear. What modern politician would be bold enough to characterize foreign policy so starkly? "Behind every great fortune there is a crime," said Balzac. Behind every great nation too. Jefferson certainly wanted to do justice to the Indians. But he knew the white man needed to instill fear in the Indian or the American experiment would fail. How characteristically Jefferson: an offhanded trope that sublimely captures the central tension of all foreign policy—that between morality and necessity, power and principle.

Jefferson could not only hold two contradictory ideas in his head, he could also act on both. Here, after all, is the great champion of small, limited government perpetrating the Louisiana Purchase, arguably the grandest exercise of extra-constitutional executive power in American history. But what else should we expect from the founder whose great vision of America was the Empire of Liberty, as profound an oxymoron as political theory can provide?

The most delightful example of the duality of the man is to be found in the library that Jefferson gave the US in 1815. Two-thirds of the books were destroyed in a fire in 1851, but now the Library of Congress has found equivalent editions and put the entire 6,487 volumes on magnificent display. The tall stacks are arranged as Jefferson had them at Monticello. What strikes you first is how brilliantly and methodically they are cataloged. Jefferson's classification system—used by the Library of Congress for 82 years—divided all knowledge into three parts: memory (history), reason (philosophy, the sciences) and imagination (art). Within these categories, he had 44(!) subcategories.

But wait. As you walk around the room, you notice something: The shelves are not of equal height. The tallest ones are at the bottom. And they are full of the tallest books. Then you understand. Jefferson, the philosopher, worshipped reason. Jefferson, the librarian, understood that sometimes you must surrender to reality and classify a book by its size.

Which is why we will be celebrating Jefferson at the next Library of Congress centenary too. He so embodies America in all its sprawling contradictory greatness: the Wilsonian idealist prepared to engage in ruthless Rooseveltian realism; the worshiper of system, order and science who is given to romance—with France, with revolution, with the American West; the practical inventor and tinkerer, yet endowed with the capacity to compose the most lyrical, most transcendent assertion of human liberty ever penned.

If Washington is father of our country, Jefferson is father of the ever restless, ever hungering American mind.

Time, May 22, 2000

Thank You, Isaiah Berlin

Not too many people can point to a specific day when they sat down with a book and got up cured of the stupidities of youth. I can. I was 19. The book was *Four Essays on Liberty*. The author was Isaiah Berlin. He died last week at 88.

Berlin was one of the great political philosophers of his time. Yet he never produced a single great tome. He left behind essays. But what essays. His most famous is "The Hedgehog and the Fox," a wonderfully imaginative division of the great thinkers of history into those who have one big idea (hedgehogs) and those who have many small ones (foxes).

Berlin was partial to foxes. He believed that single issues, fixed ideas, single-minded ideologies are dangerous, the royal road to arrogance and inhumanity. Against those who proclaimed they had found the one true path to political salvation, Berlin stood in the way, a champion of pluralism, the many-pathed way.

Four Essays on Liberty is his great argument for pluralism. Why was it such a powerful book? It came out in 1969. In 1969, to be young was heaven—and to be seized with intimations of heavenly omniscience. It was a time of grand theories and grand aspirations—liberation, revolution, historical inevitability—and we children were mightily seduced.

The temptations were many. There was, of course, Marxism; for the masochistic, there was Trotskyism; for the near-psychotic, there was Maoism. And apart from Marxism and its variants, there was the lure of such philosophers as Rousseau, the great theorist of mass democracy and the supremacy of the "popular will."

In the midst of all this craziness, along comes Berlin and says:

Look, this is all very nice, but what the monists—the believers in the one true truth, Marx and Rousseau and (by implication) such Third World deities as Mao and Ho and Castro—are proclaiming is not freedom. What they offer may be glorious and uplifting and just. But freedom is something very different. Freedom is being left alone. Freedom is a sphere of autonomy, an inviolable political space that no authority may invade.

In fact, said Berlin, these other "higher" pseudo-freedoms peddled by the monist prophets are very dangerous. They proclaim one true value above all else—equality in Marx, fraternity in Rousseau—and in the end the individual with his freedom is crushed underfoot. Heads roll. Millions of them.

And another thing, said Berlin: Historical inevitability is bunk, a kind of religion for atheists.

And one more thing, he said (in the fourth and final essay of the book): The true heart of the liberal political tradition is the belief that no one has the secret as to what is the ultimate end and goal of life. There are many ends, each deserving respect, and it is out of this very pluribus that we get freedom.

I read this book and a great fog—made of equal parts youthful enthusiasm, hubris and naïveté—lifted. I was forever enlisted on the side of limited, constitutional government—flawed as it was and despised at the time as "the system."

Berlin's argument seems blindingly obvious now. But the anti-"system" ravings of, say, the Unabomber, which seem grotesque today, were common fare on the campuses of 1969. Today history has buried Marxism's pretensions. In 1969, when history had not quite played itself out, Berlin's book was a tonic.

It was not without its flaws. It was brilliant in deconstructing the political romantics. But it did have its logical conundrum. Philosopher Leo Strauss, in his essay "Relativism," surgically exposed the central paradox of Berlin's position: that it made

pluralism—the denial of one supreme, absolute value—the supreme, absolute value.

This paradox and Berlin's fecund, restless mind—which moved from one idea to another (often in the same sentence!)—prevented him from establishing a grand intellectual edifice of his own. He remained forever a fox.

But just as there are hedgehogs and foxes, there are creators and there are curers. Berlin was one of our great curers.

Four Essays is available everywhere. Buy it. Make your children read it before they go to college, the last redoubt of romantic neo-Marxism. If they think the book is obvious, you have raised them well. If they don't, Berlin will challenge their complacency.

And keep one copy at home. The idea of limited government has triumphed. But the moment may not last. The pluralism Berlin championed will be challenged again. Whether by religious fundamentalism, by some reconstructed Marxism, or by an ideology whose outlines and ugliness we cannot even imagine today, it will be challenged. When that day comes, Berlin and his *Four Essays* will be needed again.

The Washington Post, November 14, 1997

John Paul II

The Power of Faith

It was Stalin who gave us the most famous formulation of that cynical (and today quite fashionable) philosophy known as "realism"—the idea that all that ultimately matters in the relations among nations is power: "The pope? How many divisions does he have?"

Stalin could have said that only because he never met John Paul II. We have just lost the man whose life was the ultimate refutation of "realism." Within 10 years of his elevation to the papacy, John Paul II had given his answer to Stalin and to the ages: More than you have. More than you can imagine.

History will remember many of the achievements of John Paul II, particularly his zealous guarding of the church's traditional belief in the sanctity of life, not permitting it to be unmoored by the fashionable currents of thought about abortion, euthanasia and "quality of life." But above all, he will be remembered for having sparked, tended and fanned the flames of freedom in Poland and the rest of Eastern Europe, leading ultimately and astonishingly to the total collapse of the Soviet empire.

I am not much of a believer, but I find it hard not to suspect some providential hand at play when the white smoke went up at the Vatican 27 years ago and the Polish cardinal was chosen to lead the Catholic Church. Precisely at the moment that the West most desperately needed it, we were sent a champion. It is hard to remember now how dark those days were. The 15 months following the pope's elevation marked the high tide of Soviet communism and the nadir of the free world's post-Vietnam collapse.

It was a time of one defeat after another. Vietnam invaded Cambodia, consolidating Soviet hegemony over all of Indochina. The Khomeini revolution swept away America's strategic anchor in the Middle East. Nicaragua fell to the Sandinistas, the first Soviet-allied regime on the mainland of the Western Hemisphere. (As an unnoticed but ironic coda, Marxists came to power in Grenada too.) Then, finally, the Soviets invaded Afghanistan.

And yet precisely at the time of this free-world retreat and disarray, a miracle happens. The Catholic Church, breaking nearly 500 years of tradition, puts itself in the hands of an obscure non-Italian—a Pole who, deeply understanding the Eastern European predicament, rose to become, along with Roosevelt, Churchill and Reagan, one of the great liberators of the 20th century.

John Paul II's first great mission was to reclaim his native Eastern Europe for civilization. It began with his visit to Poland in 1979, symbolizing and embodying a spiritual humanism that was the antithesis of the soulless materialism and decay of late Marxism-Leninism. As millions gathered to hear him and worship with him, they began to feel their own power and to find the institutional structure—the vibrant Polish church—around which to mobilize.

And mobilize they did. It is no accident that Solidarity, the leading edge of the Eastern European revolution, was born just a year after the pope's first visit. Deploying a brilliantly subtle diplomacy that never openly challenged the Soviet system but nurtured and justified every oppositional trend, often within the bosom of the local church, John Paul II became the pivotal figure of the people-power revolutions of Eastern Europe.

While the success of these popular movements demonstrated

the power of ideas and proved realism wrong, let us have no idealist illusions either: People power can succeed only against oppression that has lost confidence in itself. When Soviet communism still had enough sense of its own historical inevitability to send tanks against people in the street—Hungary 1956, Czechoslovakia 1968—people power was useless.

By the 1980s, however, the Soviet sphere was both large and decadent. And a new pope brought not only hope but political cunning to the captive nations yearning to be free. He demonstrated what Europe had forgotten and Stalin never knew: the power of faith as an instrument of political mobilization.

Under the benign and deeply humane vision of this pope, the power of faith led to the liberation of half a continent. Under the barbaric and nihilistic vision of Islam's jihadists, the power of faith has produced terror and chaos. That contrast alone, which has dawned upon us unmistakably ever since September 11, should be reason enough to be grateful for John Paul II. But we mourn him for more than that. We mourn him for restoring strength to the Western idea of the free human spirit at a moment of deepest doubt and despair. And for seeing us through to today's great moment of possibility for both faith and freedom.

The Washington Post, April 4, 2005

George Weidenfeld

Syrian Christians and the English Jew

Christianity, whose presence in the Middle East predates Islam's by 600 years, is about to be cleansed from the Middle East. Egyptian Copts may have found some respite under President Abdel Fattah el-Sisi, but after their persecution under the previous Muslim Brotherhood government, they know how precarious their existence in 90% Muslim Egypt remains. Elsewhere, it's much worse. Twenty-one Copts were beheaded by the Islamic State affiliate in Libya for the crime of being Christian. In those large swaths of Syria and Iraq where the Islamic State rules, the consequences for Christians are terrible—enslavement, exile, torture, massacre, crucifixion.

Over the decades, many Middle Eastern Christians, seeing the rise of political Islam and the intensification of savage sectarian wars, have simply left. Lebanon's Christians, once more than half the population, are now estimated at about a third. The number of Christians under Palestinian Authority rule in the West Bank has dwindled—in Bethlehem, for example, dropping by half. (The exception, of course, is Israel, where Christians, Arab and non-Arab, enjoy not just protection but civil rights. Their numbers are increasing. But that's another story.)

Most endangered are the Christians of Syria. Four years ago they numbered about 1.1 million. By now 700,000 have fled. Many of those remaining in country are caught either under radical Islamist rule or in the crossfire between factions. As the larger Christian world looks on passively, their future, like the future of Middle Eastern Christianity writ large, will be determined by Iran, Hezbollah, the Assad dynasty, the Islamic State, Jabhat al-Nusra, various other local factions and by regional powers seeking advantage.

Meanwhile, on a more limited scale, there are things that can be done. Three weeks ago, for example, 150 Syrian Christians were airlifted to refuge and safety in Poland.

That's the work of the Weidenfeld Safe Havens Fund. It provided the flight and will support the refugees for as long as 18 months as they try to remake their lives.

The person behind all this is Lord George Weidenfeld: life peer, philanthropist, publisher (Weidenfeld & Nicolson, established 1949), Europeanist (founder of the Institute for Strategic Dialogue to promote classically liberal European values), proud public Jew (honorary vice president of the World Jewish Congress), lifelong Zionist (he once served as the chief of cabinet to Israel's first president, Chaim Weizmann) and, as he will delightedly tell you, the last person to fight a duel at the University of Vienna—with sabers, against a Nazi. (No one died.)

Weidenfeld, now 95, once invoked *Torschlusspanik*, "a German phrase which roughly translates as the 'panic before the closing of the doors,'" to explain why "I'm a man in a hurry." Remarkably healthy and stunningly energetic (as distant cousins, we are often in touch), he appears nowhere near any exit doors. But he is aware of and deeply troubled by the doors closing in on a community in Syria largely abandoned by the world.

In context, the scale of the initial rescue is tragically small. The objective is to rescue 2,000 families. Compared to the carnage in Syria wrought by the pitiless combatants—230,000 dead, half the 22 million population driven from their homes—it's a paltry sum. But these are real people who will be saved. And for Weidenfeld, that counts.

Yet he has been criticized for rescuing just Christians. In fact, the US government will not participate because the rescue doesn't extend to Yazidis, Druze or Shiites.

This comes under the heading of no good deed going unpunished. It's a rather odd view that because he cannot do everything, he should be admonished for trying to do something. If Weidenfeld were a man of infinite means, the criticism might be valid. As it is, he says rather sensibly, "I can't save the world." The Arab states, particularly the Gulf monarchies, are surely not without resources. With so few doing so little for so many, he's doing what he can.

And for him, it's personal. In 1938, still a teenager, he was brought from Vienna to London where the Plymouth Brethren took him in and provided for him. He never forgot. He is trying to return the kindness, he explains, to repay the good that Christians did for him 77 years ago. In doing so, he is not just giving hope and a new life to 150 souls, soon to be thousands. He has struck a blow for something exceedingly rare: simple, willful righteousness.

The Washington Post, July 31, 2015

Postscript: Lord Weidenfeld died just six months after the publication of this column, on January 20, 2016. He was buried on the Mount of Olives in Jerusalem, Israel.

Meg Greenfield

My Editor, My Friend

Meg Greenfield, who died last week at 68, was not just one of the best journalists of our time. In my view, she was the best editorial page editor of our time. For 20 years, she made the editorial page of the *Washington Post* the best in the country. She did it by applying the same talents that served her so well as a writer and columnist: a quick and deep intellect, a fine pen and a total allergy to spin and bull. She had more antibodies to pap, flacks and fakes than anyone in Washington. She was immune.

Indeed, one of her great talents in her own writing was her ability to cut through the fog produced by professional fog makers in this town—politicians and bureaucrats, journalists and publicists—to expose the ironies, the foibles, the vanities, the poses that inevitably attend the politics of a great capital.

And yet she did it—and this was the distinct Greenfield touch—without condescension, without ever letting criticism turn into contempt. That is because she had great respect for what Washington does: weigh deep and often ancient arguments and try from that to fashion action. She had respect for the difficulty of this Sisyphean task and for the fallibility of the men and women engaged in it. Nonetheless, she never flinched from subjecting everything and everyone to the two great Greenfield criteria: intellectual rigor and social decency.

She was a great student, critic, analyst, debunker and in the end, shaper of power. She could expose the innards of the

Washington game without ever losing her appreciation of its more noble possibilities. She had the gift of seeing—she delighted in—both the high and the low, the sublime and the ridiculous. And she could navigate between the two with the ease that comes to those blessed with a deep and understanding humanity.

But I knew Meg not just as a writer and editor but as a friend. I knew her for 15 years. During half of those years she, George Will and I had lunch every Saturday at the Chevy Chase Lounge, a long-gone, rundown local eatery (now home to an upscale Italian "osteria"). It was wall-to-wall Formica, linoleum, canned tuna and cholesterol. Meg loved the place.

For a few months, while the Lounge was being renovated (as I recall, repairing damage suffered from the firebomb thrown into the offices of the Chinese restaurant upstairs) we looked for a suitable substitute. Meg gave the nod to Cafe Roma, another little spot (also long gone) of the same distinguished decor and menu, but with an added touch: Its walls groaned with the mounted heads of the big game that one of the early owners had bagged on safari. Our lunch guests, often senators, ambassadors or cabinet members, thought the choice droll.

It was at these lunches that I got to see Meg at her most vivid and to revel in her wit. And what a wit it was: wicked, quick, mordant and above all, subtle.

But Meg was more than that. She was a great friend: wise, generous, loyal and kind. The last of these qualities is often overlooked. Her obituaries talk of her toughness. And tough she was: She delighted in telling grandees of all stripes and nationalities where to get off, especially when they dared lay territorial claim to a column-inch of her pages. That toughness—the impossibility of pushing her around, which is what made her such a paragon of editorial and intellectual integrity—often obscured the kindness, which consisted of a bedrock decency uncontaminated by a trace of sentimentality. She never emoted. But she always did the right thing, undemonstratively.

When my father was dying, he asked me to bury him beside his parents in Israel. Knowing how difficult it is for me to travel abroad (I am in a wheelchair), we decided that, during my lifetime, he would be temporarily buried in Washington, where I could visit his grave. But that meant a funeral in a town where he knew no one (he lived in New York), and that meant a funeral lonely and sadly small for a man who had lived such a large, robust, friend-filled life. At the cemetery, there were just a few family and almost no one else—except Meg. She'd come to bury a man she'd never met simply because the son who loved him was her friend. A small act of infinite loving kindness.

Meg Greenfield was a wonderful journalist, editor and writer. Washington, journalism and American politics will sorely miss her mind and pen. I will too. But, above all, I will miss her heart.

The Washington Post, May 18, 1999

CHAPTER 2

CUSTOMS AND CULTURE

Why I Love Australia

In the Australian House of Representatives last month, opposition member Julia Gillard interrupted a speech by the minister of health thusly: "I move that that sniveling grub over there be not further heard."

For that, the good woman was ordered removed from the House, if only for a day. She might have escaped that little time-out if she had responded to the speaker's demand for an apology with something other than "If I have offended grubs, I withdraw unconditionally."

God, I love Australia. Where else do you have a shadow health minister with such, er, starch? Of course I'm prejudiced, having married an Australian, but how not to like a country, in this age of sniveling grubs worldwide, whose treasurer suggests to any person who "wants to live under *sharia* law" to try Saudi Arabia and Iran, "but not Australia." He was elaborating on an earlier suggestion that "people who . . . don't want to live by Australian values and understand them, well then they can basically clear off." Contrast this with Canada, historically and culturally Australia's commonwealth twin, where last year Ontario actually gave serious consideration to allowing its Muslims to live under sharia.

Such things don't happen in Australia. This is a place where, when the remains of a fallen soldier are accidentally switched with those of a Bosnian, the enraged widow picks up the phone late at night, calls the prime minister at home in bed and delivers a furious, unedited rant—which he publicly and graciously accepts as fully deserved. Where Americans today sue, Australians slash and skewer.

For Americans, Australia engenders nostalgia for our own past, which we gauzily remember as infused with John Wayne plain-spokenness and vigor. Australia evokes an echo of our own frontier, which is why Australia is the only place you can unironically still shoot a Western.

It is surely the only place where you hear officials speaking plainly in defense of action. What other foreign minister but Australia's would see through "multilateralism," the fetish of every sniveling foreign policy grub from the Quai d'Orsay to Foggy Bottom, calling it correctly "a synonym for an ineffective and unfocused policy involving internationalism of the lowest common denominator"?

And with action comes bravery, from the transcendent courage of the doomed at Gallipoli to the playful insanity of Australian-rules football. How can you not like a country whose trademark sport has Attila-the-Hun rules, short pants and no padding—a national passion that makes American football look positively pastoral?

That bravery breeds affection in America for another reason as well. Australia is the only country that has fought with the United States in every one of its major conflicts since 1914, the good and the bad, the winning and the losing.

Why? Because Australia's geographic and historical isolation has bred a wisdom about the structure of peace—a wisdom that eludes most other countries. Australia has no illusions about the "international community" and its feckless institutions. An island of tranquility in a roiling region, Australia understands that peace and prosperity do not come with the air we breathe but are maintained by power—once the power of the British Empire, now the power of the United States.

Australia joined the faraway wars of early-20th-century Europe not out of imperial nostalgia but out of a deep understanding that its fate and the fate of liberty were intimately bound with that of the British Empire as principal underwriter of the international system. Today the underwriter is America, and Australia understands that an American retreat or defeat—a chastening consummation devoutly, if secretly, wished by many a Western ally—would be catastrophic for Australia and for the world.

When Australian ambassadors in Washington express support for the United States, it is heartfelt and unalloyed, never the "yes, but" of the other allies, perfunctory support followed by a list of complaints, slights and sage finger-wagging. Australia understands America's role and is sympathetic to its predicament as reluctant hegemon. That understanding has led it to share foxholes with Americans from Korea to Kabul. Not every engagement has ended well. But every one was strenuous, and many quite friendless. Which is why America has such affection for a country whose prime minister said after September 11, "This is no time to be an 80% ally" and actually meant it.

The Washington Post, June 23, 2006

Rampway to Heaven

Having been in a wheelchair since I was 22, I have become a connoisseur of ramps. I have, my readers may have noticed, opinions on everything. But this—access—I know. I know what works and I know what doesn't.

I know, for example, that retrofitting to make a building wheelchair accessible is hard and often very expensive. In fact, so expensive that no owner of, say, a modest second-story restaurant should have to bankrupt himself building an elevator. The Americans with Disabilities Act has the good sense to require only "readily achievable" retrofits. It is unreasonable to ask that every establishment be accessible. Some places—why, some of my friends' homes—are simply out of reach. It is a fact of life. Big deal. Some people have allergies to places and things, and they don't make a federal case of it.

But then there are places that can be reasonably adapted and are not. The problem here is often not recalcitrance but a simple lack of imagination. There are two basic ways to stairlessly bridge an elevation: ramps and lifts. Lifts, which are becoming ubiquitous in theaters and other public places, are almost always the wrong choice.

They are chosen because they are easy. You buy it off the rack and call in a contractor. He bolts it into place, gives you the key and there you are. For the user, however, lifts are a horror.

One of the newest movie theaters in Washington, for example, needlessly bridges a five-step drop with one of these contraptions. (A ramp was easily doable.) You've seen them. They are essentially a cage, like the pen from which the bull is released at the rodeo. You go in one end, they slam the door behind you, send you on your agonizingly slow and loud ascent (the machine runs on a massive metal screw) and, when the spectacle is over—and a spectacle it is—you are released out the other end.

What's wrong with this picture? First, the indignity. The most embarrassing visual of Bill Clinton's entire presidency was the picture of him in Helsinki being lowered from his plane in a Finnair food cart. (His knee injury had landed him in a wheelchair.) There is nothing more mortifying than being hauled around like freight.

Second, lifts are almost always unnecessary. Nearly every architectural space that is bridged by a lift can be bridged by a ramp. (And Clinton should have been given a jetway.) No need to find the usher with the keys. No physical confinement. No interminable ride. No excruciating noise. Just silence and freedom.

There is a right way to design access for wheelchairs. It involves the imaginative use of ramps. And if you want to see such imagination on display, visit the brilliantly renovated Concert Hall at the Kennedy Center in Washington, DC.

The Concert Hall was redesigned for two reasons: to improve the acoustics and to improve the access. My ear for music is untrained, but my eye for accessible design is well-honed. I know elegance and subtlety when I see it, and I saw it at the Concert Hall.

Every possible elevation—to orchestra, boxes, even the stage—is ramped, but given that the Concert Hall floor is one big inclined plane anyway, the effect appears perfectly natural. So natural, in fact, that on opening night, the ramps were as crowded with able-bodied patrons as were the stairs. (Full disclosure: I was asked to consult with the designers at an early stage in the renovation, but my contribution, apart from suggesting what might and might not work, was minuscule.)

Subtlety is a function not of money but of thought. You've seen those spaces in movie theaters where a seat or two has been torn out to make room for a wheelchair. The intention is good, but these spaces are perfectly useless. Most wheelchairs won't fit, and even if after endless maneuvering it finally does, you find yourself blocking the view of a half-dozen people behind you.

What did the Kennedy Center do? It removed a full row of orchestra seats and replaced them with identical-looking but movable chairs. Brilliant: serviceable for as many disabled and non-disabled as necessary. And—my favorite touch—the floor is ever so slightly depressed, so the folks sitting behind you don't spend the evening gazing at the back of a head with an oboe coming out one ear.

For the disabled, the new Concert Hall is a marvel: You go in on your own, you go out on your own: no one to ask, no one to thank, nothing to do but, like everyone else, enjoy. For those in wheelchairs, having an everyone-else experience in a public building is a rare thing indeed. The Kennedy Center has created the model for how to make it happen.

The Washington Post, November 7, 1997

Junk Rights

If you thought the Founding Fathers blessed you with all the rights you need, you're wrong. I bring good news. The first 10 amendments and the next 16 haven't filled your quota. That is, not if you live in my neighborhood and shop at my supermarket, whose walls are graced with a huge poster proclaiming the "Consumer Bill of Rights."

There, I discovered, you are endowed with certain inalienable rights, among which are the right "to be heard" (above the Muzak?), "to redress" (without petition) and "to choose" (and what, faced with 11 varieties of noodle, was I entitled to before the Bill?). These are yours by walking in the door. No social contract here. No need to pledge your life, your fortune or your sacred honor. You don't even need a validated parking ticket. Pick a pepper and you're endowed.

Rights have been busting out all over, and I have started collecting them. A couple of months ago during a hospital stay, I discovered that I was the beneficiary of a "Patients' Bill of Rights," promising all the things one has just learned to live without in hospitals. The first thing you notice about the "right to every consideration of . . . privacy" and "right to expect that within its capacity a hospital must make reasonable response to the request of a patient for services" is the clever drafting: These rights are designed for non-enforcement. And besides, what are you supposed to do? Call for a hearing in X-ray?

I'm not complaining, of course, about the lack of rights, but about the pretense. A hospital is a place to get well, and if you want to benefit from the wonders of modern scientific—impersonal—

medicine, you've got to expect that your rights, like your trousers, will be left at the door. To pretend otherwise is silly, and telling. The proliferation of rights always signals the loss of the powers and prerogatives of the individual. It is precisely because hospitals have become so stark and impersonal that the poor soul marooned on a bedpan and ringing frantically for a nurse is supposed to make do with his paper rights.

All this rights talk is undoubtedly part of the current mania for seeing everything in legal, adversarial terms. It is evidence too of the fallen state of political language. Rights once meant the claims of the individual against the state. In the postwar era the notion has been stretched to include benefits demanded from the state: a job, medical care, "welfare rights."

Thus stretched, the idea of rights thins. It would be in better shape if, for example, the United Nations (in its 1967 International Covenant on Economic, Social and Cultural Rights) and the American Catholic Bishops (in their 1984 draft Pastoral Letter on the US economy) did not insist on calling economic needs rights. Nevertheless, work, medicine, even welfare are legitimate demands. Call them supplementary rights perhaps. In contrast, what you find on display today at the supermarket or hospital is junk rights.

And as with junk bonds and junk food, you get what you pay for. *The Father Book*, a best-seller at my local maternity shop, has some available for $8.95. On page 20: "A Bill of Rights for the Father-to-be," including the right to "determine what is best for you" and to "express or withhold your feelings about the childbirth experience." Ah, the land of the free. Is there anything that cannot qualify as a right?

Rights language, however, is not the only political language to be debased. Raids on the lexicon of democracy are not new. Normally, however, the raiders are foreigners, and their purpose—disguising tyranny—lofty. Take the word *democratic*. The most unfree governments won't let their name be uttered without making you pronounce the word. At Olympics time, Jim McKay will always respectfully say *German Democratic Republic* when he means East Germany. Among the few countries less democratic than East Germany are Cambodia and South Yemen. When the roll is called, alphabetically, at the UN, these workers' paradises come under "D," so insistent are they on being Democratic Kampuchea and Democratic Yemen.

Or take *president*, a nice word that once had democratic implications. Haiti has just elected its oxymoronic "president for life" by the comfortable margin of more than 2 million to 449. Which brings up the state of the word *election*. Albania held one in 1982 and the official tally was a Communist Party victory of—I kid you not—1,627,959 to 1. (The one has not been identified. They are still looking.)

If hypocrisy is the homage that vice pays to virtue, language theft is a compliment that tyrants pay to democrats. That's what makes the debasement of political language by dictators tolerable.

But by supermarkets? Litter the newspapers, the UN, the Olympics with Orwellian euphemism, if you will. But in the frozen-meat department give me peace, not rights.

The Washington Post, September 6, 1985

Genius, Insanity, Innocence

Everyone knows that madness and genius go together. The mad scientist (Dr. Frankenstein), the mad artist (van Gogh) have long been staples of the popular imagination. But the idea that the great are "touched" is more than popular prejudice. It is the subject of serious scientific study.

The latest is Kay Redfield Jamison's *Touched with Fire*, a superb new study of the connection between artistic temperament and manic-depressive disease. It concludes with a terrifying appendix listing a pantheon of writers, composers and artists from Antonin Artaud to Virginia Woolf who suffered serious psychiatric illness (often to the point of suicide).

Which is why any celebration of sane, untormented genius is such unexpected and welcome pleasure. Last year we had James Gleick's biography of the prodigiously gifted physicist, Richard Feynman. Feynman had his eccentricities—one of his principal recreations while working on the atomic bomb at Los Alamos was safe-cracking—but at the same time was gloriously, uproariously sane.

This year we have *Searching for Bobby Fischer*, a splendid new movie about a gifted chess prodigy, Josh Waitzkin. It is the true story of a seven-year-old who learns the game by watching the chess hustlers in New York's Washington Square Park and begins playing with such extraordinary depth and brilliance that he comes to be seen as the possible successor to the greatest chess genius of all, Bobby Fischer.

The movie is a brilliantly acted, beautifully modulated story of a young boy with a gift and of four adults—two parents, two teachers—struggling with the paradoxes and dangers of balancing a normal happy life against a gift so terrible.

The gift is especially terrible because it is chess, and chess enjoys a not wholly undeserved reputation for psychic derangement. It is an endeavor associated, when not with frank madness, with oddness and isolation. I remember a psychiatrist friend visiting me at a chess club in downtown Boston once. He walked in, sat down, looked around and said, "Jeez, I could run a group here."

Derangement is a well-known chess hazard. The greatest player of the 19th century, Paul Morphy, returned from his 1858–59 tour of Europe where he beat the best in the world and abruptly quit the game. He subsequently went quite mad. Bobby Fischer, the only other American world champion, disappeared after winning the prize in 1972. Twenty years later he reappeared, raving, in Yugoslavia.

Fischer is the looming presence behind this movie. He appears only in black-and-white newsreel footage, but he is the hinge of the story. The film's tension is between Waitzkin, who is young, gifted and normal, and Fischer, who was once young and gifted too, but, as his gift flourished, became increasingly unhinged.

Fischer is the living embodiment of what can happen to a man for whom, as he once famously declared, "Chess is life." Josh is the opposite. He has a life. He has friends and school and sports. He is sweet and kind. He is well-adjusted, a normal child in every respect except one: He is the best, the very best, at something extremely difficult and demanding.

The film is effective because the matching of the chess monster and the chess angel is no fictional contrivance. Both stories are true. Fischer's is well known. Until this movie, Waitzkin's story—he is today 16 and the highest-rated American chess player of his age—was not.

At a time when it is hard enough to find intelligence in any film, it is a treat to find one that deals intelligently and movingly with the problem of genius. To find one that at the same time is filled with subtle visual humor and beautifully drawn characters is even more surprising.

Most surprising of all, director Steven Zaillian has managed the ultimate cinematic feat: thrilling chess. The games, played at lightning speed, the moves punctuated by the slamming of pieces and the punching of clocks, have the tempo and furious excitement of a middleweight boxing match.

I admit that I come to this movie somewhat prejudiced. The subject is chess, with which I have had a patzer's romance for 20 years. My favorite magazine, I confess, is *Chess Life* (an oxymoron, a friend once observed). And the film's hero is played by an angelic eight-year-old boy. I admit to having one of my own.

Having fully disclosed my bias, I freely dispense my judgment. *Searching for Bobby Fischer* is a wonder: both a delicate exploration of genius and the most thrilling evocation of the glories of competition since *Chariots of Fire*. See it twice.

The Washington Post, August 20, 1993

Two Cromwells: Separate and Independent Realities

*W*olf Hall, the Man Booker Prize–winning historical novel about the court of Henry VIII—and, most dramatically, the conflict between Thomas Cromwell and Sir Thomas More—is now a TV series (presented on PBS). It is maddeningly good.

Maddening because its history is tendentiously distorted, yet the drama is so brilliantly conceived and executed that you almost don't care. Faced with an imaginative creation of such brooding, gripping, mordant intensity, you find yourself ready to pay for it in historical inaccuracy.

And *Wolf Hall*'s revisionism is breathtaking. It inverts the conventional view of the saintly More being undone by the corrupt, amoral, serpentine Cromwell, the king's chief minister. This is fiction as polemic. Author Hilary Mantel, an ex- and anti-Catholic ("the Catholic Church is not an institution for respectable people"), has set out to rehabilitate Cromwell and defenestrate More, most especially the More of Robert Bolt's beautiful and hagiographic *A Man for All Seasons*.

Who's right? Neither fully, though *Wolf Hall*'s depiction of More as little more than a cruel heretic-burning hypocrite is particularly provocative, if not perverse. To be sure, More worship is somewhat overdrawn, as even the late Cardinal Francis George warned at a 2012 convocation of bishops. More had his flaws. He may have been a man for all seasons, but he was also a man of his times. And in those times of merciless contention between Rome and the Reformation, the pursuit and savage persecution of heresy were the norm.

Indeed, when Cromwell achieved power, he persecuted Catholics with a zeal and thoroughness that surpassed even More's persecution of Protestants. *Wolf Hall*'s depiction of Cromwell as a man of great sensitivity and deep feeling is, therefore, even harder to credit. He was cruel and cunning, quite monstrous both in pursuit of personal power and wealth, and in serving the whims and wishes of his royal master.

Nonetheless, Cromwell's modern reputation will be enhanced by Mark Rylance's brilliant and sympathetic cinematic portrayal, featuring a stillness and economy of expression that is at once mesmerizing and humanizing. The nature of the modern audience helps too. In this secular age beset by throat-slashing religious fanatics, we are far more disposed to despise excessive piety and celebrate the pragmatic, if ruthless, modernizer.

Which Cromwell was, as the chief engineer of Henry's Reformation. He crushed the Roman church, looted the monasteries and nationalized faith by subordinating clergy to king. That may flatter today's reflexive anticlericalism. But we do well to remember that the centralized state Cromwell helped midwife did prepare the ground, over the coming centuries, for the rise of the rational, willful, thought-controlling, indeed all-controlling, state.

It is perhaps unfair to call Cromwell (and Henry) proto-totalitarian, as some critics have suggested, essentially blaming them for what came after. But they did sow the seed. And while suppressing one kind of intolerance, they did little more than redefine heresy as an offense against the sovereignty not of God but of the state.

However, *Wolf Hall* poses questions not just political, but literary. When such a distortion of history produces such a wonderfully successful piece of fiction, we are forced to ask: What license are we to grant to the historical novel?

For all the learned answers, in reality it comes down to temporal proximity. If the event is in the recent past, you'd better be accurate. Oliver Stone's paranoid and libelous *JFK* will be harmless in 50 years, but it will take that long for the stench to dissipate. On the other hand, does anyone care that Shakespeare diverges from the record (such as it is) in his Caesar or Macbeth or his Henrys?

Time turns them to legend. We don't feel it much matters anymore. There is the historical Caesar and there is Shakespeare's Caesar. They live side by side.

The film reviewer Stanley Kauffmann said much the same about David Lean's *Lawrence of Arabia* vs. the real T. E. Lawrence. They diverge. Accept them each on their own terms, as separate and independent realities. (After all, Lawrence's own account, *Seven Pillars of Wisdom*, offers magnificent prose but quite unreliable history as well.)

So with the different versions of More and Cromwell. Let them live side by side. *Wolf Hall* is utterly compelling, but I nonetheless refuse to renounce *A Man for All Seasons*. I'll live with both Mores, both Cromwells. After all, for centuries we've accepted that light is both wave and particle. If physics can live with maddening truths, why can't literature and history?

<hr>

The Washington Post, May 1, 2015

Parenthesis to History

Those of us who publicly opposed placing the National World War II Memorial on the Mall in Washington argued that doing so was a prescription for failure. If the memorial were to respect the sight lines, symmetries and elegance of the Mall, it would be too small to do justice to the grandeur of the Second World War. And if the memorial were large enough to reflect the majesty of its subject, it would overpower and ruin the delicate harmonies of the Mall.

The World War II memorial has just opened, and it is indeed a failure. The good news is that the Mall survives. The bad news is that for all its attempted monumentality, the memorial is deeply inadequate—a busy vacuity, hollow to the core.

The memorial is a parenthesis, quite literally so—two semicircular assemblies of pillars cupping the Rainbow Pool on the invisible axis that connects the Lincoln Memorial to the Washington Monument.

The pool, with its fountains, makes a nice space for tourists and toddlers to dip their feet on a hot summer's day. But as a remembrance of the most momentous event of the 20th century, it is a disaster.

Where does one start? The memorial's major feature—56 granite pillars 17 feet high, adorned with wreaths and marked with the names of the states and US territories—is a conception of staggering banality. One descends the main entry to the monument and the pillar to the left is marked American Samoa; on the right, the Virgin Islands.

What do the states have to do with World War II? What great chapter of that struggle was written by the Virgin Islands (or Kentucky, for that matter)?

The Civil War was very much a war of states. Its battles were defined by state militias that fought and died as units. But World War II was precisely the opposite. Its glory was its transcendence of geography—and class and ethnicity. Its fighting units mixed young men from every corner of America. Your classic World War II movie features the now-clichéd platoon of the Polish mill-worker from Chicago, the Jewish kid from Brooklyn, the Appalachian woodsman and the Iowa farm boy bonding and fighting and dying for each other as a band of brothers.

And yet it is these gigantic soulless pillars, each mutely and meaninglessly representing a state or territory, that define this memorial. What in God's name were they thinking? Did not one commission that passed on this project ask: "Why states?"

But that is just the beginning of the banality. The monument is strewn with quotations inscribed in stone, meant to inspire. You descend into the parenthesis from street level and the first large stone panel on your right reads: "Women who stepped up were measured as citizens of the nation, not as women . . . this was a people's war, and everyone was in it."

"Stepped up"? "Everyone was in it"? Is this the best we can do? Are we not embarrassed to put such pedestrian prose by the biblical cadences of the Gettysburg Address and the second inaugural speech carved in stone at the Lincoln Memorial just a few hundred yards down the Reflecting Pool?

And then, alas, the ultimate banality. The centerpiece of the monument is a low curved wall, closing the top of the parenthesis, as it were, straddling the central axis of the Mall and adorned with 4,000 gold stars.

The gold star, of course, was given to those who had lost a son in the war. Why 4,000 stars? To represent the more than 400,000 American dead: Each star represents a hundred.

Why a hundred? Did they die in units of a hundred? Did they fight as centurions? The number is entirely arbitrary, a way to get the stars to fit the wall.

Four thousand stars is both too few and too many. Too few to represent the sheer mass, the unbearable weight of 400,000 dead. And too many—and too abstract—to represent the suffering of the mother of a single fallen hero.

This wall has the feel of a bureaucratic compromise between commemorating every individual (as does the Vietnam Memorial) and representing loss as a whole (as do tombs of the unknown soldiers). The solution—take 400,000 and divide it by 100—is nothing but sheer imaginative laziness.

I feel sorry for the old veterans who came with war brides and grandchildren to make their pilgrimage to the monument's opening this Memorial Day weekend. They deserve to be celebrated. They deserve their memorial. And they will no doubt celebrate this one because it is all that they have. They will lend it the dignity and power of their own experience. But once again, it is they who will have done the work. They should not have to. They deserve better, far better.

The Washington Post, May 28, 2004

The Cold War Memorials

Americans have war on their minds. Not real war, like the one in Bosnia, about which we have only sporadic interest, but long-ago wars whose memories haunt us still.

We are now in the midst of a nationwide orgy of revisionism regarding the dropping of the atomic bomb. Hiroshima guilt, coupled with a desire not to bruise the feelings of the modern Japanese, who have never come to terms with their own past and resent those who insist they do, has led to the muting of upcoming V-J Day celebrations. Indeed, the very term V-J (Victory in Japan) is in disfavor, giving way to the politically correct End of the War in the Pacific (or EOWP—I kid you not—in the official listing of the events the president will attend in Hawaii, September 1–3)—as if the whole thing just ended with some let's-call-it-off handshake between MacArthur and Hirohito on Okinawa.

In the midst of this depressing demonstration of a generation that lacks the nerve even to honor the nerve of its fathers came, by coincidence and in pleasant contrast, the dedication of the Korean War Memorial. On July 27, the 42nd anniversary of the Korean armistice, Washington hosted a heartfelt and respectful recognition of the forgotten veterans and victims of the first Cold War war.

The memorial is measured and deeply moving. Set on the Mall at the foot, as it were, of the Lincoln Memorial, its principal feature is a triangular field on which stand 19 slightly larger-than-life sculptures, Korean War grunts in full gear, traversing some uncertain terrain in staggered, harmonious array. Tensely they scan, listening for danger; some are gesturing, hollering, warning one another. Their faces betray the gaunt, weary urgency of the foot soldier of a war that swept back and forth over unforgiving land and ended exactly where it began on the 38th parallel. Nearby is a long, polished granite wall in which are etched faces—real faces culled from Korean War archives—of the many others, the gunners and fliers and nurses and divers, who stood behind the men on the dangerous ground.

Standing alone, the memorial is highly evocative. But it is doubly evocative for its placement just a few hundred yards away and directly across the Reflecting Pool from its Cold War twin, the Vietnam Memorial, with which it shares an odd and imperfect symmetry. Together the two represent a single—the only—memorial to the Cold War. Here, side by side, lie the two terrible eruptions of the long twilight struggle. When you visit the one, you must visit the other.

Mark the differences. At the Vietnam Memorial, foreground and background are reversed. The wall is dominant, the figures (Frederick Hart's three beautifully rendered soldiers) are complement. At the Korean Memorial, the figures are central, the wall complement. The Vietnam Memorial envelopes you in war's aftermath, its legacy of loss; the Korean Memorial thrusts you into war's actuality, its crucible of fear and courage. The one memorializes death, numberlessly multiplied; the other struggle, faithfully rendered.

At the Vietnam Memorial, the flag is peripheral. At the Korean Memorial, it is central. And the Korean Memorial does not flinch about purpose. The inscription at its apex reads: "Our nation honors her sons and daughters who answered the call to defend a country they never knew and a people they never met." One could say exactly the same about the Vietnam dead. But we do not. The inscription at the Vietnam Memorial reads instead: "Our nation honors the courage, sacrifice and devotion to duty and country of its Vietnam veterans." And "In honor of the men and women of the armed forces of the United States who served in the Vietnam War." Served whom? Served why? Failure to achieve our purpose does not mean we never had one.

Naturally, these differences reflect the different natures and outcomes of the two wars. One would expect a memorial to tragedy and waste for a war that ended in defeat, and a memorial to grit and endurance for a war that ended in partial victory, that fell short of its goals but did secure the freedom of an otherwise lost people.

However, the two memorials reflect not just a difference in history. They reflect above all a difference in us. The Vietnam Memorial was a vessel for saying: This is war. Never again. The Korean Memorial, dedicated 13 years later, reflects a different sensibility. In the interim, the horrors of Rwanda and Bosnia have made even those once most adamantly anti-war rethink and indeed reverse themselves. Thirteen years later, we are not so sure that "learning war no more" is a good idea. Thirteen years later, we agree: There are battles worth fighting; they should be chosen with great care and fought with great purpose, but there are purposes worth fighting for. Korea was one.

The Washington Post, August 4, 1995

CHAPTER 3

CONTESTS

Suffering a Relapse, and Loving It

David Brooks of the *New York Times* wonders whether, as a lifelong Mets fan, he is morally permitted to jump ship and pledge allegiance to the new team of his (relatively) new hometown, the Washington Nationals (née Montreal Expos).

It's a charming dilemma, but it raises a more fundamental question: What is with this rooting business in the first place?

It is one thing to root for your son's Little League team. After all, he is your kid and you paid for his glove—and uniform, helmet, bat and, when he turns nine, cup. You have a stake in him and, by extension, his team.

But what possible stake do grown men have in the fortunes of 25 perfect strangers, vagabond mercenaries paid obscene sums to play a game for half the year?

The whole thing is completely irrational. For me, this is no mere abstract question. I have been a baseball fan most of my life. I could excuse the early years, the Mantle-Maris era, as mere childish hero worship. But what excuse do I have now? Why should I care about these tobacco-spitting, crotch-adjusting multimillionaires who have never heard of me and would not care if I was dispatched to my maker by an exploding scoreboard?

Why? I have no idea. True, my interest cooled for a decade when, at age 15, I discovered girls. But then one day, when I was living in Boston and almost totally indifferent to the game, life took a fatal turn. I tuned in to the 1975 World Series and happened upon the single greatest game ever played. By the time Game 6 was over, I was hooked. Again.

Carlton Fisk's 12th-inning home run dance was just the icing. I was hooked by the improbable glory of what came before: Dewey Evans' spectacular catch off Joe Morgan in the top of the 11th, George Foster nailing Denny Doyle at the plate in the bottom of the ninth, and the most improbable home run I'd ever seen: Bernie Carbo's three-run pinch tater—after a couple of flailing swings—to tie the game in the bottom of the eighth with two outs, two strikes and hopelessness in the air.

That did it. For the next 10 years, I was a fan again—straining nights to catch West Coast late games on a Sony transistor, checking box scores first thing in the morning.

Then came the 1986 World Series and the Great Buckner Collapse. At that point, I figured I'd suffered enough. I got a divorce. Amicable, but still a divorce. With a prodigious act of will, I resolved to follow the Sox—but at an enforced distance. I refused to live or die with them. Which is how I got through Grady's Blunder—leaving Pedro in too long—in Game 7 of the 2003 Red Sox-Yankees playoff.

It was a hard fall for Sox fans, but I came through it beautifully—feeling delighted, indeed somewhat superior, at my partial emancipation from the irrationality of fandom (far more troubling than the pain). Thus a free man, almost purged of all allegiance, I watched with near-indifference as the Montreal Expos moved to Washington. Little did I know.

The Washington Nationals are born. I do not know a thing about them. I do not know a single player on the team. I have no residual allegiance to them—even though I grew up in Montreal and remember well their opening 1969 season at absurdly chintzy Jarry Park—because I never cared about the Expos.

But it is a new home team. And I am a bit curious. So I'm listening to their second game, a come-from-behind win in which no-name center fielder Brad Wilkerson hits for the cycle. Next day, a nifty comeback: Jose Vidro hits a game-winning homer in the 10th.

I'm beginning to ask the Butch Cassidy question: Who *are* those guys? Then another comeback, another game-winning dinger, this time by Jose Guillen, a refugee from the Anaheim Angels, shipped out after, let us say, an altercation with his manager. And then yet another surprise victory against the fearsome Atlanta Braves, a ridiculously impossible comeback with two outs in the ninth.

Presto. It is 1975 all over again. I begin to care. I want them to win. Why? I have no idea. I begin following *day* games on the internet. I've punched not one but two preset Nationals stations onto my car radio. I'm aghast. I'm actually invested in the day-to-day fortunes of 25 lunkheads I never heard of until two weeks ago.

This is crazy. I've relapsed, and I like it so much I've forsworn all medication.

Go Nats.

The Washington Post, April 15, 2005

The Tyranny of Chess

Not all chess players are crazy. I'm willing to venture that. But not much more. Eccentricity does reign in our precincts. In my 20s, I used to hang out at the Boston Chess Club. The front of the club was a bookstore in which you'd mill around, choose a partner, put your money down with the manager and go to the back room—20 or so boards set up in utter barrenness—for some action. (At five bucks an hour it was cheaper than a bordello, but the principle seemed disturbingly similar to me.)

I remember one back room encounter quite vividly. The stranger and I sat down to the board together. I held out my hand and said, "Hi, I'm Charles." He pushed his white king's pawn and said, "I'm white," fixing me with a glare that said, "Don't you dare intrude into my space with names." It was dead silence from then on.

A psychiatrist colleague of mine came by to fetch me a few hours later. He surveyed the clientele—intense, disheveled, autistic—and declared, "I could run a group in here."

Don't get me wrong. Most chess players are sane. In fact, a group of the saner ones, mostly journalists and writers, meets at my house every Monday night for speed chess. (You make all your moves in under nine minutes total, or you lose.) But all sane chess players know its dangers. Chess is an addiction. Like alcohol, it must be taken in moderation. Overindulgence can lead to a rapid downward spiral.

Vladimir Nabokov (a gifted creator of chess problems and a fine player, by the way) wrote a novel based on the premise of the psychic peril of too close an encounter with "the full horror and abysmal depths" of chess, as he called its closed, looking-glass world. (Nabokov's chess champion hero, naturally, goes bonkers.)

Chess players, says former US champion Larry Christiansen, inhabit a "subterranean, surreal world. It is not the real world, not even close." So what happens when a creature of that nether world seizes political power?

Impossible, you say: Sure, there have been dictators—Lenin, for example—who played serious chess, but there has never been a real chess player who became a dictator.

And no wonder, considering the alarming number of great players who were so certifiably nuts they'd have had trouble tying their shoelaces, let alone running a country. Wilhelm Steinitz, the first world champion, claimed to have played against God, given Him an extra pawn, and won. Bobby Fischer had the fillings in his teeth removed to stop the radio transmissions.

Well, in some Godforsaken corner of the Russian empire, Kalmykia on the Caspian, where the sheep outnumber people two to one, the impossible has happened. A chess fanatic has seized power. Kirsan Ilyumzhinov, former boy chess champion, current president of the International Chess Federation, was elected president of Kalmykia two years ago on the promise of a cell phone for every sheepherder and $100 for every voter in his destitute republic.

Naturally, nothing came of these promises. But once elected, he seized all the instruments of power including the police, the schools and the media.

Result? Ilyumzhinov calls it the world's first "chess state." God help us. Compulsory chess classes in all schools. Prime-time chess on TV. And in the midst of crushing poverty, a just-erected "Chess City," a surreal Potemkin village topped by a five-story glass-pavilioned chess palace where Ilyumzhinov has just staged an international chess tournament.

This scene (drolly described by Andrew Higgins in the *Wall Street Journal*) would be Groucho running Fredonia if it weren't for the little matter of the opposition journalist recently murdered after being lured to a meeting where she was promised evidence of Ilyumzhinov's corruption. (Ilyumzhinov denies involvement. Perhaps it depends on how you define the word "involve.") Kalmykia is beginning to look less like Woody Allen's *Bananas* than Nurse Ratched's *Cuckoo's Nest*.

Ilyumzhinov rides around in his Rolls-Royces, presiding over a state that specializes in corruption and tax evasion. The *Washington Post* reports that he paved the road from the airport to the capital and painted every building along the way, but only the side that faces the road.

So now the world knows what chess players have known all along: A passion for chess, like a drug addiction or a criminal record, should be automatic disqualification for any serious public activity. Column writing excepted, of course.

The Washington Post, October 16, 1998

Revenge, American-Style

Vengeance is mine, sayeth the Lord. And although retribution shall surely come in the fullness of time, a ballplayer can only wait so long.

Accordingly, when Boston slugger David Ortiz came to bat against Tampa Bay's David Price at the end of May—for the first time this season—Price fired the very first pitch, a 94-mile-an-hour fastball, square into Ortiz's back.

Ortiz was not amused. Hesitation, angry smile, umpire's warning. Managers screaming, tempers flaring. Everyone knew this was no accident.

On October 5, 2013, Ortiz had hit two home runs off Price. Unusual, but not unknown. Except that after swatting the second, Ortiz stood at home plate seeming to admire his handiwork, watching the ball's majestic arc into the far right field stands—and only then began his slow, very slow, trot around the bases.

This did not sit well with Price. Cy Young winners don't take kindly to being shown up in public. He yelled angrily at Ortiz to stop showboating and start running.

But yelling does not quite soothe the savage breast. So, through the fall and long winter, through spring training and one-third of the new season, Price nursed the hurt. Then, as in a gentleman's pistol duel, at first dawn he redeemed his honor.

Except that the other guy had no pistol.

Which made for complications: further payback (Tampa Bay star Evan Longoria received a close retaliatory shave and two other players were hit before the game was done); major mayhem in the form of the always pleasing, faintly ridiculous, invariably harmless bench-clearing brawl; and all-around general ill feeling. After the game, Ortiz declared himself at war with Price, advising the louse to prepare for battle at their next encounter.

Price feigned innocence. As did his Yoda-like manager, Joe Maddon, who dryly observed that a slugger like Ortiz simply has to be pitched inside, then added with a twinkle, "Of course, that was a little bit too far inside."

Yeah, like two feet.

What is so delightful about this classic act of revenge is both the length of the fuse—eight months!—and the swiftness of the execution: one pitch, one plunk, one message delivered. Revenge as it was meant to be: cathartic, therapeutic, clean, served cold. No talking it through. No sublimation by deep breathing, reason or anything in between. No arbitration, no mediation. "Direct action," as the left might put it.

Think of it, compact and theatrical, as a highly abridged *Count of Monte Cristo*, still the most satisfying revenge novel of all time. There the fuse is deliciously long—the 14 years our betrayed hero suffers and broods on an island prison before escaping—and the execution is spectacularly elaborate: the decade developing a new identity with which to entrap his betrayers and bring each to a tortured demise.

I suspect what makes revenge so satisfying in both literature and sport is that, while the real thing can turn rather ugly, revenge thusly mediated can be experienced not just vicariously but schematically.

After all, there is nothing satisfying about watching a well-armed real-world thug like Vladimir Putin chew up neighboring countries to avenge the Soviet collapse of 1991. Or the Crimean giveaway of 1954. Or was it Czar Nicholas' misadventure of 1917–18?

Even benign dreams of restoration can be a bit unsettling.

Ever seen a Quebec license plate? *"Je me souviens."* In English, "I remember." What? The Battle of the Plains of Abraham, marking the fall of Quebec to Britain—in 1759.

The response became known centuries later as *"la revanche des berceaux."* Revenge of the cradles. They multiplied. Quietly. Determinedly. A serious exercise in making love, not war.

But the amorous Quebecois are the exception. More common are the savage retributive habits of the more tribal elements of the human family. The Serbs, for example, waging late 20th-century war suffused with fury at the Turkish conquest of Kosovo in 1389. Or Ayman al-Zawahiri calling for infidel blood with an invocation of Andalusia, lost to Islam in 1492.

We Americans, children of so young a country, can barely fathom such ineradicable grievances. We did give the world Tonya Harding and the Godfather's horse's head in the bed, but the best we can do outside sport and fiction is "Remember the Alamo." Wonderful sentiment, but with Mexico now a best buddy, hardly a battle cry.

No. We'll do our vengeance on the playing field, thank you, where unwritten rules apply and the frisson can be enjoyed with Bud in hand. So mark your calendar. Next Sox-Rays encounter: July 25. Here's hoping Price is pitching.

The Washington Post, June 13, 2014

Man vs. Computer: Still a Match

Scoff if you will, but I stayed home Tuesday to watch a chess game. I don't get ESPN in my office, and I was not about to miss the tiebreaking final game of the man vs. machine epic: the best humanity has to offer, Garry Kasparov vs. the best in silicon, X3D Fritz.

To most folks, all of this man-vs.-computer stuff is anticlimax. After all, the barrier was broken in 1997 when man was beaten, Kasparov succumbing to Deep Blue in a match that was truly frightening. Frightening not so much because the computer won but because of how it won, making at some points moves of subtlety. And subtlety makes you think there might be something stirring in all that silicon.

It seems to me obvious that machines will achieve consciousness. After all, we did, and with very humble beginnings. In biology, neurons started firing millions of years ago, allowing tiny mindless organisms to move about, avoid noxious stimuli, etc. But when enough of those neurons were put together with enough complexity, all of a sudden you got . . . us. A cartoon balloon pops up above that mass of individually unconscious neurons and says, "I exist."

In principle, why should that not eventually occur with silicon? The number of chips and complexity of their interaction will no doubt be staggering and may require centuries to construct. But I do not see why silicon cannot make the same transition from unconsciousness to consciousness that carbon did.

That's the bad news. In the meantime, the good news is that the latest man-machine chess matches are reason for some relief.

We assume that as computers get better, they are going to pull away from us, beating us more and more easily, particularly in such circumscribed logical exercises as chess. Not so. Since 1997 machines have gotten so much stronger that even off-the-shelf ones now routinely massacre the ordinary player. But the great players are learning to adapt. Genius is keeping up.

Given Moore's Law (computers double in power every 18 months), you would have expected that six years after Deep Blue's epic victory, humans would be helpless. In fact, they are not. Earlier this year, Kasparov played a match against Deep Junior and drew. And his four-game match with Fritz, the strongest chess program in the world, ended dead even: two draws and a win each.

Interestingly, in each game that was won, the loser was true to his nature. Kasparov lost Game 2 because, being human, he made a tactical error. Computers do not. When it comes to tactics, they play like God. Make one error, just one, and you're toast. The machine's exploitation of the error will be flawless and fatal.

In Game 3 the computer lost because, being a computer, it has (for now) no imagination. Computers can outplay just about any human when the field is open, the pieces have mobility and there are millions of possible tactical combinations. Kasparov therefore steered Game 3 into a position that was utterly static—a line of immobile pawns cutting across the board like the trenches of the First World War.

Neither side could cross into enemy territory. There was, "thought" Fritz, therefore nothing to do. It can see 20 moves deep, but even that staggering foresight yielded absolutely no plan of action. Like a World War I general, Fritz took to pacing up and down behind its lines.

Kasparov, on the other hand, had a deep strategic plan. Quietly and methodically, he used the bit of space he had on one side of the board to align his pieces, preparing for the push of a single pawn down the flank to queen—and win.

Meanwhile, Fritz was reduced to shuffling pieces back and forth. At one point, it moved its bishop one square and then back again on the next move. No human would ever do that. Not just because it is a waste of two moves. It is simply too humiliating. It is an open declaration to your opponent that you have no idea what you're doing, and that maybe checkers is your game.

The observers loved it. "This move showed that the computer doesn't feel any embarrassment," said grandmaster Gregory Kaidanov. It was a moment to savor. Eventually, sons of Fritz will feel embarrassment and much more, and why not: We are just cleverly arranged carbon and we feel—but that's still centuries (decades?) away. In the meantime, Kasparov is showing that while we can't out-calculate machines, we can still outsmart them.

It even appears that we—the best of us humans, that is—will be able to hold our own for a while. We're safe. For now.

The Washington Post, November 21, 2003

The Greatness Gap

There is excellence, and there is greatness—cosmic, transcendent, Einsteinian. We know it when we see it, we think. But how to measure it? Among Tiger Woods' varied contributions to contemporary American life is that he shows us how.

As just demonstrated yet again at the US Open, Woods is the greatest golfer who ever lived. How do we know? You could try Method 1: Compare him directly with the former greatest golfer, Jack Nicklaus. For example, take their total scores in their first 22 major championships (of which Nicklaus won seven, Woods eight). Nicklaus was 40 strokes over par; Tiger was 81 under—an astonishing 121 strokes better. But that is not the right way to compare. You cannot compare greatness directly across the ages. There are so many intervening variables: changes in technology, training, terrain, equipment and often rules and customs.

How then do we determine who is greatest? Method 2: the Gap. Situate each among his contemporaries. Who towers? Who is, like the US today, a hyperpower with no second in sight?

The mark of true transcendence is running alone. Nicklaus was great, but he ran with peers: Palmer, Player, Watson. Tiger has none. Of the past 11 majors, Woods has won seven. That means whenever and wherever the greatest players in the world gather, Woods wins twice and the third trophy is distributed among the next, oh, 150.

In 2000–01, Woods won four majors in a row. The *Washington Post*'s Thomas Boswell found that if you take these four and add the 2001 Players Championship (considered the next most important tournament), Tiger shot a cumulative 1,357 strokes—55 strokes better than the next guy.

To find true greatness, you must apply the "next guy" test. Then the clouds part and the deities appear. In 1921 Babe Ruth hit 59 home runs. The next four hit 24, 24, 23 and 23. Ruth alone hit more home runs than half the teams in the major leagues.

In the 1981–82 season, Wayne Gretzky scored 212 points. The next two guys scored 147 and 139. Not for nothing had he been known as the Great One—since age nine.

Gaps like these are as rare as the gods that produce them. By 1968, no one had ever long-jumped more than 27 ft. 4¾ in. In the Mexico City Olympics that year, Bob Beamon jumped 29 ft. 2½ in.—this in a sport in which records are broken by increments of a few inches, sometimes fractions. (Yes, the air is thin in Mexico City, but it was a legal jump and the record stood for an astonishing 23 years.)

In physics, a quantum leap means jumping to a higher level without ever stopping—indeed, without even traveling through—anywhere in between. In our ordinary understanding of things, that is impossible. In sports, it defines greatness.

Not only did Michael Jordan play a game of basketball so beautiful that it defied physics, but he racked up numbers that put him in a league of his own. Jordan has averaged 31 points a game, a huge gap over the (future) Hall of Famers he played against (e.g., Karl Malone, 25.7; Charles Barkley, 22.1).

The most striking visual representation of the Gap is the photograph of Secretariat crossing the finish line at the Belmont Stakes, 31(!) lengths ahead of the next horse. You can barely see the others—the fastest horses in the world, mind you—in the distance.

In 1971, Bobby Fischer played World Championship elimination rounds against the best players on the planet. These were open-ended matches that finished only when one player had won six games. Such matches could take months, because great chess masters are so evenly matched that 80% of tournament games end in draws. Victories come at rare intervals; six wins can take forever. Not this time. Fischer conducted a campaign unrivaled since Scipio Africanus leveled Carthage. He beat two challengers six games in a row, which, combined with wins before and after, produced a streak of 20 straight victories against the very best—something never seen before and likely never to be seen again.

That's a Gap. To enter the pantheon—any pantheon—you've got to be so far above and beyond your contemporaries that it is said of you, as Jack Nicklaus once said of Tiger Woods, "He's playing a game I'm not familiar with."

The biologist and philosopher Lewis Thomas was asked what record of human achievements he would launch into space to be discovered one day by some transgalactic civilization. A continual broadcast of Bach would do, Thomas suggested, though "that would be boasting."

Why not make it a music video? A Bach fugue over Tiger hitting those miraculous irons from the deep rough onto the greens at Bethpage Black. Nah. The aliens will think we did it all with computer graphics.

Time, July 1, 2002

Why Do They Even Play the Game?

In mathematics, when you're convinced of some eternal truth but can't quite prove it, you offer it as a hypothesis (with a portentous capital H) and invite the world, future generations if need be, to prove you right or wrong. Often, a cash prize is attached.

In that spirit, but without the cash, I offer the Krauthammer Conjecture: In sports, the pleasure of winning is less than the pain of losing. By any Benthamite pleasure/pain calculation, the sum is less than zero. A net negative of suffering. Which makes you wonder why anybody plays at all.

Winning is great. You get to hoot and holler, hoist the trophy, shower in champagne, ride the open parade car and boycott the White House victory ceremony (choose your cause).

But, as most who have engaged in competitive sports know, there's nothing to match the amplitude of emotion brought by losing. When the Cleveland Cavaliers lost the 2015 NBA Finals to Golden State, LeBron James sat motionless in the locker room, staring straight ahead, still wearing his game jersey, for 45 minutes after the final buzzer.

Here was a guy immensely wealthy, widely admired, at the peak of his powers—yet stricken, inconsolable. So it was for Ralph Branca, who gave up Bobby Thomson's shot heard 'round the world in 1951. So too for Royals shortstop Freddie Patek, a (literal) picture of dejection sitting alone in the dugout with his head down after his team lost the 1977 pennant to the New York Yankees.

In 1986, the *Today Show* commemorated the 30th anniversary of Don Larsen pitching the only perfect game in World Series history. They invited Larsen and his battery mate, Yogi Berra. And Dale Mitchell, the man who made the last out. Mitchell was not amused. "I ain't flying 2,000 miles to talk about striking out," he fumed. And anyway, the called third strike was high and outside. It had been 30 years and Mitchell was still mad. (Justly so. Even the Yankee fielders acknowledged that the final pitch was outside the strike zone.)

For every moment of triumph, there is an unequal and opposite feeling of despair. Take that iconic photograph of Muhammad Ali standing triumphantly over the prostrate, semiconscious wreckage of Sonny Liston. Great photo. Now think of Liston. Do the pleasure/pain calculus.

And we are talking here about professional athletes—not even the legions of Little Leaguers, freshly eliminated from the play-offs, sobbing and sniffling their way home, assuaged only by gallons of Baskin-Robbins.

Any parent can attest to the Krauthammer Conjecture. What surprises is how often it applies to battle-hardened professionals making millions.

I don't feel sorry for them. They can drown their sorrows in the Olympic-sized infinity pool that graces their Florida estate. (No state income tax.) I am merely fascinated that, despite their other substantial compensations, some of them really do care. Most interestingly, often the very best.

Max Scherzer, ace pitcher for the Washington Nationals, makes $30 million a year. On the mound, forget the money. His will to win is scary. Every time he registers a strikeout, he stalks off the mound, circling, head down, as if he's just brought down a mastodon.

On June 6, tiring as he approached victory, he began growling—yes, like a hungry tiger—at Chase Utley as he came to the plate. "It was beautiful," was the headline of the blog entry by the *Washington Post*'s Scott Allen. Nats broadcaster and former ballplayer F. P. Santangelo was so thrilled by the sheer madness of it that he said "I want to run down there and put a uni' on . . . I mean, I've got goose bumps right now."

When Scherzer gets like that, managers are actually afraid to go out and tell him he's done. He goes Mad Max. In one such instance last year, as Scherzer labored, manager Dusty Baker came out to the mound. Scherzer glared.

"He asked me how I was feeling," Scherzer recounted, "and I said I still feel strong . . . I still got one more hitter in me."

Asked Baker, demanding visual confirmation: "Which eye should I look at?"

Scherzer, who famously has one blue and one brown eye, shot back: "Look in the [expletive] brown eye!"

"That's the pitching one," he jokingly told reporters after the game.

Baker left him in.

After losing her first ever UFC match, mixed martial artist Ronda Rousey confessed that she was in the corner of the medical room, "literally sitting there thinking about killing myself. In that exact second, I'm like, 'I'm nothing.'" It doesn't get lower than that.

Said Vince Lombardi, "Winning isn't everything. It's the only thing." To which I add—conjecture—yes, but losing is worse.

The Washington Post, June 30, 2017

Jim Dickson's Triumph

Jim Dickson, a blind man, tried to sail the Atlantic alone. He didn't make it. He did, however, make it to Bermuda. Curiously, this has led to a debate. Columnist William F. Buckley disapproves of the venture on the grounds that there is no point to a blind man's trying to sail. It is against nature. "[I]f you cannot see the water and the skies, why are you going on a sailboat to begin with?"

Dickson is trying "to do that which [his] handicap inherently proscribes." Sailing is an experience simply not accessible to the blind, says Buckley. Dickson may think he is sailing, using instruments to substitute for sight. But that is "self-delusion," an exercise in false consciousness. Might as well take a deaf man to the symphony or a blind man to the Grand Canyon.

The analogy, like the argument, is inept. A concert is a hearing experience, the Grand Canyon a seeing experience. If you lack the required sense, you miss the experience entirely. Sailing is different. It engages all the senses, not just one. (Indeed sailing's most physiologically significant sensory experience—against which nature so rebels that it invented seasickness to discourage the practice—is motion.) Moreover, unlike a concert, sailing is not merely a passive sensory experience. To sail a boat requires actions of mind and hand—plotting the course, trimming the sails—that are both difficult and pleasing.

Sight is, of course, a large part of the sailing experience. But it is not all of it. If it were, then when Buckley sails into a pea soup fog in which he can no more see water and sky than can Dickson, one would have to say that Buckley is not sailing—when in fact he is.

There is a simple test of the reality of one's experience: Ask the person in question what happened. If you ask a deaf man for an account of the symphony, he can tell you nothing of the music. Ask Dickson to account for his trip to Bermuda and he has a thrilling story to tell. A deaf man at the symphony has missed the experience. A blind man at sea has a diminished experience.

Buckley's case against Dickson comes down to this: The diminished experience is not worth having. It can't be enjoyed. It can't be experienced. It doesn't even exist. "People who can't see have really no business sailing, for the reason that they are simply engaging in a challenge . . . unrelated to the experience of sailing."

Nonsense. Buckley is confusing diminished experience with non-experience. When Buckley reads Dostoevsky in translation, he is missing the rhythm and the music of the original. Moreover, not having grown up Russian, he lacks the cultural feel, the sensitivity to nuance with which even the humblest Muscovite is endowed. Reading Dostoevsky in translation is a diminished experience. Does that mean the experience is inauthentic or the enjoyment delusive?

A more correct analogy to the blind man sailing is not the deaf man at the symphony but the deaf man at the ballet. Certainly the experience is diminished. But is it right to say that it does not exist? Again the test: Can he give you an account of what happened? Yes, a partial account. Missing is the rush of the music, but certainly there is an apprehension—diminished but real—of the dance.

The first half of the objection to Dickson's feat is thus metaphysical: Whatever Dickson engaged in, it was not "sailing." The other half of the objection is practical: The venture has no point, it is a mere stunt. Now, it is true that blind men are not meant to sail the Atlantic alone. But neither are ladies (or gentlemen, for that matter) meant to swim the Bering Strait. Lynne Cox did so two weeks ago. Heretofore that stunt had been reserved for seals. And it is certainly against nature to walk to the North Pole or swim the English Channel. If it weren't, nature would have equipped man with fur and fins.

Yet people undertake such "stunts" and are rightly celebrated for it. Why? People don't swim the Channel or walk to the Pole in order to encourage others to do the same. They do so to stretch our idea of what man can do. They show the way, not literally but metaphorically. The point of a blind man sailing the Atlantic is not to get other blind men to follow. Dickson's contribution was to show that the blind can do things—such as sail to Bermuda alone—that people thought the blind could not do. Funny thing is, Dickson's already done it and some people would still like to argue that he can't.

The Washington Post, August 21, 1987

CHAPTER 4

COSMOS

In Sorrow and Glory We Find Our Common Humanity

O ur betters, religious and secular, like to instruct us on the virtues of universal brotherhood. But it is hard enough to overcome selfishness; harder still to overcome ties of family and tribe and nation. How are we to feel for all humanity?

Our efforts to institutionalize universalism have been disappointing. The UN, intended to be the parliament of man, has instead become a cockpit of rivalries that often sharpen, not lessen, feelings of national and racial hostility. Our other famous attempt, the Olympics, has also fallen short. The opening and closing ceremonies can be sweet celebrations of our oneness. But sandwiched in between are two weeks of doping, cheating, clawing and jousting to earn you a flag-draped victory lap and gold to bring home to the tribe.

These noble failures suggest that self-conscious attempts at creating community simply don't work. Our divisions are too profound. True expressions of our common humanity are more spontaneous, if infrequent. And they generally emerge in response to two kinds of phenomena: disaster and discovery.

It is a particular kind of disaster, however, that moves us to recognize global solidarity. Epidemics are simply too slow. And localized catastrophes, such as the mudslides and floods in the US last week or even the Iranian earthquake of 2003, are usually too parochial in their victimization to catch the attention of all humanity. It takes a multicontinental cataclysm—instantaneous, catastrophic, widely spread—to shake the world from its self-absorption. The tsunami that destroyed thousands of lives from Sumatra to Somalia engendered an instant, near-universal outpouring of concern, shared grief and charitable giving. Ronald Reagan once startled the UN by suggesting in a speech that humanity would unite and forget its petty divisions if we were attacked from outer space. This elicited widespread head scratching, but the point was unassailable: External threats do exactly that—not little green men but forces closer to home, forces we often assume we have tamed.

Comes the tsunami and we realize to our horror that Nature has merely to shrug, to flick a finger, as it were, and hundreds of thousands of us are broken, entire nations thrown into chaos and grief. It is the ultimate reminder of our common fragility, of just how precarious our species' ridiculously brief sojourn on this earth really is.

The other, more ennobling reminder of our common humanity is scientific discovery, which reveals not our vulnerability but our genius, not our weakness but our glory. The most universal of these inspirations have come, literally, from outer space, from our few distant glimpses of the uniqueness of our tiny earthly habitat and the brilliance of the species that could contrive to get up, out and beyond it. Indeed, the birth of our modern "whole earth" consciousness can be traced to a single act of exploration: *Apollo 8*'s circumnavigation of the moon and the astonishing photo—"Earthrise," that vision of a little blue planet—that it sent back.

Just two days before the tsunami, the *Cassini* spacecraft or-biting Saturn received instructions from this frail little spe-cies three planetary orbits away, and proceeded to detach and launch its *Huygens* probe to fly suicidally down to the giant moon Titan—measuring, sensing, learning and teaching through its final descent. All for one purpose: to satisfy the hunger for knowl-edge of a species three-quarters of a billion miles away.

Huygens carried no passengers, only the product of thousands of years of the accumulated knowledge of a race of beings that is, until proved otherwise, the crown of all creation. Even as Earth is tossing us about like toys, our own little proxies, a satellite and a probe, dare disturb Saturn and Titan. What a piece of work is man!

And yet how frail. The most famous reaction to disaster is that poignant cry from a radio reporter sent to cover the landing of the airship *Hindenburg* in New Jersey in 1937. Suddenly it goes up in flames. Bodies burn and fall pitiably. "Oh, the humanity!" Everyone has heard the cry, but it is puzzling. It has little logical meaning. It is but the primal expression of anguished fellow feel-ing for the fate of unknown human forms falling from the sky. At times like that we literally feel the humanity.

And at one other time too. Beside the sorrow of our frail hu-manity there is also the glory of our genius. Amid the shock and grief at our common helplessness before a cruel ocean, there is also this: when *Huygens* sent back those wondrous pictures from the surface of Titan this past Friday, we were reminded once again of our stubborn little common human greatness.

Time, January 24, 2005

Front-Page Physics: Why the News
From Beyond Is Beyond Us

The news from physics is not good. It seems that an X-ray satellite has detected evidence of enormous amounts of "dark matter" in the far reaches of space, perhaps enough to stop the expansion of the universe and cause its eventual extinction in the Big Crunch, a spectacular reversal of our birth in the Big Bang.

Some people find this news depressing because it foretells the End. Not me. After all, the expanding universe is no picnic either. It too ends—in a state of infinite, frozen dissipation. Given the choice between fire and ice, I hold with those who prefer the world to end in fire.

What I find more depressing than the prospect of the End is the epistemological void illuminated by these flashes from physics. Front-page physics is noteworthy less for the new knowledge it imparts the layman than for the invincible ignorance in which it leaves him.

What, after all, is "dark matter"? The *New York Times* blithely, and no doubt accurately, refers to it as "invisible material of an unknown kind." What possibly can that mean? The fact that there might be 10 times as much of this invisible stuff around as ordinary chairs and tables does not make it any more solid or comprehensible.

Consider another recent piece of physics news: 315 scientists using a massive atom smasher whose detector alone cost $65 million were unable to find the squarks and gluinos required for the theory of "supersymmetry." Interesting news, with serious policy implications—Congress is planning to spend $8.2 billion on an even stronger squark-hunting gizmo in Texas. But what does it mean? Supersymmetry—a way to unify theories of electromagnetism, the weak and strong nuclear forces—is even more opaque a notion than dark matter, which at least has some analogue in magic.

Why is physics so difficult? The reason is that at its heart is math of astonishing complexity. One either devotes a lifetime to penetrating the math—two winters ago I worked my way through a 700-page calculus text in preparation for an assault on Everest, before capitulating in exhaustion at Base Camp 1—or one tries the shortcut of metaphor.

Problem is, metaphor doesn't work. Stephen Hawking's best-selling *A Brief History of Time* is all metaphor and, as anyone who has read it can tell you (I read it twice), entirely incomprehensible. A recently done film version of the book is engaging but even less illuminating.

Or take James Gleick's wonderful new biography of the great physicist Richard Feynman. Gleick, perhaps the country's finest science writer, is a master of metaphor. (My favorite: batches of cards in a primitive computing system passing each other "like impatient golfers playing through.") He illuminates for us the life of a man who for amusement picked the locks of his co-workers' safes while working on the atomic bomb at Los Alamos. But what is there to understand about Feynman's theory of quantum electrodynamics, which won him the Nobel Prize in 1965? When asked by newsmen about his discovery, Feynman was tempted to say: "Listen, buddy, if I could tell you in a minute what I did, it wouldn't be worth the Nobel Prize." In fact, even Gleick cannot really tell you in a book.

Why is any of this important? For reasons of policy, obviously—$8 billion is real money. But even more for reasons of theology. In the age of science, physics is a form of revelation. For Einstein it was the purest form: God's rulebook. Einstein saw in the order and the beauty of the universe evidence of a benign Intelligence. Other physicists have been driven to contrary conclusions. It was said of the great physicist and atheist Paul Dirac, "There is no God, and Dirac is His prophet." It would be nice for ordinary mortals to be able to mediate between these views, or even to understand them. But they remain impenetrable to laymen.

The layman's only comfort is that just as he cannot penetrate physics, physics cannot penetrate theology. "It seems as though science will never be able to raise the curtain on the mystery of creation," writes astronomer Robert Jastrow at the close of his book *God and the Astronomers*. "For the scientist . . . the story ends like a bad dream. He has scaled the mountains of ignorance; he is about to conquer the highest peak; as he pulls himself over the final rock, he is greeted by a band of theologians who have been sitting there for centuries."

Jastrow is a scientist with, one might say, a layman's appreciation of the mystery of physics, its deeper meaning being as hidden from the physicist as the underlying equations are from the layman. He puts his hopes in a current NASA experiment listening for signs of sentient life in the universe. He calculates that any intelligence capable of signaling us must be millions, perhaps billions of years more advanced than us. Enough time, Jastrow reckons, to have worked out, for the sharing, the theological conundrums that bedevil us.

So he proposes his own shortcut to true knowledge: Check the mail. Got a better idea?

The Washington Post, January 8, 1993

What Sputnik Launched

Fifty years ago this week, America was shaken out of techno-logical complacency by a beeping 180-pound aluminum ball orbiting overhead. *Sputnik* was a shock because we had always assumed that Russia was nothing but a big, lumbering and all-brawn bear. He could wear down the Nazis and produce moun-tains of steel but had none of our savvy or sophistication. Then one day we wake up and he has beaten us into space, placing over-head the first satellite to orbit Earth since God placed the moon where it could give us lovely sailing tides.

At the time, all thoughts were about the Soviets overwhelming us technologically. But the panic turned out to be unwarranted. *Sputnik* was not subtle science. The Soviets were making up for their inability to miniaturize nuclear warheads—something that does require sophistication—by developing massive rockets. And they had managed to develop one just massive enough to hurl a ball into Earth orbit.

We had no idea how lucky we were with *Sputnik*. The subse-quent panic turned out to be an enormous boon. The fear of fall-ing behind the Communists induced the federal government to pour a river of money into science and math education. The result was a vast cohort of scientists who gave us not only Apollo and the moon, but the sinews of the information age—for example, ARPA (established just months after *Sputnik*) created ARPA-NET, which became the internet—that have ensured American technological dominance to this day.

There was another lucky outcome of *Sputnik*. Two years earlier, President Dwight D. Eisenhower had proposed "Open Skies," under which the United States and Russia would permit spy-plane overflights so each would know the other's military capabilities. The idea was to reduce mutual uncertainty and strengthen deterrence. Soviet leader Nikita Khrushchev rejected the idea out of hand.

The advent of the orbiting satellite circumvented the objection. By 1960, we had launched our first working spy satellite. But our greatest luck was the fact that the Soviets got to space first. *Sputnik* orbiting over the United States—and Eisenhower never protesting a violation of US sovereignty—established forever the principle that orbital space is not national territory but is as free and open as the high seas. Had we beaten the Russians into orbit—and we were only a few months behind—Khrushchev might very well have protested our presence over sovereign Soviet territory and reserved the right to one day (the technology was still years away) shoot us down.

Sputnik and the space age it launched had one other curious, wholly unexpected effect. Before *Sputnik*, while still dreaming about outer space in science fiction, we always assumed that one step would create the hunger for the next—ever outward from Earth orbit to the moon to Mars and beyond.

Not so. It took only 12 years to go from *Sputnik* to the moon, which we jumped about on for a brief interlude and then, amazingly, abandoned.

There are technological, budgetary and political reasons to explain this. But the most profound is psychological. It's cold out there. *In the Shadow of the Moon* is a magnificent new documentary of the remembrances of some of those very few human beings who have actually gone to the moon. They talk, as you'd expect, about the wonder and beauty and grandeur of the place. But some also recall the coldness of that desolation. One astronaut tells how on the moon's surface he was seized with the realization that he and his crewmate were utterly alone *on an entire world*.

On Earth, you can be wandering a forbidding desert but always with the hope that there might be something human over the horizon. On the moon there is nothing but dust and rock, forever. And then—just about all the astronauts talk about this—you look up and see this beautiful blue marble, warm and fragile, hanging in the black lunar sky. And you long for home.

The astronauts brought back that image in the famous photo "Earthrise"—and, with it, that feeling of longing. That iconic image did not just help spur the environmental movement. With surpassing irony, it created at the very dawn of the space age a longing not for space but for home.

This is perhaps to be expected for a 200,000-year-old race of beings leaving its crib for the first time. We will, however, outgrow that fear. It was 115 years from Columbus to the Jamestown colony. It will take about that same span of time for a new generation—ours is too bound to Earth—to go out and not look back.

The Washington Post, October 5, 2007

Pluto and Us

We need a pick-me-up. Amid the vandalizing of Palmyra, the imminent extinction of the northern white rhino, the disarray threatening Europe's most ambitious attempt ever at peaceful unification—amid plague and pestilence and, by God, in the middle of Shark Week—where can humanity turn for uplift?

Meet *New Horizons*, arriving at Pluto in five days. Small and light, the fastest spacecraft ever launched, it left Earth with such velocity that it shot past our moon in nine hours. A speeding bullet the size of a Steinway, it has flown nine and a half years to the outer edges of the solar system.

To Pluto, the now-demoted "dwarf planet" that lives beyond the Original Eight in the far distant "third zone" of the solar system—the Kuiper Belt, an unimaginably huge ring of rocks and ice and sundry debris where the dwarf is king.

After three billion miles, *New Horizons* will on Tuesday shoot right through Pluto's mini-planetary system of five moons, the magnificently named Charon, Styx, Nix, Hydra and Kerberos.

Why through? Because, while the other planets lie on roughly the same plane, Pluto and its moon system stick up at an angle to that plane like a giant archery target. *New Horizons* gets one pass, going straight by the bull's eye. No orbiting around, no lingering for months or even years to photograph and study.

No mulligans. And no navigating. Can't do that when it takes four and a half hours for a message from Earth to arrive. This is a preprogrammed, single-take, nine-day deal.

For what? First, for the science, the coming avalanche of new knowledge. Remember: We didn't even know there was a Pluto until 85 years ago when astronomer Clyde Tombaugh found a strange tiny dot moving across the star field.

Today, we still know practically nothing. In fact, two of the five moons were not discovered until after *New Horizons* was launched. And yet next week we will see an entirely new world come to life. "We're not planning to rewrite any textbooks," said principal investigator Alan Stern in a splendid *New York Times* documentary on the mission. "We're planning to write them from scratch."

Then there's the romance. The Pluto fly-by caps a half-century of solar system exploration that has yielded staggering new wonders. Such as Europa, one of Jupiter's moons, with its vast subterranean ocean under a crust of surface ice, the most inviting potential habitat for extraterrestrial life that human beings will ever reach.

Yes, ever. Promising exoplanets—the ones circling distant stars that we deduce might offer a Goldilocks zone suitable for water-based life—are being discovered by the week. But they are unreachable. The journey to even the nearest would, at *New Horizons* speed, take 280,000 years. Even mere communication would be absurdly difficult. A single exchange of greetings—"Hi there," followed by "Back at you, brother"—would take a generation.

It's the galactic version of the old Trappist monastery joke where every seven years one monk at one meal is allowed one remark. A young novice arrives and after seven years a monk stands up at dinner and says: "The soup is cold."

Seven years of silence. Then another monk stands and says: "The bread is stale."

Seven years later, the now-aging novice rises and says: "If you don't stop this bickering, I'm outta here."

Which is what a conversation with Klingons would be like, except with longer intervals. Which is why we prefer to scour

our own solar system. And for more than just the science, more than just the romance. Here we are, upright bipeds with opposable thumbs, barely down from the trees, until yesterday unable to fly, to communicate at a distance, to reproduce a sound or motion or even an image—and even today barely able to manage the elementary decencies of civilization—taking close-up pictures and chemical readings of a mysterious world nine and a half years away.

One final touch. Every ounce of superfluous weight has been stripped from *New Horizons* to give it more speed and pack more instruments. Yet there was one concession to poetry. *New Horizons* is carrying some of Clyde Tombaugh's ashes. After all, he found the dot. Not only will he fly by his netherworldly discovery, notes Carter Emmart of the American Museum of Natural History, he will become the first human being to have his remains carried beyond the solar system.

For the wretched race of beings we surely are, we do, on occasion, manage to soar.

The Washington Post, July 10, 2015

Space: The Visionaries Take Over

Fractured and divided as we are, on one thing we can agree: 2015 was a miserable year. The only cheer was provided by Lincoln Chafee and the Pluto flyby (two separate phenomena), as well as one seminal aeronautical breakthrough.

On December 21, Elon Musk's SpaceX, after launching 11 satellites into orbit, returned its 15-story booster rocket, upright and intact, to a landing pad at Cape Canaveral. That's a $60 million mountain of machinery—recovered. (The traditional booster rocket either burns up or disappears into some ocean.)

The reusable rocket has arrived. Arguably, it arrived a month earlier when Blue Origin, a privately owned outfit created by Amazon chief executive Jeff Bezos, launched and landed its own booster rocket, albeit for a suborbital flight. But whether you attribute priority to Musk or Bezos, the two events together mark the inauguration of a new era in spaceflight.

Musk predicts that the reusable rocket will reduce the cost of accessing space a hundredfold. This depends, of course, on whether the wear and tear and stresses of the launch make the refurbishing prohibitively expensive. Assuming it's not, and assuming Musk is even 10% right, reusability revolutionizes the economics of spaceflight.

Which both democratizes and commercializes it. Which means space travel has now slipped the surly bonds of government—presidents, Congress, NASA bureaucracies. Its future will now be driven far more by a competitive marketplace with its multiplicity of independent actors, including deeply motivated, financially savvy and visionary entrepreneurs.

To be sure, the enterprise is not entirely free of government. After all, SpaceX's Falcon 9 rocket landed on a Cape Canaveral pad formerly used to launch Air Force Atlas rockets. Moreover, initial financing for these ventures already depends in part on NASA contracts, such as resupplying the space station.

That, however, is not much different from the growth of aviation a century ago. It hardly lived off air-show tickets or Channel-crossing prize money. What really propelled the infant industry was government contracts. For useful things like mail—and bomb—delivery.

The first and most visible consequence of the new entrepreneurial era will be restoring America as a spacefaring nation. Yes, I know we do spectacular robotic explorations. But our ability to toss humans into space disappeared when NASA retired the space shuttle—without a replacement.

To get an astronaut into just low Earth orbit, therefore, we have to hitch a ride on Russia's Soyuz with its 1960s technology. At $82 million a pop. Yet, today, two private companies already have contracts with NASA to send astronauts to the space station as soon as 2017.

The real prize, however, lies beyond Earth orbit. By now, everyone realizes that the space station was a colossal mistake, a white elephant in search of a mission. Its main contribution is to study the biological effects of long-term weightlessness. But we could have done that in *Skylab*, a modest space station that our political betters decided four decades ago to abandon.

With increasing privatization, such decisions will no longer be exclusively Washington's. When President Obama came into office, the plan was to return to the moon by 2020. A year later, he decided we should go to an asteroid instead. Why? Who knows.

Today future directions are being set by private companies with growing technical experience and competing visions. Musk is fixated on colonizing Mars, Bezos on seeing millions of people living and working in space and Richard Branson on space tourism by way of Virgin Galactic (he has already sold 700 tickets to ride at $250,000 each). And Moon Express, another private enterprise, is not even interested in hurling about clumsy, air-breathing humans. It is bent on robotic mining expeditions to the moon. My personal preference is a permanent manned moon base, which would likely already exist had our politicians not decided to abandon the moon in the early 1970s.

We have no idea which plan is more likely to succeed and flourish. But the beauty of privatization is that we don't get just one shot at it. Our trajectory in space will now be the work of a functioning market of both ideas and commerce. It no longer will hinge on the whims of only tangentially interested politicians.

Space has now entered the era of the Teslas, the Edisons and the Wright brothers. From now on, they will be doing more and more of the driving. Which means we are actually—finally—going somewhere again.

The Washington Post, January 1, 2016

Redeeming Columbia

The remembrances of the *Space Shuttle Columbia* astronauts were deeply moving, dignified in their restraint. The president's eulogy at the Johnson Space Center recalled each of them individually, gave the simple reassurance that "America's space program will go on," and modestly offered the "respect and gratitude of the people of the United States."

The mood of grief felt so keenly upon hearing the news passed far more quickly than one would have expected—and far more quickly than it did after the *Challenger* accident. Of course, *Challenger* was the first fatal in-flight accident in the history of the American space program—the kind of thing you might imagine but are never quite prepared for. *Challenger* was accompanied by feelings of unreality. *Columbia* was accompanied by feelings of sad déjà vu, rather crudely captured by the *Newsweek* headline "Not Again."

There was, however, a deeper, subtler reason that the sorrow was somewhat muted, even mitigated. The *Columbia* astronauts died on their way back, not on their way there. The unstated theme of the president's memorial address was that these people had fulfilled their dream, and died doing it. Not died trying to do it, on the way to doing it, failing to do it. *Columbia* died coming home. Death here had an Odyssean quality, and thus a hint of redemption. President Reagan's eulogy for the *Challenger* astronauts spoke of having "slipped the surly bonds of Earth." *Challenger* had the additional tragedy of never having done so.

In the longer run, however, a nagging realization will temper the redemptive sense of a mission nearly accomplished. The

Columbia astronauts, as President Bush pointed out, were only minutes away from home. But what did the rest of the trip amount to? That, it seems to me, is the deepest part of this tragedy: the waste. For, whatever the joy felt by the astronauts during their 16 days aloft, one has to ask what they were doing up there in the first place or, more precisely, what we were doing sending them up in such a fragile vehicle on such a hazardous journey.

It turns out that their 16-day mission was spent conducting scientific experiments, most of which are relatively trivial, and many of which could have been done either on the space station or by unmanned spacecraft. That's all *Columbia* did, or could do (with the notable exception of repairing *Hubble*). That, and running cargo to and from the space station, is all any of the shuttles do. And, as we now realize, at astonishing peril. *Challenger* at first and now *Columbia* are stirring us to finally face the central truth about our current manned space program: the enormous imbalance between risk and reward.

The most difficult part of space travel is the first 150 miles escaping gravity and navigating the atmosphere. Beyond that, space travel gets relatively easy. And it is also beyond that that space travel gets glorious—and interesting. Once you escape the atmosphere, you no longer have to fight the heat and friction and gravitational stresses that can tear spacecraft to pieces. You no longer need absolute precision to balance all the forces necessary to keep catastrophe at bay. An astronaut who had flown on three shuttle missions averred in a post-*Columbia* interview that on every flight he was terrified on takeoff, apprehensive on landing, but calm and relaxed in space. And yet, since Apollo, we have inexplicably reduced the entire manned space program to endlessly traversing the most terror-inducing, and yet most scientifically and spiritually mundane, part of space.

Within hours of *Columbia*'s crash, the first recourse of critics was to pin the tragedy on inadequate funding. This is probably right, but how could the funding ever be adequate for such a program? It is hugely expensive—in large part to cover minimal safety requirements—and yet has no appeal to the popular imagination. And popular imagination determines how much of the country's resources go to projects that are at root romantic rather than utilitarian.

No one had ever heard of *Columbia* or its crew before the disaster. That is not a failure of the popular imagination. That is a failure of those—politicians and scientists—who have reduced the manned space program to spinning around in zero gravity in a space station, and sending a space truck (a beautiful and complicated one to be sure, but a truck, nonetheless) back and forth to service it.

This is an enormous risk for very little payoff. As I wrote in *The Weekly Standard* three years ago ("On to Mars," January 31, 2000), the entire shuttle/station idea was a wrong turn. The space station, for all of its beauty, is a failure. It does not serve as a waystation and landing base on the way to the moon and Mars—as it was originally envisioned a generation ago. No one even pretends that it is doing serious science. Under the Clinton administration it metamorphosed into yet another project in "interdependence," yet another institution to foster cooperative activity with the Russians and the Europeans.

Well, there's nothing wrong with cooperative activity with the Russians and the Europeans (in moderation), but not at the absurd cost of the space station and the absurd risk of the space shuttle.

What to do? Should we shut them down completely? No. There's too much already invested. And we do have contractual obligations to the other countries that signed up in good faith for the station. But not a penny more for its expansion. We should do just enough to sustain it with its three-astronaut crew, the minimum required to keep it going. We should forget about expanding it to house the seven astronauts and the larger living space that were originally intended. Keep it alive for the next few years. And send the shuttle up just for changes of crew, which would require no more than two or three trips a year. We can use unmanned Russian vehicles for cargo. Why risk seven human lives to lug stuff?

Right now, the shuttle is our only vehicle for getting humans into space, and the space station is their only destination. For now, keep them on life support. We dare not let them die completely lest we lose for decades the will to do anything at all in space. But a radically toned down shuttle and space station program should be a holding action as we prepare for a return to our true destiny: leaving Earth, not spinning around it. When we take the risk of sending people through that first 150 miles of terror, of killing atmosphere and gravity, it should be worth it. It should be for going farther and deeper into the glory regions. It should be for the great journeys: returning to the moon, establishing a permanent lunar presence and sending a human expedition to Mars.

What most people don't realize is that today these things are doable. It makes a lot more sense than low Earth orbit, which is the limit of the horizon for both the shuttle and the space station. Low Earth orbit, after all, is a desert. There's nothing there. It's literally a vacuum. You have to support everything by hauling it up and bringing it back. On the moon and on Mars you can live off the land. There's limited gravity to anchor you. There's soil. And most blessedly, there's water, which is the stuff of both life and power: oxygen for life support, hydrogen for propellant. All the necessities can be pre-positioned by machines sent ahead so that the humans can travel light. And when you get there, you can build things, mine things, find things, perhaps even grow things—at first a base, then a habitat and then ultimately a civilization.

February 2003 is not the time for a president to propose such a vast new enterprise. We have just watched our current space technology fall to Earth. Moreover, we are in economic hard times. We are in the midst of war. We have terrestrial dangers that call upon us right now. But this moment will pass. And when it does, it will be time for real leadership to point us, as John Kennedy did, upward and outward.

To glory. That, in the end, was Kennedy's purpose. That, in the end, is the only purpose that will sustain popular support for space. Yes, then as now, there will be the usual chorus pointing out that we have problems on earth that demand our attention and resources before we go adventuring. But this complaint is disingenuous: These problems, being perennial, are a perennial excuse for going nowhere, for dreaming nothing.

The real objection comes from those who simply can't understand why we need to venture into the void in the first place. The cheap, disgraceful answer to such an objection is to dangle Tang and Teflon and tout the great spinoffs. That misses the point and, by the way, misrepresents the facts. There's not a crystal we will ever grow in space—no matter how perfect—that will ever justify the billions of dollars and the dozens of lives it will have cost. At this point in human history it is no more practical to go into space than it was for the Wright brothers to zip around Kitty Hawk. The plain fact is that we are not doing this for the utility but for the romance.

And that is reason enough. You and I are the improbable winners of the most miraculous intergenerational lottery: After uncounted generations of human beings, we have the unique privilege of living in a time when man has the capacity to travel to other worlds. Anyone who can remain unhumbled by the majesty of the enterprise, dead to the transcendent promise of his own time, should have his citizenship in the 21st century revoked. The rest of us need to get to work—on a new space program, revised, revived and back on course.

The Weekly Standard, February 17, 2003

CHAPTER 5

THE DOCTOR IS IN

A Doctor's Duty

Around the world, hearts were broken when news came that the conjoined Bijani twins had died on the operating table. Having lived in tortured unity for 29 years, they traveled from their native Iran to Singapore for the surgery meant to set them free. The doctors who performed it were devastated. When you lose a patient, particularly when the patient dies at your own hand, the heartbreak mixes with unbearable guilt. The doctors are asking themselves the same question everyone else is asking: Should they have done it?

The doctors certainly knew the risk. They knew that, with the women's shared circulatory systems, the risk was great. They might have underestimated the technical challenges, but they did not deceive their patients. The sisters, highly educated and highly motivated, knew full well the risk of never waking up from the surgery.

Indeed, they never did. Should the surgeons have attempted such a risky procedure on patients who were not dying, and, in fact, were not even sick?

For all the regrets and second guesses, it is hard to see how the answer could have been anything but yes. The foundation of the medical vocation is that the doctor is servant to the patient's will. Not always, of course. There are times when the doctor must say no. This was not such a time.

Consider those cases in which outside values trump the patient's expressed desire. The first is life. Even if the patient asks you to, you may not kill him. In some advanced precincts—Holland and Oregon, for example—this is thought to be a quaint idea, and the state permits physicians to perform "assisted suicide." That is a terrible mistake, for the state and for the physician. And not only because it embarks us on a slippery slope where putting people to death in the name of some higher humanity becomes progressively easier.

Even if there were no slippery slope, there is a deeply important principle at stake: Doctors are healers, not killers. You cannot annihilate the subject you are supposedly serving—it is not just a philosophical absurdity, it constitutes the most fundamental violation of the Hippocratic oath. You are not permitted to do any harm to the patient, let alone the ultimate harm.

There are other forms of self-immolation, less instantaneous and less spectacular, to which doctors may not contribute. Drug taking, for example. One could say: The patient wants it, and he knows the risks—why not give him what he wants? No. The doctor is there to help save a suffering soul from the ravages of a failing body. He is not there to ravage a healthy body in the service of a sick and self-destructive soul.

Doctors are not just biotechnicians. They must make judgments about, yes, the soul. Before serving a patient's will, doctors have to decide whether it is perverse and self-destructive. One has to ask what kind of plastic surgeon would repeatedly do his work on Michael Jackson. Or on the Manhattan socialite, known now as the cat woman, who had her face tweaked so many times that it changed inexorably into that of a feline.

Do sex-change operations fall into this category? Some doctors believe that prospective transsexuals really are born into the wrong body; the surgery is therefore corrective. Others argue with equal force that gender dysphoria, as it is known, is a psychiatric affliction and that mutilating the body to fit the afflicted psyche is to inflict a double injury on the patient. The area is gray enough, and the controversy serious enough, to leave the matter, as we have, to the conscience of the individual physician.

But we ought never leave the decision to the individual physician when we come to the two redlines: no assistance in self-destruction (whether gradual or immediate) and no assistance in mutilation.

That is all, however. Beyond that, the patient is sovereign and the physician's duty is to be the servant. Which is why the doctors in Singapore were right to try to separate the twins. They were not seeking self-destruction; they were seeking liberation. And they were trying to undo a form of mutilation imposed on them by nature. The extraordinary thing about their request was that it was so utterly ordinary. They were asking for nothing special, nothing superhuman, nothing radically enhancing of human nature. They were only seeking to satisfy the most simple and pedestrian of desires: to live as single human beings.

The twins suffered from an error of nature, a mistake in individuation. They were asking for nothing more than the possibility of solitude. To risk everything for this was perfectly rational—indeed, an act of nobility and great courage. Their doctors were assisting heroism, not suicide. They should feel no guilt, only sorrow that victory once again went to nature, in all its cruelty.

Time, July 21, 2003

Why Doctors Quit

About a decade ago, a doctor friend was lamenting the increasingly frustrating conditions of clinical practice. "How did you know to get out of medicine in 1978?" he asked with a smile.

"I didn't," I replied. "I had no idea what was coming. I just felt I'd chosen the wrong vocation."

I was reminded of this exchange upon receiving my med-school class' 40th-reunion report and reading some of the entries. In general, my classmates felt fulfilled by family, friends and the considerable achievements of their professional lives. But there was an undercurrent of deep disappointment, almost demoralization, with what medical practice had become.

The complaint was not financial but vocational—an incessant interference with their work, a deep erosion of their autonomy and authority, a transformation from physician to "provider."

As one of them wrote, "My colleagues who have already left practice all say they still love patient care, being a doctor. They just couldn't stand everything else." By which he meant "a never-ending attack on the profession from government, insurance companies, and lawyers ... progressively intrusive and usually unproductive rules and regulations," topped by an electronic health records (EHR) mandate that produces nothing more than "billing and legal documents"—and degraded medicine.

I hear this everywhere. Virtually every doctor and doctors' group I speak to cites the same litany, with particular bitterness about the EHR mandate. As another classmate wrote, "The introduction of the electronic medical record into our office has created so much more need for documentation that I can only see about three-quarters of the patients I could before, and has prompted me to seriously consider leaving for the first time."

You may have zero sympathy for doctors, but think about the extraordinary loss to society—and maybe to you, one day—of driving away 40 years of irreplaceable clinical experience.

And for what? The newly elected Barack Obama told the nation in 2009 that "it just won't save billions of dollars"—$77 billion a year, promised the administration—"and thousands of jobs, it will save lives." He then threw a cool $27 billion at going paperless by 2015.

It's 2015 and what have we achieved? The $27 billion is gone, of course. The $77 billion in savings became a joke. Indeed, reported the Health and Human Services inspector general in 2014, "EHR technology can make it easier to commit fraud," as in Medicare fraud, the copy-and-paste function allowing the instant filling of vast data fields, facilitating billing inflation.

That's just the beginning of the losses. Consider the myriad small practices that, facing ruinous transition costs in equipment, software, training and time, have closed shop, gone bankrupt or been swallowed by some larger entity.

This hardly stays the long arm of the health-care police, however. As of January 1, 2015, if you haven't gone electronic, your Medicare payments will be cut, by 1% this year, rising to 3% (potentially 5%) in subsequent years.

Then there is the toll on doctors' time and patient care. One study in the *American Journal of Emergency Medicine* found that emergency-room doctors spend 43% of their time entering electronic records information, 28% with patients. Another study found that family-practice physicians spend on average 48 minutes a day just entering clinical data.

Forget the numbers. Think just of your own doctor's visits, of how much less listening, examining, even eye contact goes on, given the need for scrolling, clicking and box checking.

The geniuses who rammed this through undoubtedly thought they were rationalizing health care. After all, banking went electronic. Why not medicine?

Because banks deal with nothing but data. They don't listen to your heart or examine your groin. Clicking boxes on an endless electronic form turns the patient into a data machine and cancels out the subtlety of a doctor's unique feel and judgment.

Why did all this happen? Because liberals in a hurry refuse to trust the self-interested wisdom of individual practitioners, who were already adopting EHR on their own, but gradually, organically, as the technology became ripe and the costs tolerable. Instead, Washington picked a date out of a hat and decreed: Digital by 2015.

As with other such arbitrary arrogance, the results are not pretty. EHR is health care's big-government boondoggle. Many, no doubt, feasted nicely on the $27 billion, but the rest is waste: money squandered, patients neglected, good physicians demoralized.

Like my old classmates who signed up for patient care—which they still love—and now do data entry.

The Washington Post, May 29, 2015

Sick, Tired and Not Taking It Anymore

Surgeons in West Virginia have gone on strike to protest the exorbitant cost of malpractice insurance. Good for them. Don't talk to me about the ethics of doctors going on strike. So long as they agree to treat emergency cases, they have as much right to strike as anybody else. The premise of a free market is that people can withhold their labor if they find the conditions under which they work intolerable.

Many doctors do. Many, especially those in the inherently risky specialties, such as surgery or obstetrics, have been forced out of business by malpractice premiums or hounded out by malpractice litigation. A totally irresponsible legal system, driven by a small cadre of lawyers who have hit the mother lode, has produced perhaps the most dysfunctional medical-liability system in the world. Juries hand out millions of dollars not just for lost earnings but also in capricious punitive damages in which the number of zeros attached to the penalty seems to be chosen at random.

As a result, innocent doctors who have devoted their lives to their patients are required to spend tens, even hundreds, of thousands of dollars a year on insurance. In effect, we are making doctors give up an entire chunk of each year laboring just to work off their insurance premiums. Why? To cover for the few offenders in their midst. To compensate the lucky few victims who stumble upon the most profligate juries. And, most important, to make a few trial lawyers very, very rich. (Herewith the requisite full disclosure: I am a doctor, though I no longer practice.)

This is not a hard problem to fix. Tort reform is not rocket science. A reasonable bill passed the House of Representatives just last year but died in the Senate, where the trial-lawyer lobby rules. The elements of a fix are simple: no limit on plaintiffs' lost earnings or other costs, a reasonable cap on pain and suffering ($250,000 in the House bill), a similar cap on punitive damages, serious penalties for frivolous lawsuits.

For years, such remedies have had a tough time getting through legislatures, which are—surprise!—peopled overwhelmingly by lawyers. That is why you have never heard of a lawyers' strike. Lawyers have assured themselves pretty good working conditions. Some of my friends who graduated with me from medical school in the mid-'70s are working 50 to 60 hours a week, almost as hard as they did as interns, just to make ends meet: to pay their rent and nurses and other office expenses on the highly reduced reimbursements they get from HMOs, Medicare and Medicaid. And then a huge part of what is left over goes to pay for malpractice insurance.

But the frustration of doctors is more than a matter of money. The real blow to the profession has been the assault on autonomy. Physicians spend endless days and long years acquiring an extraordinarily specialized skill and then find themselves being told by some 23-year-old HMO administrator a thousand miles away how many minutes they can spend with a patient, how long they can keep him in the hospital and what kind of treatment they are allowed to give him. The introduction of managed care may be societally necessary to keep down costs. But we should at least recognize its cost to the dignity and effectiveness of the profession it regulates. Forgive my obsession here, but lawyers would never put up with faraway bureaucrats dictating their methods and setting their fees.

A doctor wants to strike no more than does a textile worker. But the malpractice burden—indeed, the malpractice threat—is the final assault on the implicit contract society makes with its healers: You give up the best decade of your youth, your 20s, to treat the sick and learn your craft, and we will allow you to practice it with autonomy, dignity and the kind of security—and freedom from capricious victimization—that, oh, say, lawyers enjoy.

Of course there will be medical errors. And there will be medical malefactors. The bad doctors need to be found, punished, defrocked. But why should their sins be paid for by the good doctors among them?

The current system is crazy, ruinous and unfair. And it is easily changed. By lawyers.

Time, January 13, 2003

The Twilight of Psychotherapy

It seems elementary, but a science—like the Party—must have unity, at least in the fundamentals. Chemistry cannot have two periodic tables. Physics will not permit believers in 19th-century ether. Alchemy is not an elective at MIT.

Indeed, perhaps the most important event for the development of a science is the dying away of its schools. Biology could not mature if split between Darwinian and Lamarckian schools of heredity. It was not until that battle was settled—the Lamarckians fell on their swords and were carted away—that biology could take off as a science.

Which brings us to psychotherapy, the science of the talking cure, now turning a ripe 100. Psychotherapy has had quite the opposite development. It opened for business, as it were, a century ago next spring, when Sigmund Freud opened his consulting room at Berggasse 19. What began in one great mind and one great room has proliferated wildly into . . . well, let the Great Phoenix Gathering tell the story.

A few weeks ago in Phoenix an extraordinary conference was held to mark the anniversary of the opening of Freud's office. It was called, optimistically, "The Evolution of Psychotherapy." Seven thousand psychotherapists showed up to see and hear the largest assembly of gurus in history.

It was the greatest concentration of psychotherapeutic talent to gather in one place since Freud dined alone. The leaders of every major school, more than two dozen in all, were there. Rollo May, Bruno Bettelheim, Virginia Satir, R. D. Laing, Carl Rogers. They represented every technique: Freudian therapy, family therapy, behavior therapy, existential therapy. Even Thomas Szasz was there, representing, I suppose, pseudo-therapy, since he believes that mental illness is a myth. (Szasz once outlined his approach to the patient who comes to him and says he is Jesus: "I say he is lying.") For a science, evolution means development toward some deeper unity. This jamboree of jousting sects and one-man shows might more properly have been called the devolution of psychotherapy. It showed what these hundred years have wrought: "a babel of conflicting voices," to quote Joseph Wolpe, a founder of behavior therapy.

Psychotherapy has come upon this state of confusion because, true to its healing, understanding soul, it permits too few deaths among its schools. It is incapable of killing its own. Psychotherapy is dying of dilution.

So what? Business is good and the intellectual ferment brings new techniques ("a new crop every year from California," noted Wolpe wryly) to serve new patients. Who cares whether psychotherapy is a science? Let's see. A few intellectual purists. A few nostalgics, who respect Freud's original vision of psychoanalysis as a scientific technique.

Oh, yes. And one 800-pound gorilla: the insurance companies. As psychotherapy grew more popular, it grew more expensive for insurers. By the mid-'70s, with every psychotherapy school claiming incomparable (in both senses of the word) results, and with bills mounting and premiums rising, insurers began cutting coverage. But finding no way to separate the elite from the quacks, they cut the subsidy to all the schools.

Fifteen years ago in Washington, you could get insurance to cover 80% of unlimited psychotherapy. Around then, when I told a psychiatric colleague (at the time, I was a psychiatrist) that I would be coming to Washington to work for the government, he smiled and said, "Now you can get the Big Tune-up." I was puzzled. He explained: With insurance paying 80% and no limit on visits, why not go for it: five-days-a-week psychoanalysis. Redo the engine.

I answered that my engine felt okay, and I did not want anyone poking around under the hood. But today it wouldn't matter. The Big Tune-up is gone. You can barely get a lube job. Insurers have generally cut coverage to 50%, with severe limits on visits.

As long as psychotherapies resist pressure to produce scientific evidence that they work, the economic squeeze will tighten. After all, if psychotherapy is really an art, it should be supported by the National Endowment, not by Blue Cross.

The first to face economic extinction will be the longer-term therapies, such as, ironically enough, Freudian analysis. Where it ends, though, is not clear. My hope is that society will not totally abandon support for psychotherapy as a form of treatment. In my own experience, some psychotherapies (behavior therapies, in particular) helped my patients, some dramatically. But mine is anecdotal evidence, and there is not a school that cannot produce a bagful of glowing affidavits. What is needed is real science.

Unfortunately, psychotherapy shows little sign that it is inclined to reverse the direction of its disastrous anti-scientific evolution. Phoenix didn't help. In fact, it makes clear that, as an intellectual and perhaps soon as an economic enterprise, psychotherapy in its 100th year is deep into its twilight.

The Washington Post, December 27, 1985

They Die with Their Rights On

In the liberal remake of *Casablanca*, the police captain comes upon the scene of the shooting and orders his men to "round up the usual weapons."

It's always the weapon and never the shooter. Twelve people are murdered in a rampage at the Washington Navy Yard, and before sundown Senator Dianne Feinstein has called for yet another debate on gun violence. Major opprobrium is heaped on the AR-15, the semiautomatic used in the Newtown massacre.

Turns out no AR-15 was used at the Navy Yard. And the shotgun that was used was obtained legally in Virginia after the buyer, Aaron Alexis, had passed both a state and federal background check.

As was the case in the Tucson shooting—instantly politicized into a gun-control and (fabricated) Tea-Party-climate-of-violence issue—the origin of this crime lies not in any politically expedient externality but in the nature of the shooter.

On August 7, that same Alexis had called police from a Newport, Rhode Island, Marriott. He was hearing voices. Three people were following him, he told the cops. They were sending microwaves through walls, making his skin vibrate and preventing him from sleeping. He had already twice changed hotels to escape the men, the radiation, the voices.

Delusions, paranoid ideation, auditory (and somatic) hallucinations: the classic symptoms of schizophrenia.

So here is this panic-stricken soul, psychotic and in terrible distress. And what does modern policing do for him? The cops tell him to "stay away from the individuals that are following him." Then they leave.

But the three "individuals" were imaginary, for God's sake. This is how a civilized society deals with a man in such a state of terror?

Had this happened 35 years ago in Boston, Alexis would have been brought to me as the psychiatrist on duty at the emergency room of the Massachusetts General Hospital. Were he as agitated and distressed as in the police report, I probably would have administered an immediate dose of Haldol, the most powerful fast-acting antipsychotic of the time.

This would generally have relieved the hallucinations and delusions, a blessing not only in itself, but also for the lucidity brought on that would have allowed him to give us important diagnostic details—psychiatric history, family history, social history, medical history, etc. If I had thought he could be sufficiently cared for by family or friends to receive regular oral medication, therapy and follow-up, I would have discharged him. Otherwise, I'd have admitted him. And if he refused, I'd have ordered a 14-day involuntary commitment.

Sounds cruel? On the contrary. For many people living on park benches, commitment means a warm bed, shelter and three hot meals a day. For Alexis, it would have meant the beginning of a treatment regimen designed to bring him back to himself before discharging him to a world heretofore madly radioactive.

That's what a compassionate society does. It would no more abandon this man to fend for himself than it would a man suffering a stroke. And as a side effect, that compassion might even extend to potential victims of his psychosis—in the event, remote but real, that he might someday burst into some place of work and kill 12 innocent people.

Instead, what happened? The Newport police sent their report to the local naval station, where it promptly disappeared into the ether. Alexis subsequently twice visited VA hospital ERs, but without any florid symptoms of psychosis and complaining only of sleeplessness, the diagnosis was missed. (He was given a sleep medication.) He fell back through the cracks.

True, psychiatric care is underfunded and often scarce. But Alexis had full access to the VA system. The problem here was not fiscal but political and, yes, even moral.

I know the civil libertarian arguments. I know that involuntary commitment is outright paternalism. But paternalism is essential for children because they don't have a fully developed rational will. Do you think Alexis was in command of his will that night in Newport?

We cannot, of course, be cavalier about commitment. We should have layers of review, albeit rapid. But it's both cruel and reckless to turn loose people as lost and profoundly suffering as Alexis, even apart from any potential dangerousness.

More than half of those you see sleeping on grates have suffered mental illness. It's a national scandal. It's time we recalibrated the pendulum that today allows the mentally ill to die with their rights on—and, rarely but unforgivably, take a dozen innocents with them.

The Washington Post, September 20, 2013

CHAPTER 6

MATTERS OF LIFE AND DEATH

Five Lives vs. One Principle

Brenda and Michael Winner are going to have a baby in the next few days. By next week, he will almost certainly be dead. He suffers from anencephaly, meaning he will be born with so little brain tissue that he cannot live. The Winners want some good to come out of this tragedy. They want to donate the organs of this doomed child to give life to others. Up to five other children can be made to live from the organs donated by one. But the Winners have had a hard time finding a hospital willing to accommodate them. Only Loma Linda hospital in San Francisco will do what they want.

Why? Because what they want is to remove the heart and lungs and kidneys and liver from their child before he dies. If they wait until he dies, the organs will not be in good enough shape for transplant. Unfortunately, as soon as you take these organs out of the still-living child, he dies immediately. You will have killed him. The dilemma is this: Does it matter if the child dies 24 or 48 hours before he might otherwise, particularly if that act will give life to four or five other kids?

It is a fair question. But it admits only one answer. Yes, it does matter. Loma Linda is wrong. Not because you are prohibited from ever ending a doomed life prematurely. You might do so if you are acting on behalf of the person whose life you are ending. Euthanasia might be justified if done for the benefit—to alleviate the pain and suffering—of the one who is dying.

But in this case the benefit is for others. We run up against the starkest possible test of Kantian versus utilitarian ethics. The utilitarian ethic, summed up by the slogan "the greatest good for the greatest number," would surely permit, indeed dictate, that the dying child be used as an organ donor. The Kantian ethic prohibits using—and certainly killing—one person for the sake of another.

The Kantian ethic is hard to hold to here because it means countenancing the death of organ-needy children in order to up-hold an abstract principle and, in the practical terms of this case, in order to allow a few more hours of life to a doomed child who is barely living in the first place. But the principle is important because to relinquish it is to step into the abyss.

If we can make organ farms of living anencephalics, of which about 3,000 are born every year, why not of irreversibly comatose adults? Karen Ann Quinlan lived for 10 years breathing on her own. Why not cut her up for a heart and a liver? Technology will soon allow us to grow fetuses in test tubes. In *Brave New World*, Aldous Huxley imagined breeding a subclass of babies as drones. Even he did not imagine breeding babies for spare parts. Soon the barrier to doing so will not be technology, only principle.

The Winner case pits the welfare of real kids against that ab-stract principle. But the principle is so basic that even those who want to permit this kind of transplant are driven to deny that they are violating it. They deny that they are killing anyone. They argue instead that because the anencephalic child has no higher brain functions, it is born dead.

This notion of living death is exceedingly dangerous. There are, after all, lots of humans who lack higher brain functions: some newborns with hydrocephaly (water on the brain), old people with severe Alzheimer's (senility), accident victims in irreversible comas. It is one thing to say that such people need not be kept alive by artificial means such as respirators. It is another to say that they may be killed and harvested for organs.

"Living death" means that there are categories of people who are not to be considered human and who may therefore be violated in any way. Iran, not surprisingly, has taken the idea to its most barbaric extreme. Prisoners condemned to death have, prior to execution, had their eyes removed for transplantation to war-injured soldiers.

As of now, only Loma Linda hospital—famous for another adventure in medical ethics, trying a baboon heart in a dying Baby Fae—has acceded to the Winners' request. But as the technology and the utilitarian arguments get more sophisticated, the pressure to organ farm the "living dead" will increase. After a newspaper report of a case identical to the Winners', a bill was introduced in the California Senate that would have declared living anencephalics dead at birth. That bill was later withdrawn, but a similar bill that would permit the transplantation of organs from living anencephalics is still before the New Jersey legislature.

As Professor Alexander Capron, a leading medical ethicist who helped shape our modern definition of death, has argued, this is morally catastrophic. What Loma Linda is doing is the first breach in the principle that one does not use people, however useless their life and imminent their death, as spare parts for others. On the far side of this breach lies *Coma*, the nightmare world of organ farming so ghoulishly depicted by novelist Robin Cook. It is a tragedy that the first line of defense against the nightmare is to say no to the Winners and to the children they want to help. But to say yes is a crime.

The Washington Post, December 11, 1987

Stem Cells: Mounting the Slippery Slope

I favor federal funding of stem cell research, but now I am scared to death—of my allies. The case they (and I) have made is simple: Stem cells, possessing in theory the capacity to replace almost any damaged or defective tissue in the body, have a great potential for good. Although deriving stem cells may require destroying a five-day-old human embryo, this "blastocyst" is usually taken from fertility clinics, where it is going to be discarded anyway. It's not as if—or so we have been saying—we are wantonly creating human embryos only to destroy them for research.

Not so. It turns out the Jones Institute for Reproductive Medicine in Norfolk, Virginia, has been doing exactly that: taking volunteers' sperm and eggs to create a human embryo for the sole purpose of dismembering it for its mother lode of stem cells.

Two things are disturbing here. First, while this research did not become widely known until July 11, it had been reported to fellow scientists back in October. Yet for nine months, stem cell advocates have been repeating the "only discarded embryos" mantra. What did they know, and when did they know it? Second, and equally disturbing, is the stem cell supporters' response to the Norfolk research. John Gearhart, one of the original stem cell pioneers, told the *New York Times* that he was "perplexed" by this development because "we don't think it's necessary."

Unnecessary? Had we not all agreed that it is unethical, a violation of the elementary notion that we don't make of the human embryo a thing—to be made, unmade and used as a mere instrument for others? Dr. Michael Soules of the American Society for Reproductive Medicine was even more appalling. He saw nothing wrong with the procedure, except the "timing." Meaning, I suppose, that it would have been better if this news had remained hidden until President Bush had decided whether to fund stem cell research, believing, falsely, that only discarded embryos were being used.

The other reassurance my side had been giving is that stem cell research is not about cloning. A day after the news from Norfolk we learned that a laboratory in Worcester, Massachusetts (the very same lab that three years ago produced a hybrid human-cow embryo), is trying to grow cloned human embryos to produce stem cells—but could be used to produce a full or (even more ghastly) partial human clone. What other monstrosities are going on that we don't know about?

Yes, some people oppose stem cell research because they believe human life begins at conception. But you don't have to believe that to be apprehensive that stem cell research may legitimize the mechanization of life, the making of the human fetus into the ultimate guinea pig. People are horrified when a virgin hill is strip-mined for coal; how can they be unmoved when a human embryo is created solely to be strip-mined for its parts?

What next? Today a blastocyst is created for harvesting. Tomorrow, researchers may find that a five-month-old fetus with a discernible human appearance, suspended in an artificial placenta, may be the source of even more promising body parts. At what point do we draw the line?

Let's draw it right where it is and hold it. It is a reasonable moral calculus to use and thus derive some good from an already doomed, fertility-clinic blastocyst. Moreover, federal funding would, for the first time, permit the procedure to be regulated.

But if we do decide to give society's imprimatur to stem cell research, it must be with open eyes and a troubled conscience. These new disclosures of human cloning and the creation of embryos for their deliberate destruction are well-timed reminders of how easily moral barriers can be violated. Federal regulation must therefore be strict and unbending.

— No human cloning. At any stage. For any purpose, even research. Congress should criminalize it.

— No embryos created solely to be harvested.

— Stem cell production permitted only from otherwise discarded fertility-clinic embryos or from fetal cadavers.

— A radical increase in federal support for research into adult stem cells, which present fewer moral problems and which might prove to be more genetically stable and controllable than fetal-derived stem cells.

Stem cell research will one day be a boon to humanity. We owe it to posterity to pursue it. But we also owe posterity a moral universe not trampled and corrupted by arrogant, brilliant science. It is precisely because of the glittering promise of stem cell research that we need great care, great vigilance and great restraint as we mount the slippery slope.

Time, July 23, 2001

The Abortion Debate: Just Words

A curious thing has happened to the abortion debate. It remains politically hot, but it is intellectually spent. Everyone seems to know both sides of the argument backward and forward. One reason for the exhaustion is that the abortion issue has been—and will be—decided not by the popular branches of government, Congress or the president, but by the Supreme Court, our system's concession to aristocracy. When the outcome of a struggle bears little relation to public opinion or practical politics, debate becomes increasingly autistic. With little prospect of winning converts, both sides in the abortion debate have turned to capturing words.

Terrorist. Only a few weeks ago it seemed extremely important to pro-abortionists that those who were bombing abortion clinics be called terrorists. The ostensible reason was that using the word would trigger FBI intervention, although the Bureau of Alcohol, Tobacco and Firearms appears to have done a fairly good job of rounding up suspects. The larger aim, of course, was polemical. Everyone hates terrorists. Moreover, anti-abortionists are generally conservative; conservatives make a big point of denouncing terrorism; to find terrorists in their midst would be an acute embarrassment. Touché.

Yet last month, on the weekend of the 12th anniversary of *Roe v. Wade,* activists from the National Organization for Women kept overnight vigil in some abortion clinics. The idea was to deter the bombers by putting people in the buildings after closing hours. But the very definition of a terrorist is someone who is not

112

deterred by the prospect of harming innocents. In fact, he seeks them out in order to magnify the effect of his violence. To hold a vigil at the US Embassy in Beirut, for example, would be a novel, but imprudent, defense against terrorism.

Abolition. More wordplay, this time on the other side. Everyone would like to borrow some of the glory of the anti-slavery movement. Moreover, for the anti-abortion side it offers a delicious irony. Its opponents tend to be liberals, for whom Abolition (and its 20th-century successor, the civil rights movement) is the most hallowed of causes. How better to hoist them than by appropriating their cause and portraying them as having betrayed it? Of course, this is all sleight of hand. Who is to say whether banning a social behavior constitutes Abolition or Prohibition?

Pro-life and *pro-choice.* Wordplay of a high order. It makes the opponent—against either life or choice—a denier of at least one-third of the promises of the Declaration of Independence. At the same time, these words, like all words that mean everything and nothing, are artfully empty. Pacifists, vegetarians, gun controllers, anti-smokers, Mothers Against Drunk Drivers and the air-bag lobby can equally claim the pro-life slogan. And who is against choice? It is hard to think of a cause that is not pro-choice, from legalizing marijuana to abolishing the income tax (contributions to the government to be voluntary). Suppose you are pro-lynching. Why not call yourself pro-choice? (A fair trial or a lynching: Let the people decide.) Until, that is, you are caught and condemned for a lynching. Not wanting to hang, declare yourself then to be pro-life.

Terminating a pregnancy. When the CIA says "terminate" (with or without extreme prejudice), the euphemism is so outrageous as to be comic. "Terminate a pregnancy," on the other hand, has a medical ring that endows abortion with instant moral neutrality. Yet, one really does not have to believe that abortion is murder to know that "terminating a pregnancy" is a different moral proposition from, say, removing a hangnail.

Pre-born. A favorite of Nellie Gray, leader of the March for Life. "Pre-born child" is her way, her only way, I gather, of saying fetus. The technique is to make the distinction between a fetus and a child sound like one of packaging. The point is to rig the debate: If what is at stake is a child—differently boxed, perhaps, but a child nonetheless—the entire abortion issue is nicely foreclosed.

Scream. As in *The Silent Scream*, the anti-abortion film shown Tuesday at the White House. The idea, says the film's producer, Dr. Bernard Nathanson, is to "vault over the tired, stalemated, point-counterpoint" debate—to go beyond words—by showing the ultrasound image of an actual abortion. "Scream" refers to a point in the film in which the fetus' mouth appears to open. Neurologists point out that a fetus at 12 weeks is no more capable of a scream than of experiencing pain. "Perhaps the use of the word scream is a little metaphorical," admits Nathanson. "But there is no question this child is grimacing." No matter. Just words.

Things will get worse. In an exhausted debate, all that's left to do is to rework the words. One side plumbs the lexicon of slavery and Dachau; the other speaks medicalese and clothes its opponents in every variety of political intolerance. There is not the slightest recognition on either side that abortion might be at the limits of our empirical and moral knowledge. The problem starts with an awesome mystery: the transformation of two soulless cells into a living human being. That leads to an insoluble empirical question: How and exactly when does that occur? On that, in turn, hangs the moral issue: What are the claims of the entity undergoing that transformation?

How can we expect such a question to yield answers that are not tentative and indeterminate? So difficult a moral question should command humility, or at least a little old-fashioned tolerance. Instead we get each side claiming truth by linguistic fiat. This is nothing less than a sophisticated form of lying—moral lying perhaps, but lying nonetheless. Well? "Everybody lies," says Stepan in Camus' *The Just Assassins*. "What's important is to lie well."

The Washington Post, February 15, 1985

The Price of Fetal Parts

"Thank you, Planned Parenthood. God bless you."
—*Barack Obama, address to Planned Parenthood, April 26, 2013*

Planned Parenthood's reaction to the release of a clandestinely recorded conversation about the sale of fetal body parts was highly revealing. After protesting that it did nothing illegal, it apologized for the "tone" of one of its senior directors.

Her remarks lacked compassion, admitted Planned Parenthood President Cecile Richards. As if Dr. Deborah Nucatola's cold and casual discussion over salad and wine of how the fetal body can be crushed with forceps in a way that leaves valuable organs intact for sale is some kind of personal idiosyncrasy. On the contrary, it's precisely the kind of psychic numbing that occurs when dealing daily with industrial scale destruction of the growing, thriving, recognizably human fetus.

This was again demonstrated by the release this week of a second video showing another official sporting that same tone, casual and even jocular, while haggling over the price of an embryonic liver. "If it's still low, then we can bump it up," she joked, "I want a Lamborghini."

Abortion critics have long warned that the problem is not only the obvious—what abortion does to the fetus—but also what it does to us. It's the same kind of desensitization that has occurred in the Netherlands with another mass exercise in life termination: assisted suicide. It began as a way to prevent the suffering of the terminally ill. It has now become so widespread and wanton that one-fifth of all Dutch assisted-suicide patients are euthanized without their explicit consent.

The Planned Parenthood revelations will have an effect. Perhaps not on government funding, given the Democratic Party's unwavering support and the president wishing it divine guidance. Planned Parenthood might escape legal jeopardy as well, given the loophole in the law banning the sale of fetal parts that permits compensation for expenses (shipping and handling, as it were).

But these revelations will have an effect on public perceptions. Just as ultrasound altered feelings about abortion by showing the image, the movement, the vibrant living-ness of the developing infant in utero, so too, I suspect, will these Planned Parenthood revelations, by throwing open the door to the backroom of the clinic where that being is destroyed.

It's an ugly scene. The issue is less the sale of body parts than how they are obtained. The nightmare for abortion advocates is a spreading consciousness of how exactly a healthy fetus is turned into a mass of marketable organs, how, in the words of a senior Planned Parenthood official, one might use "a less crunchy technique"—crush the head, spare the organs—"to get more whole specimens."

The effect on the public is a two-step change in sensibilities. First, when ultrasound reveals how human the living fetus appears. Next, when people learn, as in these inadvertent admissions, what killing the fetus involves.

Remember. The advent of ultrasound has coincided with a remarkable phenomenon: Of all the major social issues, abortion is the only one that has not moved toward increasing liberalization. While the legalization of drugs, the redefinition of marriage and other assertions of individual autonomy have advanced, some with astonishing rapidity, abortion attitudes have remained largely static. The country remains evenly split.

What will be the reaction to these Planned Parenthood revelations? Right now, to try to deprive it of taxpayer money. Citizens repelled by its activities should not be made complicit in them. But why not shift the focus from the facilitator to the procedure itself?

The House has already passed a bill banning abortion after 20 weeks. That's far more fruitful than trying to ban it entirely because, apart from the obvious constitutional issue, there is no national consensus about the moral status of the early embryo. There's more agreement on the moral status of the later-term fetus. Indeed, about two-thirds of Americans would ban abortion after the first trimester.

There is more division about the first trimester because one's views of the early embryo are largely a matter of belief, often religious belief. One's view of the later-term fetus, however, is more a matter of what might be called sympathetic identification—seeing the image of a recognizable human infant and, now, hearing from the experts exactly what it takes to "terminate" its existence.

The role of democratic politics is to turn such moral sensibilities into law. This is a moment to press relentlessly for a national ban on late-term abortions.

The Washington Post, July 24, 2015

What to Do for Little Charlie Gard

One cannot imagine a more wrenching moral dilemma than the case of little Charlie Gard. He is a beautiful 11-month-old boy with an incurable genetic disease. It depletes his cells' energy-producing structures (the mitochondria), thereby progressively ravaging his organs. He cannot hear, he cannot see, he can barely open his eyes. He cannot swallow, he cannot move, he cannot breathe on his own. He suffers from severe epilepsy, and his brain is seriously damaged. Doctors aren't even sure whether he can feel pain.

For months he's been at the Great Ormond Street Hospital in London. His doctors have recommended removing him from life support.

His parents are deeply opposed. They have repeatedly petitioned the courts to allow them to take Charlie for experimental treatment in the United States.

The courts have denied the parents' petition. They concluded that the proposed treatment had no chance of saving the child and would do nothing but inflict upon him further suffering. They did, however, allow the American specialist to come to London to examine Charlie. He is giving his findings to the court. A final ruling is expected on July 25.

The Telegraph of London reports that Charlie's doctors remain unconvinced by the American researcher. Indeed, the weight of the evidence appears to support the doctors and the courts. Charlie's genetic variant is different and far more devastating than the ones in which nucleoside bypass therapy has shown some improvement. There aren't even animal models for treating Charlie's condition. It's extremely unlikely that treatment can even reach Charlie's brain cells, let alone reverse the existing damage.

The parents have garnered support from thousands of petitioners and from such disparate luminaries as the pope and the president of the United States, both of whom have offered to bring Charlie to their facilities.

What to do? There is only one real question: What's best for Charlie? But because he can't speak for himself, we resort to a second question: Who is to speak for him?

The most heart-rending situation occurs when these two questions yield opposing answers. Charlie's is such a case.

Let me explain.

In my view, two truths must guide any decision: (1) The parents must be sovereign, but (2) the parents are sometimes wrong.

I believe that in this case the parents are wrong, and the doctors and judges are right. Charlie's suffering is literally unimaginable and we are simply prolonging it. This is a life of no light, no sound, no motion, only moments of physical suffering (seizures? intubation?) to punctuate the darkness. His doctors understandably believe that allowing a natural death is the most merciful thing they can do for Charlie.

As for miracle cures, I share the court's skepticism. They always arise in such cases, and invariably prove to be cruel deceptions.

And yet. Despite all these considerations, I would nevertheless let the parents take their boy where they wish.

The sovereignty of loved ones must be the overriding principle that guides all such decisions. We have no other way. The irreducible truth is that these conundrums have no definitive answer. We thus necessarily fall back on family or, to put it more sentimentally, on love.

What is best for the child? The best guide is a loving parent. A parent's motive is the most pure.

This rule is not invariable, of course. Which is why the state seizes control when parents are demonstrably injurious, even if unintentionally so, as in the case of those who, for some religious imperative, would deny their child treatment for a curable disease.

But there's a reason why, despite these exceptions, all societies grant parents sovereignty over their children until they reach maturity. Parents are simply more likely than anyone else to act in the best interest of the child.

Not always, of course. Loved ones don't always act for the purest of motives. Heirs, for example, may not the best guide as to when to pull the plug on an elderly relative with a modest fortune.

But then again, states can have ulterior motives too. In countries where taxpayers bear the burden of expensive treatments, the state has an inherent incentive (of which Britain's National Health Service has produced notorious cases) to deny treatment for reasons of economy rather than mercy.

Nonetheless, as a general rule, we trust in the impartiality of the courts—and the loving imperative of the parent.

And if they clash? What then? If it were me, I would detach the tubes and cradle the child until death. But it's not me. It's not the NHS. And it's not the European Court of Human Rights.

It's a father and a mother and their desperate love for a child. They must prevail. Let them go.

The Washington Post, July 21, 2017

PART II

MAN AND SOCIETY

CHAPTER 7

LOOK OUTWARD

Three Pieces of Sage Advice

An Address to McGill
University's Class of 1993

I

Exactly 23 years ago, in this very building, I was sitting in your seat. What I shall offer you today is a reconnaissance report from a two-decade life expedition into the world beyond McGill College Avenue. Like Marco Polo, I return—without silk, but with three pieces of sage advice.

Lesson one: Don't lose your head. I'm speaking here of intellectual fashion, of the alarming regularity with which the chattering classes, that herd of independent minds, are swept away by the periodic enthusiasms that wash over the culture.

Only a decade ago, for example, the West was seized with a near mass hysteria about imminent nuclear apocalypse. Tens of millions of my countrymen, including the intellectuals who should have known better, were in the grip of a nuclear anxiety attack. The airwaves, the bookstores, the Congress were filled with dire warnings about our headlong dash to the nuclear abyss. It was quite a scene.

A political movement rose to avert the End. It was the nuclear freeze movement and its slogan was "The freeze: Because no one wants a nuclear war," as if those who resisted the freeze were in favor of nuclear war. Indeed, those who refused to lose their heads to the hysteria were diagnosed as suffering from some psychological disorder. "Nuclearism," "psychic numbing" it was called.

Ten years later, with nuclear weapons still capable of destroying the world many times over—not a word about the coming apocalypse. The fever has passed.

But not the propensity for fever. Another day, another fever. With the end of the Cold War, with nuclear apocalypse now out of fashion, the vacuum is filled by eco-catastrophists predicting a coming doomsday of uncontrollable pollution, overpopulation and resource depletion.

Some prefer their catastrophes more mundane. For them there is economic apocalypse. It is hard to think of a time when the best-seller list did not feature a *Crash of Nineteen-something* book. The idea is the same. Only the date gets pushed back.

Do not misunderstand. There is a nuclear problem, especially in the form of nuclear proliferation. There are environmental problems. And every society has economic problems. But there is a difference between a problem and panic.

So the next time you find yourself in the midst of some national hysteria with sensible people losing their heads, with legislatures in panic and with the media buying it all and amplifying it with a kind of megaphone effect, remember this:

Remember that a people—even the most sensible people—can all lose their heads at once.

Remember the tulip craze that swept Holland three centuries ago, an orgy of panicked financial speculation in which, as historian Simon Schama tells it, "tracts of land, houses, silver and gold vessels and fine furniture were all commonly traded" for tulips. At the mania's peak, a single Semper Augustus tulip could fetch 20 townhouses.

Remember that when the people or the legislature or the media approve something with unanimity, they're probably wrong. Remember the Gulf of Tonkin resolution which essentially launched the United States into the Vietnam war. It passed the US Senate 88 to 2. It passed the House 410 to 0. That should have been a warning.

In the old Soviet Union, where the commissars would routinely rewrite and rearrange history to fit their political needs, there was a saying: In Russia, it is impossible to predict the past. In Israel, at the time of hyperinflation some years ago, it was said: In Israel, it was impossible to predict the present. Well, in the normal, bourgeois, middle-class, democratic West, one should say, when confronted with the apocalypse du jour: Here it is impossible to predict the future. So when confronted with a national riot of dread: Keep your head.

II

Lesson two: Look outward. By that I mean: Don't look inward too much. You have been taught—rightly taught—Socrates' dictum that the unexamined life is not worth living. Yet I would add: Beware the too-examined life.

Perhaps previous ages suffered from a lack of self-examination. The Age of Oprah does not. Our problem is quite the opposite.

One of the defining features of modernity is self-consciousness:

psychological self-consciousness as popularized by Freud; historical self-consciousness as introduced by Hegel and Marx; literary self-consciousness as practiced in the interior, self-absorbed, self-referential world of modern fiction.

We live in an age in which the highest moral injunction is to get in touch with one's feelings. Speaking as a psychiatrist—well, a psychiatrist in remission—I can assure you that this is a highly overrated pursuit.

The reigning cliché of the day is that in order to love others one must first learn to love oneself. This formulation—love thyself, then thy neighbor—is a license for unremitting self-indulgence, because the quest for self-love is endless. By the time you have finally learned to love yourself, you'll find yourself playing golf at Leisure World, having outlived those you might have loved.

"Love thy neighbor" was supposed to be the hard part of the biblical injunction. Sometimes it seems as if all of America is working on the "thyself" part—almost a definition of narcissism.

This obsession with self-regard has deeply affected modern pedagogy. A recent international study compared the mathematical proficiency of 13-year-olds in six advanced countries. The United States ranked last in mathematical ability, Korea first. The kids were then asked to rate how good they thought they were at math. The Americans were number one.

They couldn't add, but they felt good about themselves. In other words, they were a modern pedagogical success, the principal aim of primary education today being to instill students with self-esteem. Reading, maybe. Writing, perhaps. Arithmetic, someday. But self-esteem above all. There seems to be no conception that perhaps self-esteem follows achievement. It is what comes with a sense of mastery.

The story is told of the Sultan who awoke in the middle of the night and summoned his wizard. "Wizard," he said, "my sleep is troubled. Tell me: What is holding up the earth?"

"Majesty," replied the wizard, "the earth rests on the back of a giant elephant."

The Sultan was satisfied and went back to sleep. He then awoke in a cold sweat and called the wizard back immediately. "Wizard," he said, "what's holding up the elephant?"

The wizard looked at him and said, "The elephant stands on the back of a giant turtle. And you can stop right there, Majesty. It's turtles all the way down."

My friends, don't get lost in the study of turtles. Endless, vertiginous self-examination leads not only to a sterile moral life, but to a stilted intellectual life. Yes, examine if you must. But do it with dispatch and modesty and then get on with it. The dictum for this age should not be that the unexamined life is not worth living, but rather that the un-lived life is not worth examining. So go out and live: Act and go and seek and do. Save the psychic impact report, the memoirs and the motives for later. There will be time enough.

III

Which brings us to lesson three: When you do act and go and seek, what to do? Everything. But above all this: Save the best.

Conserving what's best in the past is, well, conservative advice. It was the advice of G. K. Chesterton, who defined tradition as the democracy of the dead. Tradition is the ultimate democracy because it extends the franchise to generations past and benefits from their hard-earned wisdom.

Now, in this country, in this city, and at this great university, saving the best means something very particular. It means saving your remarkable and almost unprecedented historical achievement in ethnic coexistence.

North America offers the world two models for ethnic coexistence. The American model is the melting pot, where all are supposed to be turned into Americans upon arrival at Ellis Island. Canada, a different place with a different history, offers a different model. It offers the model of shared sovereignty between two constituent peoples who have learned to live in sometimes fractious but respectful and fruitful proximity.

But what the American and Canadian models share—and what is so often overlooked amid the inevitable imperfections of this blessed continent—is their success. It is no accident that when boat people are found floating on some distant sea their preferred destination is almost invariably North America. Not just because of its prosperity. Not just because of its democracy. But because of its ethnic harmony. We have figured out how to live together without raging ethnic strife.

I find it deeply moving that today in the Bosnian town of Srebrenica, where 20,000 Muslims are surrounded by Orthodox Christian Serbs, where peoples that have lived in proximity to each other for centuries are now at each other's throats— in Srebrenica, that symbol of ethnic intolerance, there are today 300 Canadian soldiers sheltering the innocent. Soldiers from a country that might have been a Yugoslavia, serving as protectors in a country that is Yugoslavia.

I wish to encourage you to cherish the coexistence—no, not the coexistence, the mutual enhancement—that characterizes our countries. It is a legacy not to be thrown away. In the United States, there are those who are prepared to throw away the traditional, successful, American approach to ethnic diversity and begin counting by race. It is a dangerous and thoughtless course that we will one day regret with Balkan intensity.

Similarly the Canadian solution of dignified, respectful if sometimes disputatious coexistence between two great peoples is one too precious to be thrown away.

Save the best.

Look outward.

Don't lose your head.

End of sermon. Now go out and change the world.

Adapted from the author's commencement address at
McGill University, Montreal, Canada, June 14, 1993

CHAPTER 8

AGAINST THE GRAIN

Apocalypse, with and without God

It is not enough that the murderous ravings of David Koresh and his apocalyptic religious cult have turned into a terrible human tragedy. There seems to be a great desire to turn it into a cultural statement. The siege at Waco has occasioned a worldwide festival of commentary—and condescension—on the subject of American primitivism. An Israeli TV interviewer asked me to explain to his audience why it is that America seems to throw up these weird religious cults at such regular intervals. I pointed out that Israel sports the *Ateret Hacohanim*, a group of believers so convinced of the imminence of the Messiah who will rebuild the Temple of Solomon that they spend their days studying the ancient laws of animal sacrifice. That way they'll be—as we say—ready on Day 1.

Tut-tutting about American primitivism mixes easily with that other sport, eye rolling about religious primitivism. You know: There go those religious nuts again. In keeping with a popular culture that gives serious religion no attention but devotes endless prime time to crooked, hypocritical and otherwise deformed religiosity, the Waco wackos are getting more coverage in a week than religion does in a year.

A front-page story in the *Washington Post* looked for deeper trends. "The United States has become a land echoing with the rumble of apocalyptic prophecy," it reported on Day 5 of the siege. And the phenomenon is ecumenical: "The anticipation extends across religious lines."

True enough. But it also extends *beyond* religious lines. What the endless media chatter about the Koresh phenomenon misses completely is that millenarian thinking is hardly the property of the religious. Indeed, the most widespread and historically significant outbreaks of millenarianism in our time have been secular.

For the past half-century more than a quarter of the earth's people were controlled by political movements whose pursuit of the millennium was as fanatical as that of their religious counterparts—and far more destructive. Soviet, Cambodian, Korean, Chinese communists relentlessly drove their people to extremes of privation and repression in order to hasten the arrival of full-fledged "communism," the millennium as foretold by that 19th-century prophet Karl Marx.

In 1958, for example, Mao decided to skip the intermediate stages of "socialist construction" and go right to full communism. He called it the Great Leap Forward. It would take a million David Koreshes to kill the number of Chinese who perished (through famine, forced labor and civil unrest) to satisfy that lunge for the millennium. Two decades later, the Khmer Rouge murdered more than a million of their countrymen in an attempt, explained Khieu Samphan, to "reach total communism with one leap forward." Has any religious vision occasioned more human sacrifice than "total communism"?

As for the US, there are a handful of people who believe Koresh's loony speculations about the end of the world. But not a decade ago, tens of millions of Americans, including many who should have known better, were in the grip of a national anxiety attack about nuclear apocalypse. Jonathan Schell's panicked anticipation of nuclear destruction, modestly titled *The Fate of the Earth*, was rapturously received. *The Day After*, a re-creation of the End, was the TV event of the year. Psychologists were dispatched to help kids deal with its anticipated psychological fallout. Hundreds of thousands took to observing "Ground Zero Week," which featured the loving re-creation of every detail of the apocalypse—in the weird expectation that rehearsing the End would prevent it. Those who refused to join the hysteria were diagnosed as suffering from "nuclearism" or "psychic numbing."

With the end of the Cold War, nuclear apocalypticism has gone out of fashion. The vacuum is amply filled by the eco-catastrophists. The late '60s featured Paul Ehrlich's huge best-seller, *The Population Bomb*, an astonishingly wrongheaded prediction of the End brought on by overpopulation—by 1983. In the '70s, the Club of Rome predicted, with hilarious imprecision, a coming doomsday of uncontrollable pollution, wild overpopulation and resource depletion (by 1992, for example, no oil).

Today Al Gore writes a best seller warning that if environmentalism does not become "our new organizing principle," then "the very survival of our civilization will be in doubt." And "the potential for true catastrophe lies in the future, but the downslope that pulls us toward it is becoming recognizably steeper with each passing year." Familiar, isn't it? The yawning chasm—accompanied, as for every apocalypse, by the death struggle between the forces of light and the forces of darkness: "We now face the prospect of a kind of global civil war between those who refuse to consider the consequences of civilization's relentless advance and those who refuse to be silent partners in the destruction."

Some prefer their catastrophes more mundane. For them we have economic apocalypse. It is hard to think of a time when the best-seller list did not feature a *Crash of Nineteen-something* book.

A few years ago, it was *The Crash of '79*. Then *The Panic of '89*. (Same author!) Then the *Bankruptcy 1995*. The idea is the same. Only the date gets pushed back.

The apocalypse recedes. Yet its fascination endures. It is fine to look down one's nose at Waco. But Bible-thumping psychopaths hold no monopoly on belief in the End. Before casting stones at the easy targets, a secular society might reflect on its own ample appetite for apocalypse.

Time, March 22, 1993

When Modern Medicine Fails

I n the movie *Sleeper*, Woody Allen wakes up a couple of hundred years in the future to discover, among other things, that scientists have found that tobacco is actually good for you.

Well, not quite yet. But how about eggs? After years of egg phobia, we have learned that eggs may not be bad for you after all. And that butter is healthier than stick margarine. Every month, it seems, some accepted nutritional fact is overturned.

We have come to expect that diet fashions, though promulgated with scientific authority, change like the seasons. What we do not expect is a change in hormone fashions. Hence the shock this week when a massive study of hormone replacement therapy in postmenopausal women had to be halted three years early because the estrogen-progestin combination appeared to cause an alarming increase in invasive breast cancer, blood clots, strokes and heart attacks.

With that, the decades-old medical axiom about the protective powers of hormonal therapy was overturned in a flash. The reverberations were immediate. The company whose pill was being tested, Wyeth Pharmaceutical, lost 24% of its value in one day. Millions of women are now frantically calling their doctors for advice on whether to continue.

Most shocking, perhaps, is the simple reminder of how contingent are the received truths of modern medicine. We know how pre-modern medicine got it wrong, from centuries of leeching and bleeding to the lobotomies and shock therapies that destroyed the lives of so many psychiatric patients in the mid-20th century. But we think of modern science as infinitely more enlightened and more solid.

Not so. Less than a century ago, the most exalted scientific theory, Newtonian mechanics, was overthrown. Today its successors, general relativity and quantum mechanics, have yet to be fully reconciled. Thirty years ago, the scientific consensus was that we were headed for global cooling. Today it is global warming. The only thing I feel reasonably sure about is that 30 years from now meteorological science will have delivered yet a new theory, a new threat, a new thrall.

The problem is that even the most sophisticated scientific studies are limited by method, by modeling, by sampling and by an inevitable margin of error. Hence error and revision.

In medicine, because its solemn pronouncements are so widely propagated and so ingrained in people's lives, these revisions are particularly shocking. Yet common. When I was a kid, everyone got a tonsillectomy. It was a rite of passage. We now know that this was unnecessary surgery, indeed, worse than useless. We also routinely were given antibiotics for earaches. It now turns out that this did not hasten recovery, and in fact may have made us, and the population in general, more resistant to antibiotics.

For decades, breast cancer was treated with radical mastectomy, a disfiguring and deeply invasive surgery. The idea that many patients should instead be treated with lumpectomy was ridiculed for decades. It is now accepted medical practice.

My favorite myth is 98.6. If there was anything solid in my medical education, it was that mean body temperature was 98.6 degrees Fahrenheit. Well, in 1992 the *Journal of the American Medical Association* published a study that actually measured it. It turns out to be 98.2 degrees. Where did the 98.6 come from?

From the German doctor Carl Wunderlich. In 1868. No one had bothered to check it since then.

The myths go on and on. That infectious diseases had been conquered. (Then came HIV.) That asthma is a psychological condition. That ulcers are caused by stress or stomach acid. For decades at mid-century, at the height of the psychoanalytic fad, the cream of the New York intelligentsia was sending its healthy children to five-day-a-week psychoanalysis.

So much nonsense. So much damage. Yet science has a hard time with humility. The rage today is regenerative medicine. Stem cells. Cloning. The growing, essentially, of replacement parts. It sounds wonderful, and it may yet turn out to be.

It is well to remember, however, that this is not the first panacea to be peddled. Yesterday, it was fetal tissue transplants for degenerative diseases and angiogenesis inhibitors for the cure of cancer. All of which looked wonderful on paper but have not panned out.

This is not to say that this embryonic research will not pan out. It is only to say that when you hear Senator Dianne Feinstein tell you that the research cloning her bill would promote will do wonders for your suffering Aunt Sarah, hold on to your wallet. She's talking about the speculative benefits from the most speculative of new technologies—at a time when, until yesterday, science could not tell us the effects of *existing* postmenopausal hormone therapy on *known* medical conditions.

For now, I'll put my money on Woody Allen. *Sleeper* discovers that hot-fudge sundaes turn out to be good for you too.

The Washington Post, July 12, 2002

The Myth of "Settled Science"

I repeat: I'm not a global warming believer. I'm not a global warming denier. I've long believed that it cannot be good for humanity to be spewing tons of carbon dioxide into the atmosphere. I also believe that those scientists who pretend to know exactly what this will cause in 20, 30 or 50 years are white-coated propagandists.

"The debate is settled," asserted propagandist-in-chief Barack Obama in his latest State of the Union address. "Climate change is a fact." Really? There is nothing more anti-scientific than the very idea that science is settled, static, impervious to challenge. Take a non-climate example. It was long assumed that mammograms help reduce breast cancer deaths. This fact was so settled that Obamacare requires every insurance plan to offer mammograms (for free, no less) or be subject to termination.

Now we learn from a massive randomized study—90,000 women followed for 25 years—that mammograms may have no effect on breast cancer deaths. Indeed, one out of five of those diagnosed by mammogram receives unnecessary radiation, chemo or surgery.

So much for settledness. And climate is less well understood than breast cancer. If climate science is settled, why do its predictions keep changing? And how is it that the great physicist Freeman Dyson, who did some climate research in the late 1970s, thinks today's climate-change Cassandras are hopelessly mistaken?

They deal with the fluid dynamics of the atmosphere and oceans, argues Dyson, ignoring the effect of biology, i.e., vegetation and topsoil. Further, their predictions rest on models they fall in love with: "You sit in front of a computer screen for 10 years and you start to think of your model as being real." Not surprisingly, these models have been "consistently and spectacularly wrong" in their predictions, write atmospheric scientists Richard McNider and John Christy—and always, amazingly, in the same direction.

Settled? Even Britain's national weather service concedes there's been no change—delicately called a "pause"—in global temperature in 15 years. If even the raw data is recalcitrant, let alone the assumptions and underlying models, how settled is the science?

But even worse than the pretense of settledness is the cynical attribution of any politically convenient natural disaster to climate change, a clever term that allows you to attribute anything—warming and cooling, drought and flood—to man's sinful carbon burning.

Accordingly, Obama ostentatiously visited drought-stricken California last Friday. Surprise! He blamed climate change. Here even the *New York Times* gagged, pointing out that far from being supported by the evidence, "the most recent computer projections suggest that as the world warms, California should get wetter, not drier, in the winter."

How inconvenient. But we've been here before. Hurricane Sandy was made the poster child for the alleged increased frequency and strength of "extreme weather events" like hurricanes.

Nonsense. Sandy wasn't even a hurricane when it hit the United States. Indeed, in all of 2012, only a single hurricane made US landfall. And 2013 saw the fewest Atlantic hurricanes in 30 years. In fact, in the last half-century, one-third fewer major hurricanes have hit the United States than in the previous half-century.

Similarly tornadoes. Every time one hits, the climate-change commentary begins. Yet last year saw the fewest in a quarter-century. And the last 30 years—of presumed global warming—has seen a 30% decrease in extreme tornado activity (F3 and above) versus the previous 30 years.

None of this is dispositive. It doesn't settle the issue. But that's the point. It mocks the very notion of settled science, which is nothing but a crude attempt to silence critics and delegitimize debate. As does the term "denier"—an echo of Holocaust denial, contemptibly suggesting the malevolent rejection of an established historical truth.

Climate-change proponents have made their cause a matter of fealty and faith. For folks who pretend to be brave carriers of the scientific ethic, there's more than a tinge of religion in their jeremiads. If you whore after other gods, the Bible tells us, "the Lord's wrath be kindled against you, and he shut up the heaven, that there be no rain, and that the land yield not her fruit" (Deuteronomy 11).

Sounds like California. Except that today there's a new god, the Earth Mother. And a new set of sins—burning coal and driving a fully equipped F-150.

But whoring is whoring, and the gods must be appeased. So if California burns, you send your high priest (in carbon-belching Air Force One, but never mind) to the bone-dry land to offer up, on behalf of the repentant congregation, a $1 billion burnt offering called a "climate resilience fund."

Ah, settled science in action.

The Washington Post, February 21, 2014

Thought Police on Patrol

Two months ago, a petition bearing more than 110,000 signatures was delivered to the *Washington Post*, demanding a ban on any article questioning global warming. The petition arrived the day before publication of my column, which consisted of precisely that heresy.

The column ran as usual. But I was gratified by the show of intolerance because it perfectly illustrated my argument that the left is entering a new phase of ideological agitation—no longer trying to win the debate but stopping debate altogether, banishing from public discourse any and all opposition.

The proper word for that attitude is totalitarian. It declares certain controversies over and visits serious consequences—from social ostracism to vocational defenestration—upon those who refuse to be silenced.

Sometimes the word comes from on high, as when the president of the United States declares the science of global warming to be "settled." Anyone who disagrees is then branded "anti-science." And better still, a "denier"—a brilliantly chosen calumny meant to impute to the climate skeptic the opprobrium normally reserved for the hatemongers and crackpots who deny the Holocaust.

Then last week, another outbreak. The newest closing of the leftist mind is on gay marriage. Just as the science of global warming is settled, so, it seems, are the moral and philosophical merits of gay marriage.

To oppose it is nothing but bigotry, akin to racism. Opponents are to be similarly marginalized and shunned, destroyed personally and professionally.

Like the CEO of Mozilla who resigned under pressure just 10 days into his job when it was disclosed that six years earlier he had donated to California's Proposition 8, which defined marriage as between a man and a woman.

But why stop with Brendan Eich, the victim of this high-tech lynching? Prop 8 passed by half a million votes. Six million Californians joined Eich in the crime of "privileging" traditional marriage. So did Barack Obama. In that same year, he declared that his Christian beliefs made him oppose gay marriage.

Yet under the new dispensation, this is outright bigotry. By that logic, the man whom the left so ecstatically carried to the White House in 2008 was equally a bigot.

The whole thing is so stupid as to be unworthy of exegesis. There is no logic. What's at play is sheer ideological prejudice—and the enforcement of the new totalitarian norm that declares, unilaterally, certain issues to be closed.

Closed to debate. Open only to intimidated acquiescence.

To this magic circle of forced conformity, the left would like to add certain other policies, resistance to which is deemed a "war on women." It's a colorful synonym for sexism. Leveling the charge is a crude way to cut off debate.

Thus, to oppose late-term abortion is to make war on women's "reproductive health." Similarly, to question Obamacare's mandate of free contraception for all.

Some oppose the regulation because of its impingement on the free exercise of religion. Others on the simpler (nontheological) grounds of a skewed hierarchy of values. Under the new law, everything is covered, but a few choice things are given away free. To what does contraception owe its exalted status? Why should it rank above, say, antibiotics for a sick child, for which that same mother must co-pay?

Say that, however, and you are accused of denying women "access to contraception."

Or try objecting to the new so-called Paycheck Fairness Act for women, which is little more than a full-employment act for trial lawyers. Sex discrimination is already illegal. What these new laws do is relieve the plaintiffs of proving intentional discrimination. To bring suit, they need only to show that women make less in that workplace.

Like the White House, where women make 88 cents to the men's dollar?

That's called "disparate impact." Does anyone really think Obama consciously discriminates against female employees, rather than the disparity being a reflection of experience, work history, etc.? But just to raise such questions is to betray heretical tendencies.

The good news is that the "war on women" charge is mostly cynicism, fodder for campaign-year demagoguery. But the trend is growing. Oppose the current consensus and you're a denier, a bigot, a homophobe, a sexist, an enemy of the people.

Long a staple of academia, the totalitarian impulse is spreading. What to do? Defend the dissenters, even if—perhaps, especially if—you disagree with their policy. It is—it was?—the American way.

The Washington Post, April 11, 2014

CHAPTER 9

THE TOO-EXAMINED LIFE

Suicide ad Absurdum

On July 10, 1979, alone and off-camera, Jo Roman, a New York artist, killed herself with an overdose of sleeping pills. It was not an impulsive act. As early as 1975, she had made up her mind that she would end her life on her own terms, purposefully and "rationally." Several years later, when she learned that she had breast cancer, she moved up the date. She would do it within a year, she decided, and proceeded to tell friends, family and a TV film crew. Thus began a drama that culminated in a sensational front-page story in the *New York Times* and a harrowing one-hour documentary entitled *Choosing Suicide* that aired June 16 on PBS.

The documentary is a faithful record of the gatherings Jo held during that year to prepare for her great deed. It records the deliberations of a Greek chorus of chosen literati and hapless family relations drawn into her web as co-conspirators, spectators and participants. At these meetings, all sit in the obligatory circle. Jo, the queen bee, presides. She is quiet, controlled, in command. She is experiencing no pain or disability, but her mind is made up. No one can change her resolve, but all "acknowledge" and "respect" her feelings. There is much touching, hugging, crying and stroking. No one seems distracted by the bobbing microphones and clanking camera stands.

All the while, I am trying to figure out why they are all there. The film crew, I suppose, thinks that if she delivers they've got a hot property and, if it is done with taste, maybe an Emmy. Friends and family must feel the weight of the contemporary obligation to "be there" and share the experience. And how do you turn down an invitation to a suicide?

But what's in it for Jo? Perhaps, like Tom Sawyer, she simply wants to live the fantasy of attending, indeed directing, her own wake. Jo herself invokes loftier motives with more decidedly romantic pretensions: She considers this act a work of art, "the final brush stroke on the canvas of my life." It is a claim taken with utmost seriousness by her friends, who seem to believe that art is anything that artists do (and then proceed to frame). "This is the greatest creative act of your life," gushes one friend. An unkind reviewer, taking note of Jo's paintings and sculptures strewn around the apartment, might concur with this judgment. And because it is art, Jo Roman's son can assure her that rational suicide is not something he would recommend for the masses. He has told his friends and co-workers of Jo's plans, he says, but they are all into apple pie, baseball and religion, and they don't understand.

The masses, I infer, could begin to understand the angry crash into the highway abutment, the impulsive leap from the apartment window. They could begin to understand the everyday anguished acts of self-destruction full of killing and pain and suffering. What they would find difficult to understand is the bloodless, careless, motiveless, meaningless art of Jo Roman's rational suicide. Jo's friends, however, are awed by her innovation. After all, one friend comments, we need something more dignified than sidewalk splatter (as passé as action painting, I suppose). And Jo, in a burst of creativity, has given them the ultimate soufflé, the stylish alternative to such crude gaucheries, the artistic way to end it all. She has produced the last word in sophistication: the meticulously orchestrated, thoroughly psychoanalyzed, faithfully filmed, yearlong death watch.

Jo has other reasons for suicide besides art. She and her flock coo responsively about how all this has brought them closer together, put them in touch with their own feelings, given them a profound "learning experience." In an interview taped 12 days after Jo's death, husband Mel, looking grave and lost, reflects on how the whole year leading up to Jo's death caused him great pain and suffering. But it has been worthwhile, he says, because he has learned a lot about himself. I found this a particularly sad sight: a grown man in his bereavement seeking solace in the shallowest cliché of adolescent solipsism—the world as an instrument of one's own education. It marked the moment in the show when the banality finally transcended the pathos.

Jo herself occasionally gropes for some deeper philosophic justification for her act. She proclaims suicide as the enricher and clarifier of life. Her friends stroke her hand and nod sagely in the classic group therapy mode, but I have no idea what she meant. Another group favorite was the idea that Jo is "taking control of her own life," taking responsibility for herself, finishing a job she started. They congratulate Jo for preempting God or cancer and taking her own life. In their preoccupation with the agency of her act, however, they avoid the question of its consequences. And the documentary shows us just what these consequences are: feelings of acute loss for her friends, pain and suffering for her loved ones, bewilderment and self-doubt for her husband. When one of the pernicious seeds of her act begins to flower before her eyes—when her daughter, who also has had cancer, begins to contemplate her own suicide—Jo sees not horror but raised consciousness.

Our usual response to a victim of suicide is, as Pasternak says, to "bow compassionately before [his] suffering" because "what finally makes him kill himself is not the firmness of his resolve but the unbearable quality of his anguish." Jo Roman, however, denies us our compassion because she denies herself her anguish. She opens the film looking into the camera and calmly proclaiming that her suicide, unlike others, does not involve killing and hurting, but is a reasoned response to her life. But her very coldness persuades us that we are watching not a suicide but a murder. This is why we experience not sorrow but emptiness, why we feel not pity but anger.

The anger is directed both at the murderer and at her mesmerized accomplices. A protesting voice is difficult to find. One friend says to her "I can't understand you. If someone say at age 75 said to me 'I have arthritis and I can't type'—O.K. I can understand that, but you. . . ." Can't type! What next? Suicide as the answer to a lost backhand? To a clogged Cuisinart? The anger turns to bewilderment. What happens when these people are threatened by something worse than pain or age or travail? What happens when their children or their values are threatened? Is their reward for sophistication a capacity for self-delusion so prodigious as to turn cowardice into courage, death into creativity and suicide into art?

Not that voluntary death is either new or necessarily eccentric. History contains many acts of voluntary death from Socrates and Christ to the mother who gives up her seat on the lifeboat for her child. But they died for truth or salvation or love. They died for more than a dose of good feelings or artistic conceit. What is most pathetic about Jo Roman's death is that, in her enervated and alienated circle, she died for the illusion that her death would express some transcendent reality. Like the Dadaists, she believed that her life and death were art. But at least the Dadaists were under no illusion. They considered both equally worthless.

Choosing Suicide is disturbing because it leaves us with the feeling that the Dadaists were right after all. For all its voguish psychobabble and pseudophilosophic paradoxes, this documentary leaves us with one conviction: that on the altar of her savage household gods—art, growth, feeling, control, creativity—Jo Roman died for nothing.

The New Republic, July 5, 1980

Holiday: Living on a Return Ticket

August is holiday time. France heads for the beach, Congress for home and psychiatry for the asylum of Truro on Cape Cod. What makes for a holiday? Not time off from work. That happens on weekends, and no one calls that a holiday. Nor merely leaving home. That happens on business trips. Ask Willy Loman. On holiday one escapes more than work or home. One leaves oneself behind. The idea of holiday is a change of person, the remaking of oneself in one's own image. The baseball camp for adults where the bulky stockbroker, facing an aged Whitey Ford, can imagine himself the slugger he never was: That's a holiday.

On holiday one seeks to be what one is not. The accountant turns into a woodsman, the farmer into a city slicker. And when they all go overseas, they insist that their tourist spot be tourist-free, the better to experience the simulated authenticity of another way of life. To holiday is to go native, to be native—temporarily, of course.

Reversibility is crucial. One wants to be native only for a time. The true holiday requires metamorphosis, but, even more important, return to normality. Return is what distinguishes excursion from exile. If the change of persona becomes irreversible—if the Mardi Gras mask becomes permanently, grotesquely stuck—holiday turns to horror. One must be able to go home.

And there are many ways, besides a Cook's tour, to leave home. One cheap, popular alternative these days is the psychic holiday: the cosmos on $5 a day. The preferred mode of travel is drugs, the destination lotus land. Madness is exotic. True, it is no longer celebrated, as it was in the heyday of R.D. Laing and the "politics of experience," as the only real sanity in this world of (nuclear, capitalist, fill-in-the-blanks) insanity. But it retains a mystique, a reputation for authenticity and depth of vision. We all know that the mentally ill inhabit a terrible place, literally a place of terrors. But that makes madness, like its two-dimensional facsimile, the horror film, all the more titillating.

For some, therefore, the ideal is to go there on a visit, a trip. The most widely used drugs, in fact, promise to re-create the experience of a major mental illness. Marijuana lets you circumnavigate the land of schizophrenia; LSD parachutes you in for the day. Quaaludes and downers promise a languid overnight stay in the Lethean land of depression, cocaine in the energized hothouse of mania.

As in any holiday, however, there must be an exit. For a drug to be widely popular it must be thought to be nonaddictive. That was cocaine's early, and false, claim to fame: the perfect high, it gets you there and back. (It is only those living in utter despair who choose a drug like heroin that takes you there for good: They are seeking not to holiday, but to emigrate.) The spirit of the psychic holiday was uncannily captured by Steven Spielberg, when he called Michael Jackson's peculiar child fantasy world (Disney dolls, cartoons, asexuality) a place where "I wish we could all spend some time." Living there, like living in New York, being another matter altogether.

For others there is the thrill of the political holiday, which offers not personal but social upheaval. It is a favorite recreation of what V. S. Naipaul calls the "return-ticket revolutionary," the comfortable Westerner who craves a whiff of social chaos and will travel to find it. First we had the Venceremos Brigade, eager to swing a Cuban sickle at people's cane. Now we have the European and American kids who hang around Managua wearing combat boots and T-shirts that read NICARAGUA LIBRE. In the '70s it was

Gale Benson, the bored white English divorcee who followed the cult of Black Power Militant Michael X to Trinidad to play at a revolution. Now it is the carpenter from South Shields, England, wearing a kaffiyeh and an AK-47, who is evacuated from Tripoli after five weeks with the PLO, and tells a reporter aboard his Yemen-bound ship that he plans to fight Israel for a year or two more, then go home to England.

They will always be with us, these political truants, and you shall know them by the return tickets in their pockets. Strife, preferably war, is for them fun, or at least a relief from the boredom of civilization. And for them, though not for the natives they patronize, when things get hot there will always be England.

Foreign correspondents, who commute to war by day, then return for drinks at the Hilton, know something of the thrill the traveling revolutionary seeks. "Nothing in life is so exhilarating as to be shot at without result," said Winston Churchill, himself a war correspondent. Journalists, however, remain observers. They do not pretend to have remade themselves from a gringo into a Sandino, precisely the conceit of the return-ticket revolutionary.

Finally, there is the cheapest vacation of all: the moral holiday, when the rules are suspended and one is transformed into anything one wants. There are two ways to achieve this happy condition. One is to stay home and wait for an official suspension of the rules, an official "letting go" (that is what the Russian word for vacation means: like the Fasching in Germany or Mardi Gras in the Americas).

The other way is to travel to a place where one can make up one's own rules. Some go to Club Med to shed pinstripes for swim trunks, a billfold for beads and a metropolitan persona for any laid-back one they choose to invent. Some, like Billy Graham or the latest tour from the National Council of Churches, go to the Soviet Union and make up entirely new meanings for words like freedom. "We believe they are free," said NCC Tour Leader Bruce Rigdon of the McCormick Theological Seminary, referring to Soviet demonstrators thrown out of Moscow's Baptist Church.

And some go to the Middle East, on which they pronounce solemn, chin-tugging judgment full of right and wrong and anguished ambivalence, to make up rules—for others. There are so many of these travelers that the Middle East has become, in Saul Bellow's words, the "moral resort area" of the West: "What Switzerland is to winter holidays and the Dalmatian coast to summer tourists, Israel and the Palestinians are to the West's need for justice." The West Bank alone offers the moral tourist a sandbox full of paradoxes, ironies and ambiguities too neat, and cheap, to refuse. For the Israeli these are questions of life and death; for the traveling moralist, they are an occasion for indignation and advice, the consequences of which are to be observed safely from overseas.

In the end, it is the two-way ticket that makes the holiday of whatever type at once so safe, so pleasurable, and, literally, so irresponsible. It is a walk on the wild side, but a walking tour only; a desire to see and feel and even judge, and then leave. To stay— i.e., to be serious—is to miss the point. "A perpetual holiday," said George Bernard Shaw, "is a good working definition of hell." Getting home isn't half the fun. It's all of it.

Time, August 27, 1984

Shakespeare, Ruined

Early this century, on New York's Lower East Side, where the Yiddish theater thrived and Shakespeare was an audience favorite, the playbill for a famous Second Avenue production read: *"Hamlet, bei William Shakespeare, fartaytch un farbessert"*—*Hamlet*, by William Shakespeare, translated and improved.

The urge to translate and improve upon the master turns out, unfortunately, not to be the exclusive property of recent immigrants. It is by now the norm. One citadel of translation and improvement is Washington's renowned Shakespeare Theatre. ("The nation's foremost Shakespeare company"—the *Wall Street Journal*.)

I got hooked on the Shakespeare Theatre about four years ago, by a brilliantly staged production of *Henry V.* I was so impressed, I took out a subscription. But I have since paid a heavy price: so much translation, so much improvement, so much wincing, nay, recoiling.

I am not talking here about such conventional devices as abridging the text or using period costume. I am talking about the directorial flourishes that deliberately invade the text, often in pursuit of some crashingly banal political or social statement. Such as staging *Othello* with colors reversed, the Moor being white, Iago and Desdemona and the rest being black.

Or take this year's *The Trojan Women* (the season includes one or two non-Shakespeare classics) with costume and scenery—ominous, heavy metallic architectural forms—making loud allusion to the Holocaust. And for those who don't quite get it, there is a gratuitous opening moment before any dialogue when a woman prisoner runs naked across the stage into an open shower.

And now *King Lear*. They can't really ruin *Lear*, can they? Prepare yourself.

I don't object to the Edwardian period dress. But why, in God's name, the giant birthday cake in the opening scene? Candles lit, it is brought out to Lear and then—I'm not making this up—the whole assembly of daughters and courtiers bursts into a rendition of Happy Birthday.

The trope is then reinforced when Lear divides his kingdom among his daughters by carving a map of icing on the cake. This knowing, winking anachronism (lifted from *The Godfather II*, in which Hyman Roth similarly carves up Cuba) can only be described as camp. It's a joke on the play and the audience, in which the audience is supposed to join in taking ironic distance—that modern conceit—from the play itself.

Some of the other clang devices are by now routine for the Shakespeare Theatre: the minimalist staging (a flat set, Godot-like in its barrenness, barely changing whether it's supposed to be a raging heath or a sumptuous castle), costumes as deliberately flattened as the sets (the King of France in tux) and, once again, the ever-present coarse metallic background (the clichéd Holocaust-totalitarianism motif).

But one device is not routine at all. Even after the cake, it comes as a shock—an in-your-face, look-at-me piece of directorial arrogance. When it is the turn of Cordelia, the good daughter, to speak, she does so—in sign. She is mute. As she signs, her lines are spoken to the other characters by Fool (and later, by France).

Of all the people to be robbed of speech: Cordelia. And robbed by whom? This coup of political correctness is particularly egregious because it so contradicts Shakespeare. In his dying moments, Lear says movingly of Cordelia, "her voice was ever soft, / gentle, and low, an excellent thing in a woman."

It is one thing to take liberties with ambiguities. Or to seize upon holes in the text to drive through one's own sensibility. But to do it in contradiction to the text is sheer willfulness.

This willfulness is, of course, in perfect synchrony with the prevailing academic notion of the critic being superior to the author. Indeed, the author must be stripped of all authority over his creation, lest we lapse into authoritarianism. He loses control of the text the minute pen leaves paper. There is no real text, only what the reader makes of it. And the reader—which in this case means the director—can make of it what he wants.

Just a few months ago, the company's production of *The Merchant of Venice* totally inverted the character of Lorenzo. His every profession of love is undermined by a stage action—fingering Jessica's jewels or throwing a knowing wink—that tells the audience that he is a knave and that every word Shakespeare put in his mouth is meant to be taken ironically.

The coup de grâce occurs when one of Portia's suitors, the Prince of Arragon, arrives. Says Shakespeare: "with train." Says the Shakespeare Theatre: with dwarf, racing silently about making lewd gestures. As if modern audiences cannot take Shakespeare straight without some camp conceit for comic relief.

If this were the story of just one theater (albeit one the *Economist* calls one of the world's "three great Shakespearean theatres"), it would be an amusing curiosity. Unfortunately, the Shakespeare Theatre of Washington is not at all unique. Modern artists everywhere feel impelled to draw mustaches on the work of the great. It is, in part, an act of defiance. But it is more often a sign of desperation, an unwitting acknowledgment of the smallness of our time.

And yet, despite these travesties, the Bard still triumphs. We are still moved. He still speaks to us above and around and despite these febrile attempts at translation and improvement. That is the good news. The bad news is about us, plagued by a narcissism that forces even Shakespeare to struggle to be heard above our preening din.

Across town, the rival Folger Shakespeare Theatre is putting on a production of *Hamlet* in which the role of Hamlet is divided (within each performance) among four actors, three of whom are women in cross-dress. Says Kate Norris, one of the quarter-Hamlets, "We have so much fun on this thing." Rosencrantz and Guildenstern were executed for less.

The Weekly Standard, December 13, 1999

Illusions of Self-Love

So the Atlanta cabby tells his fare, Professor Allan Bloom, that he has just gotten out of prison where, happily, with the help of psychotherapy, he "found his identity and learned to like himself." Observes Bloom: "A generation earlier he would have found God and learned to despise himself." But rebuilding life in a spirit of humility is not the American way. The indispensable element of modern rehabilitation is the acquisition of self-love.

You would think that narcissism, excessive and exclusive self-love, might qualify as a vice. In fact, in today's America, it might be the ultimate virtue or, more accurately, the prerequisite for all virtue. It is, after all, common and endlessly repeated wisdom that one cannot begin to love others until one has come to love oneself.

In the age of *Donahue*, the commandment is: Love thyself, then thy neighbor. The formulation is a license for unremitting self-indulgence, since the quest for self-love is never finished and since the obligation to love others must be deferred while the search continues. No distractions please. First things first.

The ideology of self-love enjoyed currency during the '70s as a form of psychic recreation for the Me Generation. It has now been resurrected as a cure for the social pathologies of the '80s, for the drug and other behavioral epidemics that ravage the nation and particularly the inner cities.

The conventional wisdom is that people are acting so self-destructively because of an absence of self-worth. Until they can learn to love themselves, they will continue to damage both themselves and others. A riveting example of this kind of logic was displayed last week on Ted Koppel's three-hour extravaganza on

Washington's drug epidemic. The last speaker, a woman named Patricia Godley, took the stage and held it with a mesmerizing confessional. She confessed variously to having been a convict, an addict and a failed parent. (A son, who grew up illiterate and disabled while she was addicted, had recently been killed in the city's drug wars.)

She was struggling now to learn to value herself. She demanded help. Her plea to mayor and moderator and audience and anyone else who would listen was: "Make me know that I am worth fighting for. . . . Make me feel like I can do it." Koppel so congratulated her for "telling it like it is" that he ended the show right there, saying that there was nothing more to be said on the subject.

She had told it like it is, or at least as we would like to hear it. If the problem of the destitute is that of self-worth, then all we need is some good psychotherapy and a few "I am somebody" recitations, and we are on our way. Easier that than to seek the roots of lower-class misery in economic, social and family structures.

Senator Daniel Moynihan has pointed out recently that in the inner city there is an alarming new trend: a descent from single-parent to no-parent families as the mother is engulfed in the drug culture. We are producing a generation of orphans.

Societies have occasional success bringing up orphans, but on a large scale it is a losing proposition. The welfare state was originally called upon to supplement families. It is now called upon to substitute for them, and that is clearly impossible. The state cannot undo the devastation that comes from parental abandonment. Nor is it equipped to train parents.

Cried Patricia Godley, "What can you do to help me be something I have never been, a parent?" The answer, properly, is "almost nothing." The state can give you day care and food stamps and supplement your income, but teaching a mother to mother is not something that the state is designed to do. The culture, the community, the family have to do it. If they don't, it does not get done.

And when it does not get done, the harm that results is not undone by mantras about self-worth. Indeed, today's conventional wisdom that drug abuse and alcoholism and sexual irresponsibility come from an absence of self-worth seems to me to be precisely wrong. Drugs and sex and alcohol have but one thing in common: They yield intense and immediate pleasure. That is why people do them. Indulgence in what used to be called vices is an act of excessive self-love. It requires such regard for one's own immediate well-being as to be oblivious to any harm that indulgence might cause others, even one's own children.

The answer to Patricia Godley is, first, that there is no way the state can make you love yourself or your child. And second, that even if there were, loving yourself certainly is not the problem. Nor is loving your child. Every mother loves her child. What is hard is to sacrifice for the child. And that requires not self-love, but its opposite, self-denial.

No one has a good answer to the pathologies that wrack the inner cities. But the latest prescription so glibly dispensed—more self-love—is an illusion. Bloom calls our attention to the modern distinction between the "inner-directed and other-directed" person. It is now believed that the former is "unqualifiedly good" and that "the healthy inner-directed person will really care for others." Bloom's response is admirably concise: "If you can believe that, you can believe anything."

The Washington Post, May 5, 1989

CHAPTER 10

OUT OF MANY, ONE

Assimilation Nation

One of the reasons for the successes we've enjoyed in Afghanistan is that our ambassador there, who saw the country through the founding of a democratic government, was not just a serious thinker and a skilled diplomat but also spoke the language and understood the culture. Why? Because Zalmay Khalilzad is an Afghan-born Afghan American.

It is not every country that can send to obscure faraway places envoys who are themselves children of that culture. Indeed, Americans are the only people who can do that for practically every country.

Being mankind's first-ever universal nation, to use Ben Wattenberg's felicitous phrase for our highly integrated polyglot country, carries enormous advantage. In the shrunken world of the information age, we have significant populations of every ethnicity capable of making instant and deep connections—economic as well as diplomatic—with just about every foreign trouble spot, hothouse and economic dynamo on the planet.

That is a priceless and unique asset. It is true that other

countries, particularly in Europe, have in the past several decades opened themselves up to immigration. But the real problem is not immigration but assimilation. Anyone can do immigration. But if you don't assimilate the immigrants—France, for example, has vast, isolated exurban immigrant slums with populations totally alienated from the polity and the general culture—then immigration becomes not an asset but a liability.

America's genius has always been assimilation, taking immigrants and turning them into Americans. Yet our current debates on immigration focus on only one side of the issue—the massive waves of illegal immigrants that we seem unable to stop.

The various plans, all well-intentioned, have an air of hopelessness about them. Amnesty of some sort seems reasonable because there is no way we're going to expel 10 million–plus illegal immigrants, and we might as well make their lives more normal. But that will not stop further illegal immigration. In fact, it will encourage it, because every amnesty—and we have them periodically—tells potential illegals still in Mexico and elsewhere that if they persist long enough, they will get in, and if they stay here long enough, they can cut to the head of the line.

In the end, increased law enforcement, guest-worker programs and other incentives that encourage some of the illegals to go back home can go only so far. Which is why we should be devoting far more attention to the other half of the problem: not just how many come in but what happens to them once they're here.

The anti-immigrant types argue that there is something unique about our mostly Latin immigration that makes it unassimilable. First, that there's simply too much of it to be digested. Actually, the percentage of foreign-born people living in the United States today is significantly below what it was in 1890 and 1910—and those were spectacularly successful immigrations. And there is nothing about their culture that makes it any more difficult for

Catholic Hispanics to assimilate than the Czechs and Hungarians, Chinese and Koreans, who came decades ago.

The key to assimilation, of course, is language. The real threat to the United States is not immigration per se but bilingualism and, ultimately, biculturalism. Having grown up in Canada, where a language divide is a recurring source of friction and fracture, I can only wonder at those who want to duplicate that plague in the United States.

The good news, and the reason I am less panicked about illegal immigration than most, is that the vogue for bilingual education is waning. It has been abolished by referendum in California, Arizona and even Massachusetts.

As the results in California have shown, it was a disaster for Hispanic children. It delays assimilation by perhaps a full generation. Those in "English immersion" have more than twice the rate of English proficiency as those in the old bilingual system (being taught other subjects in Spanish while being gradually taught English).

By all means we should try to control immigration. Nonetheless, given our geography, our tolerant culture and the magnetic attraction of our economy, illegals will always be with us. Our first task, therefore, should be abolishing bilingual education everywhere and requiring that our citizenship tests have strict standards for English language and American civics.

The cure for excessive immigration is successful assimilation. The way to prevent European-like immigration catastrophes is to turn every immigrant—and most surely his children—into an American. Who might one day grow up to be our next Zalmay Khalilzad.

The Washington Post, June 17, 2005

The Tribalization of America

O ne day's news:

— A prominent Tory MP is killed by an IRA car bomb.

— Government soldiers in Liberia murder hundreds of refugees from a rival rebel tribe.

— A radical Islamic sect in Trinidad kidnaps the prime minister and his cabinet and holds them at gunpoint.

— American Indians demonstrate outside the Canadian Embassy in solidarity with Mohawks caught in a violent land dispute with Quebec (which itself is in an autonomy dispute with Canada).

What connects these unconnected events? The powerful, often ignored, global reality of tribalism. The Irish, Liberian and Trinidadian variety is more violent, but Canada illustrates best its bewilderingly regressive nature. Canadian nationalism has long sought to distinguish itself from the United States; Quebec nationalism to distinguish itself from Canada; and now here come the Mohawks with their own claim of apartness from Quebec.

Tribes within nations within empires. The world is littered with such Chinese boxes, and they make perfect tinder for conflict. Nowhere more so than in the Soviet bloc, where the decline of communism has brought a revival of tribalism (most notably in Azerbaijan and Transylvania) as savage and primitive as seen anywhere.

What is all this to Americans? A lesson and a warning. America, alone among the multi-ethnic countries of the world, has managed to assimilate its citizenry into a common nationality. We are now doing our best to squander this great achievement.

Spain still has its Basque secessionists, France its Corsicans. Even Britain has the pull of Scottish and Welsh to say nothing of Irish nationalists. But America has, through painful experience, found a way to overcome its centrifugal forces.

American unity has been built on a tightly federalist politics and a powerful melting pot culture. Most important, America chose to deal with the problem of differentness (ethnicity) by embracing a radical individualism and rejecting the notion of group rights. Of course, there was one great, shameful historical exception: the denial of rights to blacks. When that was finally outlawed in the '60s, America appeared ready to resume its destiny, a destiny celebrated by Martin Luther King Jr., as the home of a true and now universal individualism.

Why is this a destiny to be celebrated? Because it works. Because while Spain and Canada, to say nothing of Liberia and Ireland, are wracked by separatism and tribal conflict, America has been largely spared. Its union is more secure than that of any multi-ethnic nation on earth.

We are now, however, in the process of throwing away this patrimony. Our great national achievement—fashioning a common citizenship and identity for a multi-ethnic, multi-lingual, multi-racial people—is now threatened by a process of relentless, deliberate Balkanization. The great engines of social life—the law, the schools, the arts—are systematically encouraging the division of America into racial, ethnic and gender separateness.

It began with the courts, which legitimized the allocation of jobs, government contracts, admission to medical school and now TV licenses by race, gender and ethnic group.

Then education. First Stanford capitulated to separatist know-nothings and abandoned its "Western Civilization" course because of its bias toward white males. (You know: narrow-minded ethnics like Socrates, Jesus and Jefferson.) Now the push is to start kids much earlier on the road to intellectual separatism. Grade school, for example.

A proposed revision of New York State's school curriculum to rid it of "Eurocentric" bias is so clearly an attempt at "ethnic cheerleading on the demand of pressure groups" that historians Diane Ravitch, Arthur Schlesinger Jr., C. Vann Woodward, Robert Caro and 20 others were moved to issue a joint protest. Despite their considerable ideological differences, they joined to oppose the "use of the school system to promote the division of our people into antagonistic racial groups."

Even the arts have been conscripted into the separatist crusade. "Both the Rockefeller and Ford foundations," writes Samuel Lipman in *Commentary*, "intend to downgrade and even eliminate support for art based on traditional European sources and instead will encourage activity by certain approved minorities."

Countries struggling to transcend their tribal separateness have long looked to America as their model. Now, however, America is going backward. While the great multi-ethnic states try desperately to imbue their people with a sense of shared national identity, the great American institutions, from the courts to the foundations, are promoting group identity instead.

Without ever having thought it through, we are engaged in unmaking the American union and encouraging the very tribalism that is the bane of the modern world.

The Washington Post, August 6, 1990

Counting by Race

Last week the *Washington Post* reported on two Asian American children who were denied transfer from one local public school to another because of their race. The school board denied them entry to the second school, with its unique French immersion program, because the first school had only 11 Asian students. To keep their numbers up, no Asians were permitted to transfer out.

This is by no means a unique case. A white parent, writing just a few days later in the *Washington Post*, described the agonies of trying to transfer his adopted Korean-born child, a transfer denied because of its "impact on diversity," as the school board's rejection letter memorably explained.

Diversity is now the great successor to affirmative action as the justification for counting and assigning by race in America. First, diversity sounds more benign. Affirmative action has acquired a bad reputation because it implies the unfair advancement of one group over another. Diversity cheerfully promises nothing more than making every corner of America "look like America."

Moreover, diversity is a blunter instrument. Affirmative action requires an inquiry into history and justifies itself as redress for past injustice. Diversity is much simpler. It does not even try to justify itself by appeal to justice or some other value. It is an end in itself. It requires no demonstration of historical wrong, only of current racial imbalance. Too few Asians at Rock Creek Forest Elementary School? Fine. No Asian will be allowed to leave.

Because of its blithe disregard of anything—individual rights, common citizenship, past injustice—except racial numbers, the appeal to diversity represents the ultimate degeneration of the idea of counting by race. At its beginnings, affirmative action was deeply morally rooted as an attempt to redress centuries of discrimination against blacks. Yes, affirmative action did violate the principle of judging people as individuals and not by group. But it did so in the name of another high moral principle: the redress of grievous, gratuitous harm inflicted on one group because of its race.

Had affirmative action remained restricted to African Americans and to the redress of past discrimination, it would still command support in the country today. Instead it has been stretched, diluted and corrupted beyond recognition, transmuted from redress for blacks—a case of massive, official, unique injustice—to diversity for all, except, of course, white males.

By what principle should government preferentially award a contract to, say, the newly arrived son of an Argentinian businessman over a native-born American white? None. Diversity alone, in and of itself, is invoked to justify such a travesty.

Diversity, drawing on no moral argument, is morally bankrupt. It draws only on a new form of American utopianism, a multi-hued variant of an older Norman Rockwell utopianism, in which in every walk of American life, race and ethnicity are represented in exactly correct proportions.

Like all utopianisms, this one is divorced from reality. It is entirely cockeyed to expect different groups to gravitate with strict proportionality to every school, workplace and neighborhood in America.

And when they don't, this utopianism partakes of the brutality of all utopianisms and forces the fit. Individuals who obstruct the quest for the perfect post-Rockwell tableau beware.

The kindergartners denied entry to the French program at the Maryvale Elementary School in Rockville constitute such an obstruction. Yet they are hardly the most deeply aggrieved parties. That honor belongs to California's Asian American high school graduates who, alas, have excelled disproportionately in school and thus threaten to overwhelm California's best colleges.

Everyone knows that there is an unspoken quota system in the California universities and in other schools around the country that keeps Asians out because of their race. How does this shameful practice differ from the exclusion of similarly gifted Jews during the '30s and '40s? Perhaps only in the hypocrisy of those defending the practice. In the old days, the justification for anti-Jewish quotas was simple antipathy toward "pushy" Jews. Today, justification for excluding "nerdy" Asians is more highfalutin: They are an impediment to diversity.

Proponents of these appalling classifications by race prefer, of course, to pretend that they are about such grand notions as culture. Nonsense. As the white father of the untransferable Asian schoolkid notes, "I couldn't help wonder what cultural contribution my son could make [as an Asian]—he was just five months old when he left Korea." These quotas are not about culture. They are about skin color, eye shape and hair texture.

One stymied Asian American mother, desperate for a loophole, tried having her child reclassified as white because the father is white. More parents will seek such solutions. How shall we adjudicate these vexing questions of mixed blood?

Turn to the source—the modern state that produced the most exquisitely developed system of race classification. The unemployed justices who enforced the Group Areas Act of apartheid South Africa may finally find gainful work again.

The Washington Post, September 1, 1995

Redskins and Reason

In regard to the (Washington) Redskins. Should the name be changed?

I don't like the language police ensuring that no one anywhere gives offense to anyone about anything. And I fully credit the claim of Redskins owner Dan Snyder and many passionate fans that they intend no malice or prejudice and that "Redskins" has a proud 80-year history they wish to maintain.

The fact is, however, that words don't stand still. They evolve.

Fifty years ago the preferred, most respectful term for African Americans was Negro. The word appears 15 times in Martin Luther King's "I have a dream" speech. Negro replaced a long list of insulting words in common use during decades of public and legal discrimination.

And then, for complicated historical reasons (having to do with the black power and "black is beautiful" movements), usage changed. The preferred term is now black or African American. With a rare few legacy exceptions, such as the United Negro College Fund, Negro carries an unmistakably patronizing and demeaning tone.

If you were detailing the racial composition of Congress, you wouldn't say: "Well, to start with, there are 44 Negroes." If you'd been asleep for 50 years, you might. But upon being informed how the word had changed in nuance, you would stop using it and choose another.

And here's the key point: You would stop not because of the language police. Not because you might incur a presidential rebuke. But simply because the word was tainted, freighted with negative connotations with which you would not want to be associated.

Proof? You wouldn't even use the word in private, where being harassed for political incorrectness is not an issue.

Similarly, regarding the further racial breakdown of Congress, you wouldn't say: "And by my count, there are two redskins." It's inconceivable, because no matter how the word was used 80 years ago, it carries invidious connotations today.

I know there are surveys that say that most Native Americans aren't bothered by the word. But that's not the point. My objection is not rooted in pressure from various minorities or fear of public polls or public scolds.

When I was growing up, I thought "gyp" was simply a synonym for "cheat," and used it accordingly. It was only when I was an adult that I learned that gyp was short for gypsy. At which point, I stopped using it.

Not because I took a poll of Roma to find out if they were offended. If some mysterious disease had carried away every gypsy on the planet, and there were none left to offend, I still wouldn't use it.

Why? Simple decency. I wouldn't want to use a word that defines a people—living or dead, offended or not—in a most demeaning way. It's a question not of who or how many had their feelings hurt, but of whether you want to associate yourself with a word that, for whatever historical reason having nothing to do with you, carries inherently derogatory connotations.

Years ago, the word "retarded" emerged as the enlightened substitute for such cruel terms as "feeble-minded" or "mongoloid." Today, however, it is considered a form of denigration, having been replaced by the clumsy but now conventional "developmentally disabled." There is no particular logic to this evolution. But it's a social fact. Unless you're looking to give gratuitous offense, you don't call someone "retarded."

Let's recognize that there are many people of good will for whom "Washington Redskins" contains sentimental and historical attachment—and not an ounce of intended animus. So let's turn down the temperature. What's at issue is not high principle but adaptation to a change in linguistic nuance. A close call, though I personally would err on the side of not using the word if others are available.

How about Skins, a contraction already applied to the Washington football team? And that carries a sports connotation, as in skins vs. shirts in pickup basketball.

Choose whatever name you like. But let's go easy on the other side. We're not talking *Brown v. Board of Education* here. There's no demand that Native Americans man the team's offensive line. This is a matter of usage—and usage changes. If you shot a remake of 1934's *The Gay Divorcee*, you'd have to change that title too.

Not because the lady changed but because the word did.

Hail Skins.

The Washington Post, October 18, 2013

Neither Ennobling nor Degrading

Early in their training in cinematic conventions, kids learn the rule of thumb for sorting out good guys from bad guys: The good-looking guy is good, and the bad-looking guy is bad. Indeed, if the guy is positively ugly, he is the likely villain. And if he has something visibly wrong with him—a limp, a scar—he'll be an especially cruel one.

Of course, Hollywood did not invent this cultural convention. It is a tradition that goes back at least as far as Richard III, whose "deformed, unfinish'd . . . half made up" body—a hunchback, a limp—prefigured the disfigurement of his soul.

Hollywood, manufacturer of both dreams and nightmares, has always been of two minds about how to portray those who like Richard III are "rudely stamp'd." It has settled on one of two stereotypical responses: sentimentalize or demonize.

The sentimentalizing you have seen often enough: those sickly sweet movies in which the hero's physical impairment is a window onto a higher, purer, more spiritual plane of being. The perfect vehicle for this kind of schmaltz is the blind hero who invariably sees deeper and farther for having been loosed from the bonds of the physical world. *The Elephant Man*, *Simon Birch* and *Regarding Henry* (lawyer gets shot in head, becomes good person) are recent variations on the theme.

Alternating with this Hallmark beatification of disability is the more sinister convention of associating it with villainy. James Bond films are notable for adorning the villain with, say, hooks for hands or steel for teeth. In *Batman*, disfigurement in a vat of acid transforms Jack Nicholson's small-time hood into evil incarnate.

Even *The Lion King* cannot resist the convention: The bad lion is called Scar, and sports one.

A minor classic of the genre is *The Sting*. That otherwise delightful 1973 Redford-Newman vehicle felt it necessary to give Redford's nemesis (a mobster played by Robert Shaw) a limp. This is no noble wound like Captain Ahab's. It is an incidental piece of the landscape, never explained because one does not have to. Villains limp; Redford doesn't.

But if *The Sting* offers a rather subliminal link between inner and outer defectiveness, the just-opened, wildly popular *Wild, Wild West*—a Will Smith vehicle otherwise too silly to merit notice—dispenses with the subtlety, offering up the most extreme and revolting example of this convention in recent memory.

West features two villains, both embittered, crazed Confederate officers now getting their post–Civil War revenge on the Union. They're notable because the minor baddy is missing an ear and has a disfigured face, while the major baddy, played with creepy gusto by Kenneth Branagh, is missing the entire lower half of his body. With so much more missing, you know he is so much more psychotically evil than his merely earless friend.

Much fun is had with Branagh's half body, none of it funny, much of it cruel. Yet with the P.C. police so outraged at the alleged racism of George Lucas' new *Star Wars*—going so far as to locate, ridiculously, a Yiddish accent in Watto, the slave-owning merchant—it is rather odd that nothing has been said about the savage mockery of physical deformity in *West*, a blockbuster hit aimed squarely at kids.

What makes it odder still is that this is the same Hollywood that routinely gives teary standing ovations every time Christopher Reeve makes an appearance at some awards ceremony. It is the same culture that falls over itself in soppy sentimental tributes to the "inspiration" that emanates from the disabled.

Or maybe it is not so odd. The whole politically correct vogue for paying tribute to the "courage" and higher powers of the disabled—and of acquiescing to such comic linguistic conventions as calling the disabled "differently abled," as if those of us in wheelchairs have chosen some alternative lifestyle—is, in the end, a form of condescension.

To be sure, patronizing the disabled is not as offensive as the in-your-face mockery of something like *West*. But its effect is similar: to distance oneself, to give expression to the reflexive mixture of fear and pity that misfortune in others evokes in all of us.

Disability—like exile, the human condition it most resembles—neither ennobles nor degrades. It frames experience. It does not define it.

But that undramatic reality is hardly grist for Hollywood, which specializes in, and swings wildly between, fawning idealization and primitive caricature of disability. It is saint or sicko—now (as ever) playing at a theater near you.

The Washington Post, July 9, 1999

On Lowering the Flag

After a massacre like the one at Emanuel AME Church in Charleston, our immediate reaction is to do something. Something, for politicians, means legislation. And for Democratic politicians, this means gun control.

It's the all-purpose, go-to, knee-jerk solution. Within hours of the massacre, President Obama was lamenting the absence of progress on gun control. A particular Democratic (and media) lament was Congress' failure to pass anything after Sandy Hook.

But the unfortunate fact is that the post–Sandy Hook legislation would have had zero effect on the events in Charleston. Its main provisions had to do with assault weapons; the (alleged) shooter Dylann Roof was using a semiautomatic pistol.

You can pass any gun law you want. The 1994 assault weapons ban was allowed to expire after 10 years because, as a Justice Department study showed, it had no effect. There's only one gun law that would make a difference: confiscation. Everything else is for show.

And in this country, confiscation is impossible. Constitutionally, because of the Second Amendment. Politically, because doing so would cause something of an insurrection. And culturally, because Americans cherish—cling to, as Obama once had it—their guns as a symbol of freedom. You can largely ban guns in Canada where the founding document gives the purpose of confederation as the achievement of "peace, order and good government." Harder to disarm a nation whose founding purpose is "life, liberty and the pursuit of happiness."

With gun control going nowhere, the psychic national need post-Charleston to nonetheless do something took a remarkable direction: banishment of the Confederate battle flag, starting with the one flying on the grounds of the statehouse in Columbia, then spreading like wildfire to consume Confederate flags, symbols, statues and even memorabilia everywhere—from the Alabama state capitol to Walmart and Amazon.

Logically, the connection is tenuous. Yes, Roof does pose with the Confederate flag, among other symbols of racism, on his website. But does anyone imagine that if the South Carolina flag had been relegated to a museum, the massacre would not have occurred?

Politically, the killings created a unique moment. Governor Nikki Haley was surely sincere in calling for the Confederate flag's removal. But she also understood that the massacre had created a moment when the usual pro–Confederate flag feeling—and, surely, expressions of it—would be largely suppressed, presenting the opportunity to achieve something otherwise politically unachievable.

But there's a deeper reason for this rush to banish Confederate symbols, to move them from the public square to the museum. The trigger was not just the massacre itself, but even more tellingly the breathtaking display of nobility and spiritual generosity by the victims' relatives. Within 48 hours of the murder of their loved ones, they spoke of redemption and reconciliation and even forgiveness of the killer himself. It was an astonishingly moving expression of Christian charity.

Such grace demands a response. In a fascinating dynamic, it created a feeling of moral obligation to reciprocate in some way. The flag was not material to the crime itself, but its connection to the underlying race history behind the crime suggested that its removal from the statehouse grounds—whatever the endlessly debated merits of the case—could serve as a reciprocal gesture of reconciliation.

The result was a microcosm of—and a historical lesson in—the moral force of the original civil rights movement, whose genius was to understand the effect that combating evil with good, violence with grace, would have on a fundamentally decent American nation.

America was indeed moved. The result was the civil rights acts. The issue today is no longer legal equality. It is more a matter of sorting through historical memory.

The Confederate flags would ultimately have come down. That is a good thing. They are now coming down in a rush. The haste may turn out to be problematic.

We will probably overshoot, as we are wont to do, in the stampede to eliminate every relic of the Confederacy. Not every statue has to be smashed, not every memory banished. Perhaps we can learn a lesson from Arlington National Cemetery, founded by the victorious Union to bury its dead. There you will find Section 16. It contains the remains of hundreds of Confederate soldiers grouped around a modest, moving monument to their devotion to "duty as they understood it"—a gesture by the Union of soldierly respect, without any concession regarding the taintedness of their cause.

Or shall we uproot them as well?

The Washington Post, June 26, 2015

CHAPTER 11

CHURCH AND STATE

Civil Religion—and No Religion

L et us begin, on Thanksgiving, by giving thanks that we are not French. I say this with no malice. I mean it this way: We both had glorious, liberating revolutions, but ours was not cursed by excessive rationalism, nor by its twin, hatred of religion.

The French revolutionaries decided to start the world anew. They decreed not just a new state, but a new religion, a religion of pure reason to overthrow Christianity, and a new calendar to go with it. The calendar, too, would abolish everything that went before. Even the week had to be replaced—by a 10-day stretch (10 being a far more rational number than seven) called a "decade," and free of Sundays!

The purposes of the American revolution were more modest: not to recreate the universe, but to alter a few "of its arrangements." The American revolution repatriated liberty and established a new political order. But its ambitions stopped there. It left the weekend alone.

Religion, too. One result is that we have generally avoided religious wars. France's revolutionaries, bent on extirpating every remnant of the ancien régime, ushered in decades of bitter conflict between anti-clericalists and a reactionary religious right.

Sound familiar? In the United States such conflict now begins to stir. For a generation, the Supreme Court has taken the view that our public life should be not so much religion-neutral as religion-free. The result, while not exactly Jacobinic, has been impressive: a general canvassing about for religious symbols in public life and a somewhat haphazard, but effective, campaign to erase them.

Last year there seemed to be a pause in this trend when the Supreme Court ruled, five to four, that Pawtucket, Rhode Island, could sponsor the public display of a nativity scene at Christmastime. The secularists may have been disappointed, but this was no great victory for religion. The court's reason was that the crèche is not principally a religious symbol after all. It is "no more an advancement or endorsement of religion" than exhibiting "religious paintings in governmentally sponsored museums." It merely illustrates the origins of a holiday. Moreover the context—the Pawtucket display included plastic reindeer and other elements with no Christian connotation at all—shows that Pawtucket's overall intent was secular and thus did not violate the Establishment Clause of the First Amendment.

The implication is that so long as religious symbolism is secular enough—empty enough of religious meaning—it will be permitted in public life. The Ten Commandments may not be posted in public schools if the purpose is "religious admonition." They may only be considered in the context of "an appropriate study" of "ethics, comparative religion or the like." The border between church and state is to be lined with plastic reindeer.

Or as Chesterton once put it unkindly, "Tolerance is the virtue of people who do not believe anything." Yet America managed tolerance fairly well for almost two centuries under a different regime. It did then believe in, and take seriously, the idea of religion in public life. Not Protestantism or Judaism or any other particularist faith, but what has been called the American Civil Religion.

It is a creed (as its finest elaborator, sociologist Robert Bellah, has argued) that sees American history in transcendent terms and endows it with religious meaning. Its Supreme Being is Jefferson's rights-giving Creator, Washington's First Author, Lincoln's Judge—an American Providence. It has a calendar, which like the civil religion itself, is meant not to replace, but to complement, what has gone before. The calendar has its days set aside to honor the saints (Washington, Lincoln and King), and to celebrate the civic virtues as embodied in the American historical experience: the Fourth of July (liberty), Memorial Day (sacrifice), Veterans Day (service).

Its supreme holiday is Thanksgiving, originally conceived as a day for celebration of America's bounty and contemplation of America's providential destiny. Which is perhaps why it was Lincoln who, in 1864, made Thanksgiving an annual national holiday. Lincoln, perhaps more than any other president, felt the sense of transcendence of American history. And in the second inaugural, when he spoke of the agony of the Civil War as divine judgment on American life and the sin of slavery, Lincoln gave that spirituality its most profound expression.

The irony is that if we were to take Thanksgiving and the other elements of the civil religion as seriously as Lincoln did, the Supreme Court would now probably have to rule it unconstitutional. In his dissent on the Pawtucket decision, Justice Brennan asks how the religious symbolism in our national life—everything from "In God We Trust" to Thanksgiving Day—can be permitted constitutionally. Because, says Brennan, it is nothing more than "ceremonial deism," practices that have "lost through rote repetition any significant religious content."

So, a day for big turkeys and pro football passes muster. But all public devotions had better be mumbled. RELIGION PROHIBITED, EXCEPT WHERE MEANINGLESS. So reads the sign in the public square.

The French would understand.

The Washington Post, November 28, 1985

Just Leave Christmas Alone

"Holiday celebrations where Christmas music is being
sung make people feel different, and because it is such a
majority, it makes the minority feel uncomfortable."
—*Mark Brownstein, parent, Maplewood, NJ, supporting the school
board's ban on religious music in holiday concerts*

"You want my advice? Go back to Bulgaria."
—*Humphrey Bogart*, Casablanca

It is Christmastime, and what would Christmas be without the usual platoon of annoying pettifoggers rising annually to strip Christmas of any Christian content? With some success:

School districts in New Jersey and Florida ban Christmas carols. The mayor of Somerville, Massachusetts, apologizes for "mistakenly" referring to the town's "holiday party" as a "Christmas party." The Broward and Fashion malls in South Florida put up a Hanukkah menorah but no nativity scene. The manager of one of the malls explains: Hanukkah commemorates a battle and not a religious event, though he hastens to add, "I really don't know a lot about it." He does not. Hanukkah commemorates a miracle, and there is no event more "religious" than a miracle.

The attempts to de-Christianize Christmas are as absurd as they are relentless. The United States today is the most tolerant and diverse society in history. It celebrates all faiths with an open heart and open-mindedness that, compared to even the most advanced countries in Europe, are unique.

Yet more than 80% of Americans are Christian, and probably

95% of Americans celebrate Christmas. Christmas Day is an official federal holiday, the only day of the entire year when, for example, the Smithsonian museums are closed. Are we to pretend that Christmas is nothing but an orgy of commerce in celebration of . . . what? The winter solstice?

I personally like Christmas because, since it is a day that for me is otherwise ordinary, I get to do nice things, such as covering for as many gentile colleagues as I could when I was a doctor at Massachusetts General Hospital. I will admit that my generosity had its rewards: I collected enough chits on Christmas Day to get reciprocal coverage not just for Yom Kippur but for both days of Rosh Hashanah and my other major holiday, Opening Day at Fenway.

Mind you, I've got nothing against Hanukkah, although I am constantly amused—and gratified—by how American culture has gone out of its way to inflate the importance of Hanukkah, easily the least important of Judaism's seven holidays, into a giant event replete with cards, presents and public commemorations as a creative way to give Jews their Christmas equivalent.

Some Americans get angry at parents who want to ban carols because they tremble that their kids might feel "different" and "uncomfortable" should they, God forbid, hear Christian music sung at their school. I feel pity. What kind of fragile religious identity have they bequeathed their children that it should be threatened by exposure to carols?

I'm struck by the fact that you almost never find Orthodox Jews complaining about a Christmas crèche in the public square. That is because their children, steeped in the richness of their own religious tradition, know who they are and are not threatened by Christians celebrating their religion in public. They are enlarged by it.

It is the more deracinated members of religious minorities, brought up largely ignorant of their own traditions, whose religious identity is so tenuous that they feel the need to be constantly on guard against displays of other religions—and who think the solution to their predicament is to prevent the other guy from displaying his religion, rather than learning a bit about their own.

To insist that the overwhelming majority of this country stifle its religious impulses in public so that minorities can feel "comfortable" not only understandably enrages the majority but commits two sins. The first is profound ungenerosity toward a majority of fellow citizens who have shown such generosity of spirit toward minority religions.

The second is the sin of incomprehension—a failure to appreciate the uniqueness of the communal American religious experience. Unlike, for example, the famously tolerant Ottoman Empire or the generally tolerant Europe of today, the United States does not merely allow minority religions to exist at its sufferance. It celebrates and welcomes and honors them.

America transcended the idea of mere toleration *in 1790* in George Washington's letter to the Newport synagogue, one of the lesser known glories of the Founding: "It is now no more that toleration is spoken of, as if it was by the indulgence of one class of people, that another enjoyed the exercise of their inherent natural rights."

More than two centuries later, it is time that members of religious (and anti-religious) minorities, as full citizens of this miraculous republic, transcend something too: petty defensiveness.

Merry Christmas. To all.

The Washington Post, December 17, 2004

Religion as Taste

As I checked in for an outpatient test at a local hospital last week, the admissions lady asked for the usual name, rank, serial number, insurance and ailment. Then she inquired, "What is your religious preference?" I was tempted to say, "I think Buddhism is the coolest, but I happen to be Jewish."

My second impulse was to repeat what Jonah said when asked by the shipmates of his foundering skiff to identify himself: "I am a Hebrew, ma'am. And I fear the Lord, the God of Heaven, who made the sea and the dry land." But that would surely have got me sent to psychiatry rather than X-ray. So I desisted.

In ancient times, they asked, "Who is your God?" A generation ago, they asked your religion. Today your creed is a preference. Preference? "I take my coffee black, my wine red, my sex straight and my shirts lightly starched. Oh yes, and put me down for Islam."

Of course, the only reason hospital folk bother to ask about religion at all is prudence, not theological curiosity. In case they accidentally kill you or you otherwise expire on their watch, they want to be sure they send up the right clergy to usher you to the next level, as it were. We're not talking belief here. We're talking liability protection.

According to Chesterton, tolerance is the virtue of people who do not believe in anything. Chesterton meant that as a critique of tolerance. But it captures nicely the upside of unbelief: Where religion is trivialized, one is unlikely to find persecution. When it is believed that on your religion hangs the fate of your immortal soul, the Inquisition follows easily; when it is believed that

religion is a breezy consumer preference, religious tolerance flourishes easily. After all, we don't persecute people for their taste in
cars. Why for their taste in gods?

Oddly, though, in our thoroughly secularized culture, there
is one form of religious intolerance that does survive. And that is
the disdain bordering on contempt of the culture makers for the
deeply religious, i.e., those for whom religion is not a preference
but a conviction.

Yale law professor Stephen Carter calls this "the culture of
disbelief," the oppressive assumption that no one of any learning
or sophistication could possibly be a religious believer—and the
social penalties meted out to those who nonetheless are.

Every manner of political argument is ruled legitimate in our
democratic discourse. But invoke the Bible as grounding for your
politics, and the First Amendment police will charge you with
breaching the sacred wall separating church and state. Carter
notes, for example, that one is allowed to have any view on abortion so long as it derives from ethical or practical or sociological or
medical considerations. But should someone stand up and oppose
abortion for reasons of faith, he is accused of trying to impose his
religious beliefs on others. Call on Timothy Leary or Chairman
Mao, fine. Call on St. Paul, and all hell breaks loose.

So ingrained is this disdain for the religious that when Clinton aide Sidney Blumenthal called Whitewater prosecutor Hick-
man Ewing a "religious fanatic"—Ewing's sins against secularism
include daily prayer, membership in a Fundamentalist church and
a sincere belief in God—it caused barely a ripple. Blumenthal did
apologize following a bit of Republican grumbling, but there was
nothing like the uproar that routinely accompanies a public insult
regarding, say, race or gender or sexual orientation. Indeed, the
question of Ewing's alleged fanaticism so pricked the interest of
the *New York Times*, zeitgeist arbiter of the Establishment, that it

dispatched a reporter to investigate. The result is hilarious: a classic of condescension posing as judiciousness.

On the one hand, writes Francis X. Clines, the *Times'* designated anthropologist to the Bible Belt, "some critics find it revealing that his 1980 law review article 'Combatting Official Corruption by All Available Means' began with an Old Testament quotation." The horror! By that standard Martin Luther King was not just a fanatic but a raving zealot.

But Clines does find another side to the story. Associates of Ewing defend him thus: "His open Christian faith, they insist, is left at the prosecutorial door." An interesting form of exoneration. Ewing is fit to carry out his judicial duties after all. Why? Because he allows none of his Christian faith to corrupt his working life.

We've come a long way in America. After two centuries, it seems we finally do have a religious test for office. True religiosity is disqualifying. Well, not quite. Believers may serve—but only if they check their belief at the office door.

At a time when religion is a preference and piety a form of eccentricity suggesting fanaticism, Chesterton needs revision: Tolerance is not just the virtue of people who do not believe in anything; tolerance extends only to people who don't believe in anything. Believe in something, and beware. You may not warrant presidential-level attack, but you'll make yourself suspect should you dare enter the naked public square.

Time, June 15, 1998

PART III

POLITICS, FOREIGN AND DOMESTIC

CHAPTER 12

THE TWO LAST TRIBES OF ISRAEL

The Miracle, at 60

Before sending Lewis and Clark west, Thomas Jefferson dispatched Meriwether Lewis to Philadelphia to see Benjamin Rush. The eminent doctor prepared a series of scientific questions for the expedition to answer. Among them, writes Stephen Ambrose: "What Affinity between their [the Indians'] religious Ceremonies & those of the Jews?" Jefferson and Lewis, like many of their day and ours, were fascinated by the Ten Lost Tribes of Israel and thought they might be out there on the Great Plains.

They weren't. They aren't anywhere. Their disappearance into the mists of history since their exile from Israel in 722 B.C. is no mystery. It is the norm, the rule for every ancient people defeated, destroyed, scattered and exiled.

With one exception, a miraculous story of redemption and return, after not a century or two, but 2,000 years. Remarkably, that miracle occurred in our time. This week marks its 60th anniversary: the return and restoration of the remaining two tribes of Israel—Judah and Benjamin, later known as the Jews—to their ancient homeland.

Besides restoring Jewish sovereignty, the establishment of the State of Israel embodied many subsidiary miracles, from the creation of the first Jewish army since Roman times to the only re-corded instance of the resurrection of a dead language—Hebrew, now the daily tongue of a vibrant nation of seven million. As historian Barbara Tuchman once wrote, Israel is "the only nation in the world that is governing itself in the same territory, under the same name, and with the same religion and same language as it did 3,000 years ago."

During its early years, Israel was often spoken of in such romantic terms. Today, such talk is considered naïve, anachronistic, even insensitive, nothing more than Zionist myth designed to hide the true story, i.e., the Palestinian narrative of dispossession.

Not so. Palestinian suffering is, of course, real and heart-wrenching, but what the Arab narrative deliberately distorts is the cause of its own tragedy: the folly of its own fanatical leadership—from Haj Amin al-Husseini, the grand mufti of Jerusalem (Nazi collaborator, who spent World War II in Berlin), to Egypt's Gamal Abdel Nasser to Yasser Arafat to Hamas of today—that repeatedly chose war rather than compromise and conciliation.

Palestinian dispossession is a direct result of the Arab rejection, then and now, of a Jewish state of any size on any part of the vast lands the Arabs claim as their exclusive patrimony. That was the cause of the war 60 years ago that, in turn, caused the refugee problem. And it remains the cause of war today.

Six months before Israel's birth, the United Nations had decided by a two-thirds majority that the only just solution to the British departure from Palestine would be the establishment of a Jewish state and an Arab state side by side. The undeniable fact remains: The Jews accepted that compromise; the Arabs rejected it.

With a vengeance. On the day the British pulled down their flag, Israel was invaded by Egypt, Syria, Lebanon, Transjordan and Iraq—650,000 Jews against 40 million Arabs.

Israel prevailed, another miracle. But at a very high cost—not just to the Palestinians displaced as a result of a war designed to extinguish Israel at birth, but also to the Israelis, whose war losses were staggering: 6,373 dead. One percent of the population. In American terms, it would take *35* Vietnam memorials to encompass such a monumental loss of life.

You rarely hear about Israel's terrible suffering in that 1948–49 war. You hear only the Palestinian side. Today, in the same vein, you hear that Israeli settlements and checkpoints and occupation are the continuing root causes of terrorism and instability in the region.

But in 1948, there were no "occupied territories." Nor in 1967 when Egypt, Syria and Jordan joined together in a second war of annihilation against Israel.

Look at Gaza today. No Israeli occupation, no settlements, not a single Jew left. The Palestinian response? Unremitting rocket fire killing and maiming Israeli civilians. The declared casus belli of the Palestinian government in Gaza behind these rockets? The very existence of a Jewish state.

One constantly hears about the disabling complexity of the Arab-Israeli dispute. Complex it is, but the root cause is not. Israel's crime is not its policies but its insistence on living. On the day the Arabs—and the Palestinians in particular—make a collective decision to accept the Jewish state, there will be peace, as Israel proved with its treaties with Egypt and Jordan. Until that day, there will be nothing but war. And every "peace process," however cynical or well meaning, will come to nothing.

The Washington Post, May 16, 2008

The Holocaust and Jewish Identity

Bernie Sanders is the most successful Jewish candidate for the presidency ever. It's a rare sign of the health of our republic that no one seems to much care or even notice. Least of all, Sanders himself. Which prompted CNN's Anderson Cooper in a recent Democratic debate to ask Sanders whether he was intentionally keeping his Judaism under wraps.

"No," answered Sanders: "I am very proud to be Jewish." He then explained that the Holocaust had wiped out his father's family. And that he remembered as a child seeing neighbors with concentration camp numbers tattooed on their arms. Being Jewish, he declared, "is an essential part of who I am as a human being."

A fascinating answer, irrelevant to presidential politics but quite revealing about the state of Jewish identity in contemporary America.

Think about it. There are several alternate ways American Jews commonly explain the role Judaism plays in their lives.

1. Practice: Judaism as embedded in their lives through religious practice or the transmission of Jewish culture by way of teaching or scholarship. Think Joe Lieberman or the neighborhood rabbi.

2. Tikkun: Seeing Judaism as an expression of the prophetic ideal of social justice. Love thy neighbor, clothe the naked, walk with God, beat swords into plowshares. As ritual and practice have fallen away over the generations, this has become the core identity of liberal Judaism. Its central mission is nothing less than to repair the world (*"Tikkun olam"*).

Which, incidentally, is the answer to the perennial question, "Why is it that Jews vote overwhelmingly Democratic?" Because, for the majority of Jews, the social ideals of liberalism are the most tangible expressions of their prophetic Jewish faith.

When Sanders was asked about his Jewish identity, I was sure his answer would be some variation of Tikkun. On the stump, he plays the Old Testament prophet railing against the powerful and denouncing their treatment of the widow and the orphan. Yet Sanders gave an entirely different answer.

3. The Holocaust. What a strange reply—yet it doesn't seem so to us because it has become increasingly common for American Jews to locate their identity in the Holocaust.

For example, it's become a growing emphasis in Jewish pedagogy from the Sunday schools to Holocaust studies programs in the various universities. Additionally, Jewish groups organize visits for young people to the concentration camps of Europe.

The memories created are indelible. And deeply valuable. Indeed, though my own family was largely spared, the Holocaust forms an ineradicable element of my own Jewish consciousness. But I worry about the balance. As Jewish practice, learning and knowledge diminish over time, my concern is that Holocaust memory is emerging as the dominant feature of Jewishness in America.

I worry that a people with a 3,000-year history of creative genius, enriched by intimate relations with every culture from Paris to Patagonia, should be placing such weight on martyrdom—and indeed, for this generation, martyrdom once removed.

I'm not criticizing Sanders. I credit him with sincerity and authenticity. But it is precisely that sincerity and authenticity—and the implications for future generations—that so concern me. Sanders is 74, but I suspect a growing number of young Jews would give an answer similar to his.

We must of course remain dedicated to keeping alive the memory and the truth of the Holocaust, particularly when they are under assault from so many quarters. Which is why, though I initially opposed having a Holocaust museum as the sole representation of the Jewish experience in the center of Washington, DC, I came to see the virtue of having so sacred yet vulnerable a legacy placed at the monumental core of—and thus entrusted to the protection of—the most tolerant and open nation on earth.

Nonetheless, there must be balance. It would be a tragedy for American Jews to make the Holocaust the principal legacy bequeathed to their children. After all, the Jewish people are living through a miraculous age: the rebirth of Jewish sovereignty, the revival of Hebrew (a cultural resurrection unique in human history), the flowering of a new Hebraic culture radiating throughout the Jewish world.

Memory is sacred, but victimhood cannot be the foundation stone of Jewish identity. Traditional Judaism has 613 commandments. The philosopher Emil Fackenheim famously said that the 614th is to deny Hitler any posthumous victories. The reduction of Jewish identity to victimhood would be one such victory. It must not be permitted.

The Washington Post, March 11, 2016

Demystifying Judaism

The sensation surrounding the elevation of Senator Joseph Lieberman, an Orthodox Jew, to the Democrats' presidential ticket lies less in the noun than in the adjective: Jews in American public life are old news; Orthodox Jews are not.

Had Al Gore chosen, say, former Treasury Secretary Robert Rubin or Senator Dianne Feinstein as his running mate, there would have been a stir about a barrier broken. But just a stir. It would not have been much of a barrier. After all, how much of a fuss was there about Jewishness when Richard Nixon made Henry Kissinger secretary of state?

Secular Jews, for whom Jewishness is little more than a form of ethnicity, identity or perhaps just racial memory, have long been accepted in the American mainstream. Why, Jerry Seinfeld—the quintessential nominal Jew who quite cheerfully acknowledges his Jewishness but finds it so devoid of meaning that it plays no role whatsoever in his life—became the most popular figure in American popular culture. The embrace of Jews is so thorough that Irving Kristol once noted wryly regarding the alarming rates of Jewish assimilation, "The problem is that they don't want to persecute us, they want to marry us."

This embrace of the secularized Jew has not, however, extended to the Orthodox. Orthodox Jews tend still to be seen by the mainstream as eccentric, even alien. Ironically, this cultural allergy is particularly acute among nominal Jews like Woody Allen, in whose films the Orthodox Jew is invariably a bearded, black-hatted buffoon.

Enter Joe Lieberman: beardless, hatless, witty, worldly, thoroughly modern, almost hip. This is Orthodox? Yes. And because it is, his ascension to the national stage will effect a demystification of Jewishness.

"What will he do if a war breaks out on the Sabbath?" the comedians asked. The answer is simple: He will break every ritual prohibition he needs to. Jewish law, the comedians and others are learning, not only permits it. Jewish law requires it.

They will learn that the rabbis seized upon an otherwise innocuous passage in Leviticus—God instructing the Israelites to observe his commandments and "live by them"—as an injunction not to die by them, and thus a subordination of all ritual to the higher value of preserving life.

This realization undermines the centuries-old myth of Judaism as severe and unforgiving, a slave of Pharisaic ritual, as opposed to the grace and charity of its progeny religion. Lieberman will not dethrone Shylock, still the single most influential Jewish figure in Western culture, for whom the law is pitiless law. But Lieberman's prominence and practice will illuminate the little-appreciated fact that Rabbinic Judaism is an attempt to take a very stark document—the Bible—and, by interpretation and adaptation, make it habitable for fallible human beings.

The most famous example concerns the death penalty. It appears rather promiscuously in the Bible. The Talmud, however, constructs such difficult evidentiary requirements and such extraordinary protections against miscarried justice that the rabbis termed a high court that executes one person in seven years "tyrannical." Another authority, continues the Talmud, says one person in 70 years.

The other great myth awaiting demystification is that traditional Judaism eschews spirituality in favor of petty, highly detailed ritual. Hence the sport that commentators have had trying to figure out what Vice President Lieberman would do on the

Sabbath. Well, he rests on the Sabbath. The rabbis define rest in very specific ways: no traveling, no carrying, no writing, no telephones, no use of electricity.

The prohibitions appear arbitrary. Not so. They have a purpose: to provide insulation against corrosive everydayness. To build fences against invasions by the profane. To create a space for sacred time.

The effect can be quite profound. I know. I grew up in a home much like Lieberman's. We too did not use electrical devices on the Sabbath. As a result, when we sat down to the last Sabbath meal toward the end of the day, we relied for illumination on light from the windows. As the day waned, the light began to die. When it came time for the Hebrew recitation (three times) of the 23rd Psalm, there was so little light that I could no longer read. I had to follow the words of my father as he chanted the Psalm softly with eyes closed. Thus did its every phrase and cadence become forever inscribed in my memory. To this day, whenever I hear the 23rd Psalm, I am filled with the most profound memories of father and family, of tranquility and grace in gentle gathering darkness.

The rabbis knew what they were doing. The elaborate way of life they constructed would not otherwise have lasted more than 2,000 years. Nor would it have lasted had it not produced the kind of spiritual transcendence that I experienced as a boy and that Lieberman experiences today—an experience many Americans will now learn about for the first time.

Which is why Lieberman's entry onto the national stage is so significant. It not only confirms and ratifies the full entry of Jews into the higher councils of American life. It marks the entry of Judaism into the deeper recesses of the American consciousness.

Time, August 21, 2000

How to Fight Academic Bigotry

For decades, the American Studies Association labored in well-deserved obscurity. No longer. It has now made a name for itself by voting to boycott Israeli universities, accusing them of denying academic and human rights to Palestinians.

Given that Israel has a profoundly democratic political system, the freest press in the Middle East, a fiercely independent judiciary and astonishing religious and racial diversity within its universities, including affirmative action for Arab students, the charge is rather strange.

Made more so when you consider the state of human rights in Israel's neighborhood. As we speak, Syria's government is dropping "barrel bombs" filled with nails, shrapnel and other instruments of terror on its own cities. Where is the ASA boycott of Syria?

And of Iran, which hangs political, religious and even sexual dissidents and has no academic freedom at all? Or Egypt, where Christians are being openly persecuted? Or Turkey, Saudi Arabia or, for that matter, massively repressive China and Russia?

Which makes obvious that the ASA boycott has nothing to do with human rights. It's an exercise in radical chic, giving marginalized academics a frisson of pretend anti-colonialism, seasoned with a dose of edgy anti-Semitism.

And don't tell me this is merely about Zionism. The ruse is transparent. Israel is the world's only Jewish state. To apply to the state of the Jews a double standard that you apply to none other, to judge one people in a way you judge no other, to single out that one people for condemnation and isolation—is to engage in a gross act of discrimination.

And discrimination against Jews has a name. It's called anti-Semitism.

Former Harvard president Larry Summers called the ASA actions "anti-Semitic in their effect if not necessarily in their intent." I choose to be less polite. The intent is clear: to incite hatred for the largest—and only sovereign—Jewish community on earth.

What to do? Facing a similar (British) academic boycott of Israelis seven years ago, Alan Dershowitz and Nobel Prize-winning physicist Steven Weinberg wrote an open letter declaring that, for the purposes of any anti-Israel boycott, they are to be considered Israelis.

Meaning: You discriminate against Israelis? Fine. Include us out. We will have nothing to do with you.

Thousands of other academics added their signatures to the Dershowitz/Weinberg letter. It was the perfect in-kind response. Boycott the boycotters, with contempt.

But academia isn't the only home for such prejudice. Throughout the cultural world, the Israel boycott movement is growing. It's become fashionable for musicians, actors, writers and performers of all kinds to ostentatiously cleanse themselves of Israel and Israelis.

The example of the tuxedoed set has spread to the more coarse and unkempt anti-Semites, such as the thugs who a few years ago disrupted London performances of the Jerusalem Quartet and the Israeli Philharmonic.

Five years ago in Sweden, Israel's Davis Cup team had to play its matches in an empty tennis stadium because the authorities could not guarantee the Israelis' safety from the mob. The most brazen display of rising anti-Semitism today is the spread of the "quenelle," a reverse Nazi salute, popularized by the openly anti-Semitic French entertainer Dieudonné M'bala M'bala.

In this sea of easy and open bigotry, an unusual man has made an unusual statement. Russian by birth, European by residence, Evgeny Kissin is arguably the world's greatest piano virtuoso. He is also a Jew of conviction. Deeply distressed by Israel's treatment in the cultural world around him, Kissin went beyond the Dershowitz/Weinberg stance of asking to be considered an Israeli. On December 7, he became one, defiantly.

Upon taking the oath of citizenship in Jerusalem, he declared: "I am a Jew, Israel is a Jewish state. ... Israel's case is my case, Israel's enemies are my enemies, and I do not want to be spared the troubles which Israeli musicians encounter when they represent the Jewish state beyond its borders."

The persistence of anti-Semitism, that most ancient of poisons, is one of history's great mysteries. Even the shame of the Holocaust proved no antidote. It provided but a temporary respite. Anti-Semitism is back. Alas, a new generation must learn to confront it.

How? How to answer the thugs, physical and intellectual, who single out Jews for attack? The best way, the most dignified way, is to do like Dershowitz, Weinberg or Kissin.

Express your solidarity. Sign the open letter or write your own. Don the yellow star and wear it proudly.

The Washington Post, January 10, 2014

Do We Really Mean "Never Again"?

Amid the ritual expressions of regret and the pledges of "never again" on Tuesday's 70th anniversary of the liberation of Auschwitz, a bitter irony was noted: Anti-Semitism has returned to Europe. With a vengeance.

It has become routine. If the kosher-grocery massacre in Paris hadn't happened in conjunction with *Charlie Hebdo*, how much worldwide notice would it have received? As little as did the murder of a rabbi and three children at a Jewish school in Toulouse. As little as did the terror attack that killed four at the Jewish Museum in Brussels.

The rise of European anti-Semitism is, in reality, just a return to the norm. For a millennium, virulent Jew-hatred—persecution, expulsions, massacres—was the norm in Europe until the shame of the Holocaust created a temporary anomaly wherein anti-Semitism became socially unacceptable.

The hiatus is over. Jew-hatred is back, recapitulating the past with impressive zeal. Italians protesting Gaza handed out leaflets calling for a boycott of Jewish merchants. As in the 1930s. A widely popular French comedian has introduced a variant of the Nazi salute. In Berlin, Gaza brought out a mob chanting, "Jew, Jew, cowardly pig, come out and fight alone!" Berlin, mind you.

European anti-Semitism is not a Jewish problem, however. It's a European problem, a stain, a disease of which Europe is congenitally unable to rid itself.

From the Jewish point of view, European anti-Semitism is a sideshow. The story of European Jewry is over. It died at Auschwitz. Europe's place as the center and fulcrum of the Jewish world has been inherited by Israel. Not only is it the first independent Jewish commonwealth in 2,000 years. It is, also for the first time in 2,000 years, the largest Jewish community on the planet.

The threat to the Jewish future lies not in Europe but in the Muslim Middle East, today the heart of global anti-Semitism, a veritable factory of anti-Jewish literature, films, blood libels and calls for violence, indeed for another genocide.

The founding charter of Hamas calls not just for the eradication of Israel but for the killing of Jews everywhere. Hezbollah chief Hassan Nasrallah welcomes Jewish emigration to Israel—because it makes the killing easier: "If Jews all gather in Israel, it will save us the trouble of going after them worldwide." And, of course, Iran openly declares as its sacred mission the annihilation of Israel.

For America, Europe and the moderate Arabs, there are powerful reasons having nothing to do with Israel for trying to prevent an apocalyptic, fanatically anti-Western clerical regime in Tehran from getting the bomb: Iranian hegemony, nuclear proliferation (including to terror groups) and elemental national security.

For Israel, however, the threat is of a different order. Direct, immediate and mortal.

The sophisticates cozily assure us not to worry. Deterrence will work. Didn't it work against the Soviets? Well, just 17 years into the atomic age, we came harrowingly close to deterrence failure and all-out nuclear war. Moreover, godless communists anticipate no reward in heaven. Atheists calculate differently from jihadists with their cult of death. Name one Soviet suicide bomber.

Former Iranian president Ali Akbar Hashemi Rafsanjani, known as a moderate, once characterized tiny Israel as a one-bomb country. He acknowledged Israel's deterrent capacity but noted the asymmetry: "Application of an atomic bomb would not leave anything in Israel, but the same thing would just produce damages in the Muslim world." Result? Israel eradicated, Islam vindicated. So much for deterrence.

And even if deterrence worked with Tehran, that's not where the story ends. Iran's very acquisition of nukes would set off a nuclear arms race with half a dozen Muslim countries from Turkey to Egypt to the Gulf states—in the most unstable part of the world. A place where you wake up in the morning to find a pro-American Yemeni government overthrown by rebels whose slogan is "God is Great. Death to America. Death to Israel. Damn the Jews. Power to Islam."

The idea that some kind of six-sided deterrence would work in this roiling cauldron of instability the way it did in the frozen bipolarity of the Cold War is simply ridiculous.

The Iranian bomb is a national security issue, an alliance issue and a regional Middle East issue. But it is also a uniquely Jewish issue because of Israel's situation as the only state on earth overtly threatened with extinction, facing a potential nuclear power overtly threatening that extinction.

On the 70th anniversary of Auschwitz, mourning dead Jews is easy. And, forgive me, cheap. Want to truly honor the dead? Show solidarity with the living—Israel and its six million Jews. Make "never again" more than an empty phrase. It took Nazi Germany seven years to kill six million Jews. It would take a nuclear Iran one day.

The Washington Post, January 30, 2015

CHAPTER 13

KEEPING THE WORLD AT BAY

How to Deal with Countries Gone Mad

Nothing is more difficult for the reasonable, settled, status quo state than to contemplate fanaticism. Those whose politics is determined by consensus and compromise become hopelessly unsettled in the face of single-minded zeal. The tendency is then to mistake it for irrationality. Ronald Reagan once famously referred to a group of regimes that defy the rules of international conduct as the "strangest collection of misfits, Looney Tunes and squalid criminals since the advent of the Third Reich." Less than two years later it was discovered that Reagan not only had dealt with these Looney Tunes but, in the words of his former chief of staff, had been snookered by them.

Reagan's list of loonies included Iran, Libya, North Korea, Cuba and Nicaragua. In fact, this is a list of small states that have tormented the US, delivering pinpricks that America has found impossible either to tolerate or prevent. Admitting this, however, is difficult. Easier to dismiss it all as the work of crazy states. Reagan was certainly right that these countries are "united by their fanatical hatred of the United States." But that in itself is not proof of derangement. Hatred is a common, often useful, phenomenon in international relations. And fanaticism is a measure of passion, not irrationality.

But assume, for the sake of argument, that there are regimes—Hitler's Germany, Amin's Uganda, Khomeini's Iran—whose ends are irrational. It is a mistake to think that because a state has lunatic ends, it must be clumsy, erratic or incompetent in carrying them out.

The fanatic can be both wise and wily. Indeed, the fanatic has a distinct advantage in choosing means. So utterly convinced is he of the rightness of his ends that he lacks ordinary inhibiting scruples in his choice of means. He need consider only their instrumental value, not their moral valence. Not for him messy moral conflicts when matching means and ends. Everything matches.

Zealotry, in fact, produces a kind of hyperrationality of technique. The trains carrying innocents to the Holocaust ran remorselessly on time. That is fanaticism's special gift, its special horror: its ability to routinize, to rationalize, to bureaucratize murderous irrationality.

The coexistence of irrational ends and rational means is an enduring source of astonishment. It should not be. Once you decide to murder every Jew in Europe, Auschwitz follows logically. Once you have decided that the city is parasitic on the countryside (Khieu Samphan, leader of the Khmer Rouge, decided that at the Sorbonne and made it a tenet of his doctoral thesis), then the forced emptying of Cambodian cities at the cost of millions of lives follows logically. After all, the extirpation of parasites is a public service. Once you have decided, as did Ayatollah Khomeini, to redeem the Islamic world from idolatry, and once you believe, as he does, that martyrdom is the quickest way to the joys of paradise, then sending 14-year-old boys into the teeth of machine guns is by no means irrational.

This is not to say states cannot act crazily. It is to say we should not expect bizarre behavior from states just because we find their ends incomprehensible. In American dealings with Iran, for example, it is the US that has behaved erratically, even laughably. After all, who sent whom the cake?

It is not just wrong but dangerous to underestimate the rationality of regimes that profess the craziest of ends. The very designation "crazy state" inclines those sure of their own sanity to let down their guard. Europe catastrophically underestimated Hitler because he was plainly a madman. That he was. It did not prevent him from conquering Europe.

A corollary to the notion that the crazy state is incompetent is the notion that it must ultimately self-destruct. Americans keep waiting for that to happen to the mullahs, the Sandinistas and the rest of the world's zealots. It is a wan hope. This century has not been kind to the notion that fanaticism must collapse from within. Generally, the crazy state does not self-destruct. On the contrary, it must be destroyed from without: Hitler by the Allies, the Khmer Rouge by Vietnam, Idi Amin by Tanzania. (In his last years Stalin was no less irrational than Hitler, if not quite as bloody. Yet far from self-destructing, his regime, having succeeded in war, extended its hegemony over a great empire.)

The authority of the charismatic despot who drives the crazy state rests largely on a myth of invincibility. That myth is best punctured from the outside. So long as the outside world cowers, accommodates and appeases, that authority grows unchallenged. Munich is the model. Once the outside world returns fire, that shock alone can be enough to shake the foundations of the despot's power. The 1986 American air raid on Libya is the model. Its military significance was minimal. Its psychological significance was enormous. Qaddafi went into retreat. And not just on the terrorism front. Within a year, his demoralized forces were routed and expelled from Chad, perhaps the weakest state in Central Africa.

Which bodes ill for those hoping to see Iran curbed today. Iran is today's paradigmatic crazy state: its ideology extreme and archaic, its leadership implacable, its population full of passionate intensity, celebrating martyrdom and incurring it. Sightings of moderates notwithstanding, the Iran of 1987 shows no sign of collapse from within. Moreover, its prospects of being punctured from without are slim. Since crazy states tend to be destroyed from the outside, their fate is often a function of their geography. Hitler had the misfortune of being located in Central Europe; his pursuit of Lebensraum ran up against the greatest powers of the day. The Khmer Rouge's bad luck was to be living next door to an equally warlike Vietnam. Otherwise it would be killing to this day, assuming there were any Cambodians left to kill. Qaddafi had the misfortune of being hard by the Mediterranean, an American lake. And Idi Amin's butchery came to an end after he had trespassed once too often on neighboring Tanzania, which muscled its way into Uganda and threw him out.

The mullahs have wisely taken great care not to provoke their powerful northern and eastern neighbors. Iran's ambitions lie to the southwest, where, if it can just get past Iraq, it faces states so weak they hardly deserve the name. With hegemony over the Gulf, the oil and the holy places awaiting it in what is a veritable geopolitical desert, Khomeinism will push on until it encounters the shock of some irresistible outside force. Until then, Iran can be as crazy as it wants.

Time, September 21, 1987

The Iranian "Moderate"

The search, now 30 years old, for Iranian "moderates" goes on. Amid the enthusiasm of the latest sighting, it's worth remembering that the highlight of the Iran-Contra arms-for-hostages debacle was the secret trip to Tehran taken by Robert McFarlane, President Reagan's former national security adviser. He brought a key-shaped cake symbolizing the new relations he was opening with the "moderates."

We know how that ended.

Three decades later, the mirage reappears in the form of Hassan Rouhani. Strange résumé for a moderate: 35 years of unswervingly loyal service to the Islamic Republic as a close aide to Ayatollahs Khomeini and Khamenei. Moreover, Rouhani was one of only six presidential candidates, another 678 having been disqualified by the regime as ideologically unsound. That puts him in the 99th centile for fealty.

Rouhani is Khamenei's agent but, with a smile and style, he's now hailed as the face of Iranian moderation. Why? Because Rouhani wants better relations with the West.

Well, what leader would not want relief from Western sanctions that have sunk Iran's economy, devalued its currency and caused widespread hardship? The test of moderation is not what you want but what you're willing to give. After all, sanctions were not slapped on Iran for amusement. It was to enforce multiple UN Security Council resolutions demanding a halt to uranium enrichment.

Yet in his lovey-dovey *Washington Post* op-ed, his UN speech and various interviews, Rouhani gives not an inch on uranium enrichment. Indeed, he has repeatedly denied that Iran is pursuing nuclear weapons at all. Or ever has. Such a transparent falsehood—what country swimming in oil would sacrifice its economy just to produce nuclear electricity that advanced countries such as Germany are already abandoning?—is hardly the basis for a successful negotiation.

But successful negotiation is not what the mullahs are seeking. They want sanctions relief. And more than anything, they want to buy time.

It takes about 250 kilograms of 20% enriched uranium to make a nuclear bomb. The International Atomic Energy Agency reported in August that Iran already has 186 kilograms. That leaves the Iranians on the threshold of going nuclear. They are adding 3,000 new high-speed centrifuges. They need just a bit more talking, stalling, smiling and stringing along of a gullible West.

Rouhani is the man to do exactly that. As Iran's chief nuclear negotiator between 2003 and 2005, he boasted in a 2004 speech to the Supreme Cultural Revolution Council, "While we were talking with the Europeans in Tehran, we were installing equipment in parts of the [uranium conversion] facility in Isfahan.... In fact, by creating a calm environment, we were able to complete the work in Isfahan."

Such is their contempt for us that they don't even hide their strategy: Spin the centrifuges while spinning the West.

And when the president of the world's sole superpower asks for a photo-op handshake with the president of a regime that, in President Obama's own words, kills and kidnaps and terrorizes Americans, the killer-kidnapper does not even deign to accept the homage. Rouhani rebuffed him.

Who can blame Rouhani? Offer a few pleasant words in an op-ed hailing a new era of non-zero-sum foreign relations, and watch the media and the administration immediately swoon with visions of détente.

Détente is difficult with a regime whose favorite refrain, fed to frenzied mass rallies, is "Death to America." Détente is difficult with a regime officially committed, as a matter of both national policy and religious duty, to the eradication of a UN member state, namely Israel. It doesn't get more zero-sum than that.

But at least we have to talk, say the enthusiasts. As if we haven't been talking. For a decade. Strung along in negotiations of every manner—the EU3, the P5+1, then the final, very final, last-chance 2012 negotiations held in Istanbul, Baghdad and Moscow at which the Iranians refused to even consider the nuclear issue, declaring the dossier closed. Plus two more useless rounds this year.

I'm for negotiations. But only if it's to do something real, not to run out the clock as Iran goes nuclear. The administration says it wants actions, not words. Fine. Demand one simple proof of good faith: Honor the UN resolutions. Suspend uranium enrichment and we will talk.

At least that stops the clock. Anything else amounts to being played.

And about the Khamenei agent who charms but declares enrichment an inalienable right, who smiles but refuses to shake the president's hand. When asked by NBC News whether the Holocaust was a myth, Rouhani replied: "I'm not a historian. I'm a politician."

Iranian moderation in action.

And, by the way, do you know who was one of the three Iranian "moderates" the cake-bearing McFarlane dealt with at that fateful arms-for-hostage meeting in Tehran 27 years ago? Hassan Rouhani.

We never learn.

The Washington Post, September 27, 2013

Middle East Peace and the
Great Muslim Civil War

"Whom the gods would destroy, they first tempt
to resolve the Arab-Israeli conflict."
—*Irving Kristol*

The quixotic American pursuit of Middle East peace is a perennial. It invariably fails, yet every administration feels compelled to give it a try. The Trump administration is no different.

It will fail as well. To be sure, no great harm has, as yet, come from President Trump's enthusiasm for what would be "the ultimate deal." It will, however, distract and detract from remarkable progress being made elsewhere in the Middle East.

That progress began with Trump's trip to Saudi Arabia, the first of his presidency—an unmistakable declaration of a radical reorientation of US policy in the region. Message: The appeasement of Iran is over.

Barack Obama's tilt toward Iran in the great Muslim civil war between Shiite Iran and Sunni Arabs led by Saudi Arabia was his reach for Nixon-to-China glory. It ended ignominiously.

The idea that the nuclear deal would make Iran more moderate has proved spectacularly wrong, as demonstrated by its defiant ballistic missile launches, its indispensable support for the genocidal Assad regime in Syria, its backing of the Houthi insurgency in Yemen, its worldwide support for terrorism, its relentless anti-Americanism and commitment to the annihilation of Israel.

These aggressions were supposed to abate. They didn't. On

the contrary, the cash payments and the lifting of economic sanctions—Tehran's reward for the nuclear deal—have only given its geopolitical thrusts more power and reach.

The reversal has now begun. The first act was Trump's Riyadh address to about 50 Muslim states (the overwhelming majority of them Sunni) signaling a wide Islamic alliance committed to resisting Iran and willing to cast its lot with the American side.

That was objective No. 1. The other was to turn the Sunni powers against Sunni terrorism. The Islamic State is Sunni. Al-Qaeda is Sunni. Fifteen of the 9/11 hijackers were Saudi. And the spread of Saudi-funded madrassas around the world has for decades inculcated a poisonous Wahhabism that has fueled Islamist terrorism.

Saudi Arabia and the other Gulf states publicly declaring war on their bastard terrorist child is significant. As is their pledge not to tolerate any semi-official support or private donations. And their opening during the summit of an anti-terrorism center in Riyadh.

After eight years of US policy hovering between neglect and betrayal, the Sunni Arabs are relieved to have America back. A salutary side effect is the possibility of a détente with Israel.

That would suggest an outside-in approach to Arab-Israeli peace: A rapprochement between the Sunni state and Israel (the outside) would put pressure on the Palestinians to come to terms (the inside). It's a long-shot strategy but it's better than all the others. Unfortunately, Trump muddied the waters a bit in Israel by at times reverting to the opposite strategy—the inside-out—by saying that an Israeli-Palestinian deal would "begin a process of peace all throughout the Middle East."

That is well-worn nonsense. Imagine if Israel disappeared tomorrow in an earthquake. Does that end the civil war in Syria? The instability in Iraq? The fighting in Yemen? Does it change anything of consequence amid the intra-Arab chaos? Of course not.

And apart from being delusional, the inside-out strategy is at present impossible. Palestinian leadership is both hopelessly weak and irredeemably rejectionist. Until it is prepared to accept the legitimacy of the Jewish state—which it has never done in the 100 years since the Balfour Declaration committed Britain (and later the League of Nations) to a Jewish homeland in Palestine—there will be no peace.

It may come one day. But not now. Which is why making the Israel-Palestinian issue central, rather than peripheral, to the epic Sunni-Shiite war shaking the Middle East today is a serious tactical mistake. It subjects any now-possible reconciliation between Israel and the Arab states to a Palestinian veto.

Ironically, the Iranian threat that grew under Obama offers a unique opportunity for US-Arab and even Israeli-Arab cooperation. Over time, such cooperation could gradually acclimate Arab peoples to a nonbelligerent stance toward Israel. Which might in turn help persuade the Palestinians to make some concessions before their fellow Arabs finally tire of the Palestinians' century of rejectionism.

Perhaps that will require a peace process of sorts. No great harm, as long as we remember that any such Israeli-Palestinian talks are for show—until conditions are one day ripe for peace.

In the meantime, the real action is on the anti-Iranian and anti-terrorism fronts. Don't let Oslo-like mirages get in the way.

The Washington Post, May 26, 2017

The Bush Legacy

Clare Boothe Luce liked to say that "a great man is one sentence." Presidents, in particular. The most common "one sentence" for George W. Bush is: "He kept us safe."

Not quite right. With Bush's legacy being reassessed as his presidential library opens in Dallas, it's important to note that he did not just keep us safe. He created the entire anti-terror infrastructure that continues to keep us safe.

That homage was paid, wordlessly, by Barack Obama, who vilified Bush's anti-terror policies as a candidate, then continued them as president: indefinite detention, rendition, warrantless wiretaps, special forces and drone warfare, and, most notoriously, Guantanamo, which Obama so ostentatiously denounced—until he found it indispensable.

Quite a list. Which is why there was not one successful terror bombing on US soil from 9/11 until last week. The Boston Marathon attack was an obvious security failure, but there is a difference between 3,000 dead and 3. And on the other side of the ledger are the innumerable plots broken up since 9/11.

Moreover, Bush's achievement was not just infrastructure. It was war. The Afghan campaign overthrew the Taliban, decimated al-Qaeda and expelled it from its haven. Yet that success is today derogated with the cheap and lazy catchphrase—"He got us into two wars"—intended to spread to Afghanistan the opprobrium associated with Iraq.

As if Afghanistan was some unilateral Bush adventure foisted on the American people. As if Obama himself did not call it a "war of necessity" and Joe Biden the most just war since World War II.

The dilemma in Afghanistan was what to do after the brilliant nine-week victory. There was no good answer. Even with the benefit of seven years' grinding experience under his predecessor, Obama got it wrong. His Afghan "surge" cost hundreds of American lives without having changed the country's prospects.

It turned out to be a land too primitive to democratize, too fractured to unify. The final withdrawal will come after Obama's own six years of futility.

Iraq was, of course, far more problematic. Critics conveniently forget that the invasion had broad support from the public and Congress, including from those who became the highest-ranking foreign policy figures in the Obama administration—Hillary Clinton, John Kerry, Chuck Hagel and Biden.

And they forget the context—crumbling sanctions that would, in short order, have restored Saddam Hussein to full economic and regional power, well positioning him, post-sanctions, to again threaten his neighbors and restart his WMD program.

Was the war worth it? Inconclusive wars never yield a good answer. Was Korea worth it? It ended with a restoration of the status quo ante. Now, 60 years later, we face nuclear threats from the same regime that was not defeated in a war that cost 10 times as many American lives as Iraq.

The Iraq War had three parts. The initial toppling of the regime was a remarkable success—like Afghanistan, rapid and with relatively few US casualties.

The occupation was a disaster, rooted in the fundamental contradiction between means and ends, between the "light footprint" provided by the US Army and the grand reformation attempted by Coalition Provisional Authority chief Paul Bremer, who tried to change everything down to the coinage.

Finally, the surge, a courageous Bush decision taken against near-universal opposition that produced the greatest US military turnaround since the Inchon landing. And inflicted the single most significant defeat for al-Qaeda (save Afghanistan)—a humiliating rout at the hands of Iraqi Sunnis fighting side by side with the American infidel.

As with Lincoln, it took Bush years of agonizing bloody stalemate before he finally found his general and his strategy. Yet, for all the terrible cost, Bush bequeathed to Obama a strategically won war. Obama had one task: Conclude a status-of-forces agreement and thus secure Iraq as a major regional ally. He failed utterly. Iraq today is more fragile, sectarian and Iranian-influenced than it was when Bush left office—and than it had to be.

Like Bush, Harry Truman left office widely scorned, largely because of the inconclusive war he left behind. In time, however, Korea came to be seen as but one battle in a much larger Cold War that Truman was instrumental in winning. He established the institutional and policy infrastructure (CIA, NATO, the Truman Doctrine, etc.) that made possible ultimate victory almost a half-century later. I suspect history will similarly see Bush as the man who, by trial and error but also with prescience and principle, established the structures that will take us through another long twilight struggle and enable us to prevail.

The Washington Post, April 26, 2013

Iraq, Abandoned

R amadi falls. The Iraqi army flees. The great 60-nation anti-Islamic State coalition so grandly proclaimed by the Obama administration is nowhere to be seen. Instead, it's the defense minister of Iran who flies into Baghdad, an unsubtle demonstration of who's in charge—while the US air campaign proves futile and America's alleged strategy for combating the Islamic State is in freefall.

It gets worse. The Gulf states' top leaders, betrayed and bitter, ostentatiously boycott President Obama's failed Camp David summit. "We were America's best friend in the Arab world for 50 years," laments Saudi Arabia's former intelligence chief.

Note: "were," not "are."

We are scraping bottom. Following six years of President Obama's steady and determined withdrawal from the Middle East, America's standing in the region has collapsed. And yet the question incessantly asked of the various presidential candidates is not about that. It's a retrospective hypothetical: Would you have invaded Iraq in 2003 if you had known then what we know now?

First, the question is not just a hypothetical but an inherently impossible hypothetical. It contradicts itself. Had we known there were no weapons of mass destruction, the very question would not have arisen. The premise of the war—the basis for going to the UN, to the Congress and, indeed, to the nation—was Iraq's possession of WMD in violation of the central condition for the cease-fire that ended the 1991 Gulf War. No WMD, no hypothetical to answer in the first place.

Second, the "if you knew then" question implicitly locates the origin and cause of the current disasters in 2003. As if the fall of Ramadi was predetermined then, as if the author of the current regional collapse is George W. Bush.

This is nonsense. The fact is that by the end of Bush's tenure the war had been won. You can argue that the price of that victory was too high. Fine. We can debate that until the end of time. But what is not debatable is that it was a victory. Bush bequeathed to Obama a success. By whose measure? By Obama's. As he told the troops at Fort Bragg on December 14, 2011, "We are leaving behind a sovereign, stable and self-reliant Iraq, with a representative government that was elected by its people." This was, said the president, a "moment of success."

Which Obama proceeded to fully squander. With the 2012 election approaching, he chose to liquidate our military presence in Iraq. We didn't just withdraw our forces. We abandoned, destroyed or turned over our equipment, stores, installations and bases. We surrendered our most valuable strategic assets, such as control of Iraqi airspace, soon to become the indispensable conduit for Iran to supply and sustain the Assad regime in Syria and cement its influence all the way to the Mediterranean. And, most relevant to the fall of Ramadi, we abandoned the vast intelligence network we had so painstakingly constructed in Anbar province, without which our current patchwork operations there are largely blind and correspondingly feeble.

The current collapse was not predetermined in 2003 but in 2011. Isn't that what should be asked of Hillary Clinton? We know you think the invasion of 2003 was a mistake. But what about the abandonment of 2011? Was that not a mistake?

Madam Secretary: When you arrived at the State Department, al-Qaeda in Iraq had been crushed and expelled from Anbar. The Iraqi government had from Basra to Sadr City fought and defeated the radical, Iranian-proxy Shiite militias. Yet today these militias are back, once again dominating Baghdad. On your watch, we gave up our position as the dominant influence over a "sovereign, stable and self-reliant Iraq"—forfeiting that position gratuitously to Iran. Was that not a mistake? And where were you when it was made?

Iraq is now a battlefield between the Sunni jihadists of the Islamic State and the Shiite jihadists of Iran's Islamic Republic. There is no viable center. We abandoned it. The Obama administration's unilateral pullout created a vacuum for the entry of the worst of the worst.

And the damage was self-inflicted. The current situation in Iraq, says David Petraeus, "is tragic foremost because it didn't have to turn out this way. The hard-earned progress of the surge was sustained for over three years."

Do the math. That's 2009 through 2011, the first three Obama years. And then came the unraveling. When? The last US troops left Iraq on December 18, 2011.

Want to do retrospective hypotheticals? Start there.

The Washington Post, May 22, 2015

The Climate Pact Swindle

Historic. Such is the ubiquitous description of the climate agreement recently announced in Beijing between Barack Obama and Xi Jinping in which China promised for the first time to cap carbon emissions.

If this were a real breakthrough, I'd be an enthusiastic supporter. I have long advocated for a tangible global agreement to curb carbon. I do remain skeptical about the arrogant, ignorant claim that climate science is "settled," that it can predict with accuracy future "global warming" effects and that therefore we must cut emissions radically, immediately and unilaterally if necessary, even at potentially ruinous economic and social cost.

I nonetheless believe (and have written since 1988) that pumping increasing amounts of CO_2 into the atmosphere cannot be a good thing. We don't know nearly enough about the planet's homeostatic mechanisms for dealing with it, but prudence would dictate reducing CO_2 emissions when and where we can.

However, anything beyond that, especially the radical unilateralism advocated by climate alarmists, would be not just economic suicide but economic suicide without purpose. It would do nothing to reduce atmospheric CO_2 as long as China, India and the other developing nations more than make up for our cuts with their huge and increasing carbon emissions.

China alone is firing up a new coal plant every eight to 10 days. We could close every coal mine in Kentucky and West Virginia and achieve absolutely nothing except devastating Appalachia and, in effect, shipping its economic lifeblood to China.

The only way forward on greenhouse gases is global reduction by global agreement. A pact with China would be a good start.

Unfortunately, the Obama-Xi agreement is nothing of the sort. It is a fraud of epic proportions. Its main plank commits China to begin cutting carbon emissions 16 years from now. On the other hand, the United States, having already cut more carbon emissions than any nation on earth since 2005, must now double its current rate of carbon cutting to meet a new, more restrictive goal by 2025. In return for which, China will keep increasing its carbon emissions year after year throughout that period—and for five years beyond.

If this sounds like the most one-sided deal since Manhattan sold for \$24 in 1626, you heard right. It becomes even more absurd when you realize that, according to the Lawrence Berkeley National Laboratory, China was on track to plateau its carbon emissions around 2030 anyway because of a projected slowdown in urbanization, population growth and heavy industry production. We cut, they coast.

The carbon emission graph is stark. China's line is nearly vertical; America's is already inflected and headed downward. The Obama-Xi agreement simply ratifies US unilateralism—the US line declines even more steeply, while China's continues rocketing upward unmolested.

Proponents of the Obama-Xi deal will then point to a second provision: China's promise to produce 20% of its energy from non-carbon sources by 2030. But China had already been planning to begin substituting for its immense use of fossil fuels (mainly by using nuclear power) because Chinese cities are being choked to death by their traditional pollutants—sulfur dioxide, nitrogen oxide, mercury compounds, particulates, etc.

These are serious health hazards. CO_2 is not. Whatever its atmospheric effects, CO2 does not poison the air. So in return for yet another Chinese transition that has nothing to do with CO2, Obama has committed the United States to drastic CO2 cuts.

Moreover, beyond substance, there is process. Or more accurately, its absence. What's the structure to sustain and verify the agreement? Where are the benchmarks? What are the enforcement mechanisms? This is just a verbal promise. Nothing more. Sixteen years from now, China is supposed to remind the world of its commitments and begin cutting?

I repeat: I would unequivocally support a real agreement with the Chinese where they cut contemporaneously and commensurately with the United States and where there is built-in reporting and independent verification. Such a bilateral agreement would need to be internationalized by bringing in such rising powers as India, Brazil, Indonesia, etc. This would be a breakthrough.

Climate enthusiasts will say that I refuse to take yes for an answer. Of course I would take yes for an answer. But the Obama-Xi agreement is not yes. It is "check back with me in 16 years." Aren't the people advocating this deal the same garment-rending climate apocalypticists who've been warning of irreversible planetary changes beginning now, and the supreme imperative of acting immediately?

Except, you see, for China, the world's No. 1 carbon polluter. It gets a 16-year pass.

The Washington Post, November 21, 2014

Russia Rising

"The United States does not view Europe as a battleground
between East and West, nor do we see the situation in
Ukraine as a zero-sum game. That's the kind of thinking
that should have ended with the Cold War."
—*Barack Obama, March 24*

Should. Lovely sentiment. As lovely as what Obama said
five years ago to the United Nations: "No one nation can or
should try to dominate another nation."

That's the kind of sentiment you expect from a Miss America
contestant asked to name her fondest wish, not from the leader of
the free world explaining his foreign policy.

The East Europeans know they inhabit the battleground between the West and a Russia that wants to return them to its
sphere of influence. Ukrainians see tens of thousands of Russian
troops across their border and know they are looking down the
barrel of quite a zero-sum game.

Obama thinks otherwise. He says that Vladimir Putin's kind
of neo-imperialist thinking is a relic of the past—and advises
Putin to transcend the Cold War.

Good God. Putin hasn't transcended the Russian revolution.
Did no one give Obama a copy of Putin's speech last week upon
the annexation of Crimea? Putin railed not only at Russia's loss of
empire in the 1990s. He went back to the 1920s: "After the revolution, the Bolsheviks... may God judge them, added large sections of the historical South of Russia to the Republic of Ukraine."
Putin was referring not to Crimea (which came two sentences

later) but to his next potential target: Kharkiv and Donetsk and the rest of southeastern Ukraine.

Putin's irredentist grievances go very deep. Obama seems unable to fathom them. Asked whether he'd misjudged Russia, whether it really is our greatest geopolitical foe, he disdainfully replied that Russia is nothing but "a regional power" acting "out of weakness."

Where does one begin? Hitler's Germany and Tojo's Japan were also regional powers, yet managed to leave behind at least 50 million dead. And yes, Russia should be no match for the American superpower. Yet under this president, Russia has run rings around America, from the attempted ingratiation of the "reset" to America's empty threats of "consequences" were Russia to annex Crimea.

Annex Crimea it did. For which the "consequences" have been risible. Numberless 19th- and 20th-century European soldiers died for Crimea. Putin conquered it in a swift and stealthy campaign that took three weeks and cost his forces not a sprained ankle. That's "weakness"?

Indeed, Obama's dismissal of Russia as a regional power makes his own leadership of the one superpower all the more embarrassing. For seven decades since the Japanese surrender, our role under 11 presidents had been as offshore balancer protecting smaller allies from potential regional hegemons.

What are the allies thinking now? Japan, South Korea, Taiwan, the Philippines and other Pacific Rim friends are wondering where this America will be as China expands its reach and claims. The Gulf states are near panic as they see the United States play-acting nuclear negotiations with Iran that, at best, will leave their mortal Shiite enemy just weeks away from the bomb.

America never sought the role that history gave it after World War II to bear unbidden burdens "to assure the survival and the success of liberty," as movingly described by John Kennedy. We have an appropriate aversion to the stark fact that the alternative to US leadership is either global chaos or dominance by the likes of China, Russia and Iran.

But Obama doesn't even seem to recognize this truth. In his major Brussels address Wednesday, the very day Russia seized the last Ukrainian naval vessel in Crimea, Obama made vague references to further measures should Russia march deeper into Ukraine, while still emphasizing the centrality of international law, international norms and international institutions such as the United Nations.

Such fanciful thinking will leave our allies with two choices: Bend a knee—or arm to the teeth. Either acquiesce to the regional bully or gird your loins; i.e., go nuclear. As surely will the Gulf states. As will, in time, Japan and South Korea.

Even Ukrainians are expressing regret at having given up their nukes in return for paper guarantees of territorial integrity. The 1994 Budapest Memorandum was ahead of its time—the perfect example of the kind of advanced 21st-century thinking so cherished by our president. Perhaps the captain of that last Ukrainian vessel should have waved the document at the Russian fleet that took his ship.

The Washington Post, March 28, 2014

To Die for Estonia?

So what if, in his speech last week to NATO, President Trump didn't explicitly reaffirm the provision that an attack on one is an attack on all?

What's the big deal? Didn't he affirm a general commitment to NATO during his visit? Hadn't he earlier sent his vice president and secretaries of state and defense to pledge allegiance to Article 5?

And anyway, who believes that the United States would really go to war with Russia—and risk nuclear annihilation—over Estonia?

Ah, but that's precisely the point. It is because deterrence is so delicate, so problematic, so literally unbelievable that it is not to be trifled with. And why for an American president to gratuitously undermine what little credibility deterrence already has, by ostentatiously refusing to recommit to Article 5, is so shocking.

Deterrence is inherently a barely believable bluff. Even at the height of the Cold War, when highly resolute presidents, such as Eisenhower and Kennedy, threatened Russia with "massive retaliation" (i.e., all-out nuclear war), would we really have sacrificed New York for Berlin?

No one knew for sure. Not Eisenhower, not Kennedy, not Khrushchev, not anyone. Yet that very uncertainty was enough to stay the hand of any aggressor and keep the peace of the world for 70 years, the longest period without war between the Great Powers in modern history.

Deterrence does not depend on 100% certainty that the other guy will go to war if you cross a red line. Given the stakes, merely a chance of that happening can be enough. For 70 years, it was enough.

Leaders therefore do everything they can to bolster it. Install tripwires, for example. During the Cold War, we stationed troops in Germany to face the massive tank armies of Soviet Russia. Today we have 28,000 troops in South Korea, 12,000 near the demilitarized zone.

Why? Not to repel invasion. They couldn't. They're not strong enough. To put it very coldly, they're there to die. They're a deliberate message to the enemy that if you invade our ally, you will have to kill a lot of Americans first. Which will galvanize us into full-scale war against you.

Tripwires are risky, dangerous and cynical. Yet we resort to them because parchment promises are problematic and tripwires imply automaticity. We do what we can to strengthen deterrence.

Rhetorically as well. Which is why presidents from Truman on have regularly and powerfully reaffirmed our deterrent pledge to NATO. Until Trump.

His omission was all the more damaging because of his personal history. This is a man chronically disdainful of NATO. He campaigned on its obsolescence. His inaugural address denounced American allies as cunning parasites living off American wealth and generosity. One of Trump's top outside advisers, Newt Gingrich, says that "Estonia is in the suburbs of St. Petersburg," as if Russian designs on the Baltic states are not at all unreasonable.

Moreover, Trump devoted much of his Brussels speech, the highlight of his first presidential trip to NATO, to berating the allies for not paying their fair share. Nothing particularly wrong with that, or new—half a century ago Senate Majority Leader Mike Mansfield was so offended by NATO free riding that he called for major reductions of US troops in Europe.

That's an American perennial. But if you're going to berate, at least reassure as well. Especially given rising Russian threats and aggression. Especially given that Trump's speech was teed up precisely for such reassurance. An administration official had spread the word that he would use the speech to endorse Article 5. And it was delivered at a ceremony honoring the first and only invocation of Article 5—ironically enough, by the allies in support of America after 9/11.

And yet Trump deliberately, defiantly refused to simply say it: *America will always honor its commitment under Article 5.*

It's not that, had Trump said the magic words, everyone would have 100% confidence we would strike back if Russia were to infiltrate little green men into Estonia, as it did in Crimea. But Trump's refusal to utter those words does lower whatever probability Vladimir Putin might attach to America responding with any seriousness to Russian aggression against a NATO ally.

German Chancellor Angela Merkel said Sunday (without mentioning his name) that after Trump's visit it is clear that Europe can no longer rely on others. It's not that yesterday Europe could fully rely—and today it cannot rely at all. It's simply that the American deterrent has been weakened. And deterrence weakened is an invitation to instability, miscalculation, provocation and worse.

And for what?

<hr>

The Washington Post, June 2, 2017

Trump and the "Madman Theory"

A t the heart of President Trump's foreign policy team lies a glaring contradiction: On the one hand, it is composed of men of experience, judgment and traditionalism. Meaning, they are all very much within the parameters of mainstream American internationalism as practiced since 1945. Practically every member of the team—the heads of State, Homeland Security, the CIA, and most especially Defense Secretary Jim Mattis and national security adviser H.R. McMaster—could fit in a Cabinet put together by, say, Hillary Clinton.

The commander in chief, on the other hand, is quite the opposite—inexperienced, untraditional, unbounded. His pronouncements on everything from the one-China policy to the two-state (Arab-Israeli) solution, from NATO obsolescence to the ravages of free trade, continue to confound and, as we say today, disrupt.

The obvious question is: Can this arrangement possibly work? The answer thus far, surprisingly, is: perhaps.

The sample size is tiny but take, for example, the German excursion. Trump dispatched his grown-ups—Vice President Pence, Defense Secretary Mattis, Secretary of Homeland Security John Kelly and Secretary of State Rex Tillerson—to various international confabs in Germany to reassure allies with the usual pieties about America's commitment to European security. They did drop a few hints to Trump's loud complaints about allied parasitism, in particular shirking their share of the defense burden.

Within days, Germany announced a 20,000-troop expansion of its military. Smaller European countries are likely to take note of the new setup. It's classic good-cop, bad-cop: The secretaries represent foreign policy continuity but their boss preaches America First. Message: Shape up.

John Hannah of the Foundation for Defense of Democracies suggests that the push-pull effect might work on foes as well as friends. On Saturday, China announced a cutoff of all coal imports from North Korea for the rest of 2017. Constituting more than one-third of all North Korean exports, this is a major blow to its economy.

True, part of the reason could be Chinese ire at the brazen assassination of Kim Jong Un's half brother, who had been under Chinese protection. Nonetheless, the boycott was declared just days after a provocative North Korean missile launch—and shortly into the term of a new American president who has shown that he can be erratic and quite disdainful of Chinese sensibilities.

His wavering on the one-China policy took Beijing by surprise. Trump also strongly denounced Chinese expansion in the South China Sea and conducted an ostentatious love-in with Japan's prime minister, something guaranteed to rankle the Chinese. Beijing's boycott of Pyongyang is many things, among them a nod to Washington.

This suggests that the peculiar and discordant makeup of the US national security team—traditionalist lieutenants, disruptive boss—might reproduce the old Nixonian "madman theory." That's when adversaries tread carefully because they suspect the US president of being unpredictable, occasionally reckless and potentially crazy dangerous. Henry Kissinger, with Nixon's collaboration, tried more than once to exploit this perception to pressure adversaries.

Trump's people have already shown a delicate touch in dealing with his bouts of loopiness. Trump has gone on for years about how we should have taken Iraq's oil for ourselves. Sunday in

Baghdad, Mattis wryly backed off, telling his hosts that "All of us in America have generally paid for our gas and oil all along, and I am sure we will continue to do so in the future."

Yet sometimes an off-center comment can have its uses. Take Trump's casual dismissal of a US commitment to a two-state solution in the Middle East. The next day, US policy was brought back in line by his own UN ambassador. But this diversion might prove salutary. It's a message to the Palestinians that their decades of rejectionism may not continue to pay off with an inexorable march toward statehood—that there may actually be a price to pay for making no concessions and simply waiting for the US to deliver them a Palestinian state.

To be sure, a two-track, two-policy, two-reality foreign policy is risky, unsettling and has the potential to go totally off the rails. This is not how you would draw it up in advance. It's unstable and confusing. But the experience of the first month suggests that, with prudence and luck, it can yield the occasional benefit—that the combination of radical rhetoric and conventional policy may induce better behavior both in friend and foe.

Alas, there is also a worst-case scenario. It needs no elaboration.

The Washington Post, February 24, 2017

CHAPTER 14

DEMOCRACY AND ITS DISCONTENTS

In Defense of Fanatics

Drive by the world's greatest medical research facility, the National Institutes of Health in Bethesda, Maryland, and you see trouble. The bumper stickers say "Liberate Laboratory Animals," and the signs say "Honk for the Silver Spring Monkeys." The animal liberation front has arrived.

The issue is no longer freeing 15 monkeys from a Silver Spring lab, where, for the sake of understanding strokes in humans, they were subjected to brain-damaging injuries. That fight was won years ago. The monkeys were freed and the research terminated.

This fight is over the proper rest home for these monkeys. NIH first housed them in cages in Poolesville. Under pressure, it then sent them to a more open environment in Louisiana. People for the Ethical Treatment of Animals demands that the monkeys live out their days at a "primate park" (Primarily Primates, Inc.) in Texas. One demonstrator—"prepared to die"—went on a 64-day hunger strike over the issue.

I am no expert on retirement homes for monkeys, but this seems to me to be going a bit far. But then again, the animal rights crusade is about going far. Its soldiers want not just to stop the abuse of animals in the laboratory. They want to stop the use of animals in the laboratory. That is what "Liberate Laboratory Animals" means. If they had their way, the labs would be shut down, the animals freed and—a side effect—medical science devastated.

The animal rights cause is a form of fanaticism. It places one value, admittedly an important one, above all others. But there are values other than the prevention of animal suffering. One of these is the prevention of human suffering through medical advances, many of which rest indispensably on animal experimentation.

And yet we owe these fanatics a great debt. A scientific lab is a place of romance and power. Even for the best-intentioned, it is an easy place to forget about the value of lesser creatures. The extremists have had a salutary effect. If you work in an animal lab you know that they are outside demonstrating and sometimes inside infiltrating. (That is how the Silver Spring monkeys were discovered.) It makes you doubly careful about how you treat your animals.

"Extremism in the defense of liberty is no vice," said Barry Goldwater in 1964. It will probably be his epitaph, and it is certainly wrong. Extremism in the defense of anything is a vice. A personal vice. Yet for a society, the presence of extremism—or rather, a mass of contending extremisms—is a virtue. It helps produce a moderation that would otherwise be impossible.

Madison, of course, was the great theorizer of such a system of contending factions. ("By a faction I understand a number of citizens . . . actuated by some common impulse of passion, or of interest, adverse to the rights of other citizens, or to the permanent and aggregate interests of the community.") As he thought, factions do indeed constrain and moderate each other, and restrain the headlong plunges of majority enthusiasms.

Enthusiasm for nuclear power, for example. Chernobyl is the latest example of Madison's wisdom. Societies where contending extremisms—i.e., pluralism—are not permitted are subject to catastrophic headlong plunges, such as the Soviets' crash nuclear power program. Where the nuclear imperative is not constrained by busloads of Diablo Canyon anti-nuclear fanatics, safety can be ignored.

During Chernobyl, there was much self-congratulation here about American nuclear safety. Yet that was not something that those who believe (as I do) in the nuclear imperative could take credit for. Credit was due to anti-nuclear fanatics, who have argued and demonstrated and litigated and cajoled this society into nuclear safety.

Of course, if they had their way, we would have not safer nuclear power, but no nuclear power. It would be disastrous if they ever won. It would be only mildly less disastrous if they went home. The paradox for a pluralist society is that extremists must be resisted, while at the same time welcomed, even celebrated.

The same is true, for example, of the anti-pornography fanatics, feminist and bluenose alike. They are a threat to free speech. And yet their critique of pornography (particularly the feminist critique) is a valuable one. It makes us rethink perhaps not what ought to be legally permitted but what ought to be socially sanctioned.

The point is that an extremist is the last person to whom you want to give power, but the first to whom you might want to give the floor. Such is the project of political pluralism. Every fanatic—whether for monkeys or motherhood—is granted the power of petition and contention. The result is a brilliant scheme for harnessing the energy that lies at the political extremes and deflecting it to produce, paradoxically, a moderating effect.

Banning experimentation or nuclear power or pornography is a terrible idea. But we need the extremists who believe in them. They keep the rest of us honest.

The Washington Post, July 18, 1986

The Death Penalty and the Constitution

The Supreme Court has just decided that if a state wants to strap a 16-year-old or a mentally retarded murderer into the electric chair and throw the switch, the Constitution does not stand in the way. The ruling was only five to four. But it was, on any plain reading of the Constitution, correct.

The Eighth Amendment bans punishments that are "cruel and unusual." Had it just said "cruel," the justices could arbitrarily pick and choose what punishments they in their robed wisdom consider humane. But by adding "unusual," the Constitution permitted the striking down of only those punishments that, in Justice Antonin Scalia's words, "society has set its face against," that are so universally abominated that only a few recalcitrant and benighted jurisdictions still practice them.

In this case, the court found that there were 22 states that permit the execution of 16-year-olds for heinous crimes. And it found that only one death penalty state (out of 37) explicitly prohibits execution of the retarded.

Critics counter by citing public opinion polls showing that a majority of Americans oppose the death penalty for juvenile offenders and for the retarded. But apart from the fact that public opinion polls are the most ephemeral, manipulable and unserious of all expressions of public sentiment, the Constitution speaks only to unusual punishment. It says nothing about unpopular punishment. Polls may tell you what is unpopular. But it is legislative practice that tells you what is unusual.

To say that the court ruled correctly, however, is not to deny that execution of the retarded is an abomination. (The age issue seems to me less urgent: If execution is going to be permitted, fixing the minimum age at 16 rather than 18 seems no more than an exercise in line drawing.) Indeed, in my view, the death penalty itself is a cruel anachronism worthy of abolition.

There are only two possible justifications for the death penalty. The first is deterrence, an argument rarely heard these days, since it is so clearly unsupported by the evidence. Death penalty states and death penalty countries do not have lower murder rates than their neighbors. West Virginia does not have the death penalty. It is surrounded by Virginia, Kentucky, Ohio and Maryland. All have the death penalty and all have higher murder rates. The United States as a whole has a murder rate 50% higher than that of abolitionist Canada and five times that of abolitionist Britain.

If not deterrence, then what? The most powerful case in favor of capital punishment is the claim of justice: Some crimes are so heinous that the only proportionate punishment, the only fitting retribution, is death. This is not a claim to be taken lightly. One purpose of the law is that it ensure that evil be appropriately repaid, that justice be done.

The death penalty is not unjust. But it is unnecessary, and that is the key argument against it. The experience of abolitionist states and countries clearly shows that it is quite possible to maintain order without the threat and practice of execution. And one of the marks of a civilized society is that it maintain order at the lowest possible level of official violence. It is in that sense that capital punishment is uncivilized.

It is considered unfashionable, if not racist, to speak of higher or lower civilizations. But few Americans would deny the proposition that a society that cuts off the hands of thieves is less civilized than a society that deals with thievery in a less brutal and violent manner. So with murder. The end of electrocution marks an advance for any civilization.

The Supreme Court, however, is a judicial not a civilizing body. Justice Scalia was right to tell abolitionists (in Stanford) that "the audience for these arguments . . . is not this court but the citizenry of the United States." In a democracy, it is not the function of the Supreme Court to create new standards of decency. That is a job for the people.

If the people want to abolish capital punishment, they have only to go to their legislatures and do it. If they want to keep capital punishment but ban it for the mentally retarded, they can do that too. Georgia did.

The director of the National Coalition to Abolish the Death Penalty complained that the justices "are clearly not taking the lead on this issue; they are following." Precisely. The purpose of the court is to interpret the law, not lead the people. Its last great experience with leading—i.e., legislating—was *Roe v. Wade*. The court and the country have yet to recover.

The Washington Post, June 30, 1989

Finally Getting It Right on Affirmative Action

Every once in a while a great, conflicted country gets an in-soluble problem exactly right. Such is the Supreme Court's ruling this week on affirmative action. It upheld a Michigan referendum prohibiting the state from discriminating either for or against any citizen on the basis of race.

The *Schuette* ruling is highly significant for two reasons: its lop-sided majority of six to two, including a crucial concurrence from liberal Justice Stephen Breyer, and, even more important, Breyer's rationale. It couldn't be simpler. "The Constitution foresees the ballot box, not the courts, as the normal instrument for resolving differences and debates about the merits of these programs."

Finally. After 36 years since the *Bakke* case, years of endless pettifoggery—parsing exactly how many spoonfuls of racial discrimination are permitted in exactly which circumstance—the court has its epiphany: Let the people decide. Not our business. We will not ban affirmative action. But we will not impose it, as the *Schuette* plaintiffs would have us do by ruling that no state is permitted to ban affirmative action.

The path to this happy place has been characteristically crooked. Eleven years ago, the court rejected an attempt to strike down affirmative action at the University of Michigan law school. The 2003 *Grutter* decision, as I wrote at the time, was "incoherent, disingenuous, intellectually muddled and morally confused"— and exactly what the country needed.

The reasoning was a mess because, given the very wording of

the Equal Protection Clause (and of the Civil Rights Act), justifying any kind of racial preference requires absurd, often comical linguistic contortions. As Justice Antonin Scalia put it in his *Schuette* concurrence, even the question is absurd: "Does the Equal Protection Clause . . . *forbid* what its text plainly *requires*?" (i.e., colorblindness).

Indeed, over these four decades, how *was* "equal protection" transformed into a mandate for race discrimination? By morphing affirmative action into diversity and declaring diversity a state purpose important enough to justify racial preferences.

This is pretty weak gruel when compared with the social harm inherent in discriminating by race: exacerbating group antagonisms, stigmatizing minority achievement and, as documented by Thomas Sowell, Stuart Taylor and many others, needlessly and tragically damaging promising minority students by turning them disproportionately into failures at institutions for which they are unprepared.

So why did I celebrate the hopelessly muddled *Grutter* decision, which left affirmative action standing?

Because much as I believe the harm of affirmative action outweighs the good, the courts are not the place to decide the question. At its core, affirmative action is an attempt—noble but terribly flawed, in my view—at racial restitution. The issue is too neuralgic, the history too troubled, the ramifications too deep to be decided on high by nine robes. As with all great national questions, the only path to an enduring, legitimate resolution is by the democratic process.

That was the lesson of *Roe v. Wade*. It created a great societal rupture because, as Ruth Bader Ginsburg once explained, it "halted a political process that was moving in a reform direction and thereby, I believe, prolonged divisiveness and deferred stable settlement of the [abortion] issue." It is never a good idea to take these profound political questions out of the political arena. (Regrettably, Ginsburg supported the dissent in *Schuette*, which would have done exactly that to affirmative action, recapitulating *Roe*.)

Which is why the 2003 *Grutter* decision was right. Asked to abolish affirmative action—and thus remove it from the democratic process—the court said no.

The implication? The people should decide.

The people responded accordingly. Three years later, they crafted a referendum to abolish race consciousness in government action. It passed overwhelmingly, 58% to 42%.

Schuette completes the circle by respecting the constitutionality of that democratic decision. As Justice Anthony Kennedy wrote in the controlling opinion: "This case is not about how the debate about racial preferences should be resolved. It is about who may resolve it."

And as Breyer wrote: "The Constitution permits, though it does not require . . . race-conscious programs." Liberal as he is, Breyer could not accept the radical proposition of the *Schuette* plaintiffs that the Constitution demands—and cannot countenance a democratically voted abolition of—racial preferences.

This gives us, finally, the basis for a new national consensus. Two-thirds of the court has just said to the nation: For those of you who wish to continue to judge by race, we'll keep making Jesuitical distinctions to keep the discrimination from getting too obvious or outrageous. If, however, you wish to be rid of this baleful legacy and banish race preferences once and for all, do what Michigan did. You have our blessing.

The Washington Post, April 25, 2014

The Right-to-Work Dilemma

For all the fury and fistfights outside the Lansing Capitol, what happened in Michigan this week was a simple accommodation to reality. The most famously unionized state, birthplace of the United Auto Workers, royalty of the American working class, became right-to-work.

It's shocking, except that it was inevitable. Indiana went that way earlier this year. The entire Rust Belt will eventually follow because the heyday of the sovereign private-sector union is gone. Globalization has made splendid isolation impossible.

The nostalgics look back to the immediate postwar years when the UAW was all-powerful, the auto companies were highly profitable and the world was flooded with American cars. In that Golden Age, the UAW won wages, benefits and protections that were the envy of the world.

Today's angry protesters demand a return to that norm. Except that it was not a norm but a historical anomaly. America, alone among the great industrial powers, emerged unscathed from World War II. Japan was a cinder, Germany rubble and the allies—beginning with Britain and France—an exhausted shell of their former imperial selves.

For a generation, America had the run of the world. Then the others recovered. Soon global competition—from Volkswagen to Samsung—began to overtake American industry that was saddled with protected, inflated, relatively uncompetitive wages, benefits and work rules.

There's a reason Detroit went bankrupt while the southern auto transplants did not. This is not to exonerate incompetent overpaid management that contributed to the fall. But clearly the wage, benefit and work-rule gap between the unionized North and the right-to-work South was a major factor.

President Obama railed against the Michigan legislation, calling right-to-work "giving you the right to work for less money." Well, there is a principle at stake here: A free country should allow its workers to choose whether to join a union. Moreover, it is more than slightly ironic that Democrats, the fiercely pro-choice party, reserve free choice for aborting a fetus while denying it for such matters as choosing your child's school or joining a union.

Principle and hypocrisy aside, however, the president's statement has some validity. Let's be honest: Right-to-work laws do weaken unions. And de-unionization can lead to lower wages.

But there is another factor at play: having a job in the first place. In right-to-work states, the average wage is about 10% lower. But in right-to-work states, unemployment also is about 10% lower.

Higher wages or lower unemployment? It is a wrenching choice. Although, you would think that liberals would be more inclined to spread the wealth—i.e., the jobs—around, preferring somewhat lower pay in order to leave fewer fellow workers mired in unemployment.

Think of the moral calculus. Lower wages cause an incremental decline in one's well-being. No doubt. But for the unemployed, the decline is categorical, sometimes catastrophic—a loss not just of income but of independence and dignity.

Nor does protectionism offer escape from this dilemma. Shutting out China and the others deprives less well-off Americans of access to the kinds of goods once reserved for the upper classes: quality clothing, furnishings, electronics, durable goods—from the Taiwanese-manufactured smartphone to the affordable, highly functional Kia.

Globalization taketh away. But it giveth more. The net benefit of free trade has been known since, oh, 1817. (See David Ricardo and the Law of Comparative Advantage.) There is no easy parachute from reality.

Obama calls this a race to the bottom. No, it's a race to a new equilibrium that tries to maintain employment levels, albeit at the price of some modest wage decline. It is a choice not to be despised.

I have great admiration for the dignity and protections trade unionism has brought to American workers. I have no great desire to see the private-sector unions defenestrated. (Like FDR, Fiorello La Guardia and George Meany, however, I don't extend that sympathy to public-sector unions.)

But rigidity and nostalgia have a price. The industrial Midwest is littered with the resulting wreckage. Michigan most notably, where its formerly great metropolis of Detroit is reduced to boarded-up bankruptcy by its inability and unwillingness to adapt to global change.

It's easy to understand why a state such as Michigan would seek to recover its competitiveness by emulating the success of Indiana. One can sympathize with those who pine for the union glory days, while at the same time welcoming the new realism that promises not an impossible restoration but desperately needed—and doable—recalibration and recovery.

The Washington Post, December 14, 2012

Brexit: Sovereign Kingdom
or Little England?

Given their arrogance, pomposity and habitual absurdities, it is hard not to feel a certain satisfaction with the comeuppance that Brexit has delivered to the unaccountable European Union bureaucrats in Brussels.

Nonetheless, we would do well to refrain from smug condescension. Unity is not easy. What began in 1951 as a six-member European Coal and Steel Community was grounded in a larger conception of a united Europe born from the ashes of World War II. Seven decades into the postwar era, Britain wants out and the EU is facing an existential crisis.

Yet where were we Americans seven decades into our great experiment in continental confederation, our "more perfect union" contracted under the Constitution of 1787? At Fort Sumter.

The failure of our federal idea gave us civil war and 600,000 dead. And we had the advantage of a common language, common heritage and common memory of heroic revolutionary struggle against a common (British) foe. Europe had none of this. The European project tries to forge the union of dozens of disparate peoples, ethnicities, languages and cultures, amid the searing memories of the two most destructive wars in history fought among and against each other.

The result is the EU, a great idea badly executed. The founding motive was obvious and noble: to reconcile the combatants of World War II, most especially France and Germany, and create conditions that would ensure there could be no repetition. Onto that was appended the more utopian vision of a continental super-state that would once and for all transcend parochial nationalism.

That vision blew up with Brexit on June 23. But we mustn't underestimate the significance, and improbability, of the project's more narrow, but still singular, achievement—peace. It has given Europe the most extended period of internal tranquility since the Roman Empire. (In conjunction, of course, with NATO, which provided Europe with its American umbrella against external threat.)

Not only is there no armed conflict among European states. The very idea is inconceivable. (Fighting among the various nations has been subcontracted to soccer hooligans.) This on a continent where war had been the norm for a millennium.

Give the EU its due. Despite its comical faux-national para-phernalia of flag, anthem and useless parliament, it has champi-oned and advanced a transnational idea that has helped curb the nationalist excesses that culminated in two world wars.

Advanced not quite enough, however. Certainly not enough to support its disdainful, often dismissive, treatment of residual nationalisms and their democratic expressions. Despite numer-ous objections by referendums and parliaments, which it routinely either ignored or circumvented, the EU continued its relentless drive for more centralization, more regulation and thus more power for its unelected self.

Such high-handed overriding of popular sentiment could go on only so long. Until June 23, 2016, to be precise.

To be sure, popular sentiment was rather narrowly divided. The most prominent disparity in the British vote was genera-tional. The young, having grown up in the new Europe, are more comfortable with its cosmopolitanism and have come to expect open borders, open commerce and open movement of people. They voted overwhelmingly—by three to one—to Remain. Leave was mainly the position of an older generation no longer willing to tolerate European assaults on British autonomy and sovereignty.

Understandably so. Here is Britain, inventor of the liberal idea and home to the mother of parliaments, being instructed by a bunch of pastry-eating Brussels bureaucrats on everything from the proper size of pomegranates to the human rights of terrorists.

Widely mentioned, and resented, was the immigration directive to admit other EU citizens near-automatically. But what pushed the Leave side over the top was less policy than primacy. Who runs Britain? Amazingly, about half of the laws and regulations that govern British life today come not from Westminster but from Brussels.

Brexit was an assertion of national sovereignty and an attempt, in one fell swoop, to recover it.

There is much to admire in that impulse. But at what cost? Among its casualties may be not just the European project (other exit referendums are already being proposed) but possibly the United Kingdom itself. The Scots are already talking about another vote for independence. And Northern Ireland, which voted to remain in the EU, might well seek to unite with the Republic.

Talk about a great idea executed badly. In seeking a newly sovereign United Kingdom, the Brits might well find themselves having produced a little England.

The Washington Post, July 1, 2016

Trump Derangement Syndrome: You Can't Govern by Id

Having coined Bush Derangement Syndrome more than a decade ago, I feel authorized to weigh in on its most recent offshoot. What distinguishes Trump Derangement Syndrome is not just general hysteria about the subject, but additionally the inability to distinguish between legitimate policy differences on the one hand and signs of psychic pathology on the other.

Take President Trump's climate-change decision. The hyperbole that met his withdrawal from the Paris agreement—a traitorous act of war against the American people, America just resigned as leader of the free world, etc.—was astonishing, though hardly unusual, this being Trump.

What the critics don't seem to recognize is that the Paris agreement itself was a huge failure. It contained no uniform commitments and no enforcement provisions. Sure, the whole world signed. But onto what? A voluntary set of vaporous promises. China pledged to "achieve the peaking of [carbon dioxide] emissions around 2030." Meaning that they rise for another 13 years.

The rationale, I suppose, is that developing countries like India and China should be given a pass because the West had a two-century head start on industrialization.

I don't think the West needs to apologize—or pay—for having invented the steam engine. In fact, I've long favored a real climate-change pact, strong and enforceable, that would impose relatively uniform demands on China, India, the United States, the European Union and any others willing to join.

Paris was nothing but hot air. Withdrawing was a perfectly

plausible policy choice (the other being remaining but trying to reduce our carbon dioxide-cutting commitments). The subsequent attacks on Trump were all the more unhinged because the president's other behavior over the past several weeks provided ample opportunity for shock and dismay.

It's the tweets, of course. Trump sees them as a direct, "unfiltered" conduit to the public. What he doesn't quite understand is that for him—indeed, for anyone—they are a direct conduit from the unfiltered id. They erase whatever membrane normally exists between one's internal disturbances and their external manifestations.

For most people, who cares? For the president of the United States, there are consequences. When the president's id speaks, the world listens.

Consider his tweets mocking the mayor of London after the most recent terrorist attack. They were appalling. This is a time when a president expresses sympathy and solidarity—and stops there. Trump can't stop, ever. He used the atrocity to renew an old feud with a minor official of another country. Petty in the extreme.

As was his using London to support his misbegotten travel ban, to attack his own Justice Department for having "watered down" the original executive order (ignoring the fact that Trump himself signed it) and to undermine the case for it just as it goes to the Supreme Court.

As when he boasted by tweet that the administration was already doing "extreme vetting." But that explodes the whole rationale for the travel ban—that a 90-day moratorium on entry was needed while new vetting procedures were developed. If the vetting is already in place, the ban has no purpose. The rationale evaporates.

And if that wasn't mischief enough, he then credited his own interventions in Saudi Arabia for the sudden squeeze that the Saudis, the UAE, Egypt and other Sunni-run states are putting on Qatar for its long-running dirty game of supporting and arming terrorists (such as the Muslim Brotherhood and Hamas) and playing footsie with Iran.

It's good to see our Sunni allies confront Qatar and try to bring it into line. But why make it personal—other than to feed the presidential id? Gratuitously injecting the US into the crisis taints the endeavor by making it seem an American rather than an Arab initiative and turns our allies into instruments of American designs rather than defenders of their own region from a double agent in their midst.

And this is just four days' worth of tweets, all vainglorious and self-injurious. Where does it end?

The economist Herb Stein once quipped that "if something cannot go on forever, it will stop." This really can't go on, can it? But it's hard to see what, short of a smoking gun produced by the Russia inquiry, actually does stop him.

Trump was elected to do politically incorrect—and needed—things like withdrawing from Paris. He was not elected to do crazy things, starting with his tweets. If he cannot distinguish between the two, Trump Derangement Syndrome will only become epidemic.

The Washington Post, June 9, 2017

Revolt of the Attorneys General

Among the many unintended legacies of Barack Obama, one has gone largely unnoticed: the emergence of a novel form of resistance to executive overreach, a check and balance improvised in reaction to his various presidential power grabs.

It's the revolt of the state attorneys general, banding together to sue and curb the executive. And it has outlived Obama.

Normally one would expect Congress to be the instrument of resistance to presidential trespass. But Congress has been supine. The Democrats in particular, approving of Obama's policy preferences, allowed him free rein over Congress' constitutional prerogatives.

Into that vacuum stepped the states. Florida and 12 others filed suit against Obamacare the day it was signed. They were later joined by 13 more, making their challenge the first in which a majority of states banded together to try to stop anything.

They did not always succeed, but they succeeded a lot. They got Obamacare's forced Medicaid expansion struck down, though Obamacare as a whole was upheld. Later, a majority of states secured stays for two egregious EPA measures. One had given the feds sovereignty over the generation and distribution of electricity (the Clean Power Plan), the other over practically every ditch and pond in America (the waters of the United States rule).

Their most notable success was blocking Obama's executive order that essentially would have legalized four million illegal immigrants. "If Congress will not do their job, at least we can do ours," said Obama. Not your job, said the courts.

Democrats noticed. And now with a Republican in the White

House, they've adopted the technique. Having lost control of Congress, they realize that one way to curb presidential power is to go through the states. They just did on President Trump's immigration ban. Taking advantage of the courts' increased willingness to grant standing to the states, Washington and Minnesota got a district court to issue an injunction against Trump's executive order and got it upheld by the Ninth Circuit. Where the ban died.

A singular victory. Democratic-run states will be emboldened to join together in opposing Trump administration measures issuing from both the agency rulings (especially EPA and the Education Department) and presidential executive orders.

Is this a good thing? Regardless of your party or policy preferences, you must admit we are witnessing a remarkable phenomenon: the organic response of a constitutional system in which the traditional barriers to overreach have atrophied and a new check and balance emerges almost ex nihilo.

Congress has allowed itself to become an increasingly subordinate branch. Look at how reluctant Congress has been to even consider a new authorization for the use of force abroad, an area in which, constitutionally, it should be dominant. Look at today's GOP Congress, having had years to prepare to govern, now appearing so tentative, almost paralyzed. "Many Republican members," reports the *Washington Post*, "are eager for Trump to provide clear marching orders." The president orders, Congress marches—that is not how the Founders drew it up.

Hence the state attorneys general rise to check the president and his functionaries. This is good.

Not because it necessarily produces the best policy outcomes. It often doesn't.

Not because judicial grants of standing are always correct. The Ninth Circuit, in effect, granted Minnesota and Washington standing to represent the due process rights of Yemeni nationals who've never set foot in the United States—an imaginary harm to states that presupposes imaginary rights for Yemenis.

And not because it's necessarily good for the judicial system to acquire, through this process, yet more power. This really should be adjudicated by the elected branches. Problem is: Congress has abdicated.

Nonetheless, the revolt of the attorneys general is to be celebrated. It is a reassuring sign of the creativity and suppleness of the American Constitution, of its amphibian capacity to grow a new limb when an old one atrophies.

This is, of course, not the first time the states have asserted themselves against federal power. There was Fort Sumter, 1861, when the instruments employed were rather more blunt than the multistate lawsuit. All the more reason to celebrate this modern device.

I'm sure conservatives won't like many of the outcomes over the next four years, just as many liberals deeply disapproved of the Obama-blocking outcomes of the recent past.

The point, however, is not outcome but process. Remarkably, we have spontaneously developed a new one—to counter executive willfulness. There's a reason that after two and a half centuries the French are on their Fifth Republic and we are still on our first.

The Washington Post, March 3, 2017

American Democracy:
Not So Decadent After All

U nder the big gray cloud, amid the general gloom, allow me to offer a ray of sunshine. The last two months have brought a pleasant surprise: Turns out the much feared, much predicted withering of our democratic institutions has been grossly exaggerated. The system lives.

Let me explain. Donald Trump's triumph last year was based on a frontal attack on the Washington "establishment," that all-powerful, all-seeing, supremely cynical, bipartisan "cartel" (as Ted Cruz would have it) that allegedly runs everything. Yet the establishment proved to be Potemkin empty. In 2016, it folded pitifully, surrendering with barely a fight to a lightweight outsider.

At which point, fear of the vaunted behemoth turned to contempt for its now-exposed lassitude and decadence. Compounding the confusion were Trump's intimations of authoritarianism. He declared "I alone can fix it" and "I am your voice," the classic tropes of the demagogue. He unabashedly expressed admiration for strongmen (most notably, Vladimir Putin).

Trump had just cut through the grandees like a hot knife through butter. Who would now prevent him from trampling, caudillo-like, over a Washington grown weak and decadent? A Washington, moreover, that had declined markedly in public esteem, as confidence in our traditional institutions—from the political parties to Congress—fell to new lows.

The strongman cometh, it was feared. Who and what would stop him?

Two months into the Trumpian era, we have our answer. Our checks and balances have turned out to be quite vibrant. Consider:

1. The courts.

Trump rolls out not one but two immigration bans, and is stopped dead in his tracks by the courts. However you feel about the merits of the policy itself (in my view, execrable and useless but legal) or the merits of the constitutional reasoning of the Ninth Circuit Court of Appeals (embarrassingly weak, transparently political), the fact remains: The president proposed and the courts disposed.

Trump's pushback? A plaintive tweet or two complaining about the judges—that his own Supreme Court nominee denounced (if obliquely) as "disheartening" and "demoralizing."

2. The states.

Federalism lives. The first immigration challenge to Trump was brought by the attorneys general of two states (Washington and Minnesota) picking up on a trend begun during the Barack Obama years when state attorneys general banded together to kill his immigration overreach and the more egregious trespasses of his Environmental Protection Agency.

And beyond working through the courts, state governors—Republicans, no less—have been exerting pressure on members of Congress to oppose a Republican president's signature health-care reform. Institutional exigency still trumps party loyalty.

3. Congress.

The Republican-controlled Congress (House and Senate) is putting up epic resistance to a Republican administration's health-care reform. True, that's because of ideological and tactical disagreements rather than any particular desire to hem in Trump. But it does demonstrate that Congress is no rubber stamp.

And its independence extends beyond the perennially divisive health-care conundrums. Trump's budget, for example, was instantly declared dead on arrival in Congress, as it almost invariably is regardless of which party is in power.

4. The media.

Trump is right. It is the opposition party. Indeed, furiously so, often indulging in appalling overkill. It's sometimes embarrassing to read the front pages of the major newspapers, festooned as they are with anti-Trump editorializing masquerading as news.

Nonetheless, if you take the view from 30,000 feet, better this than a press acquiescing on bended knee, where it spent most of the Obama years in a slavish *Pravda*-like thrall. Every democracy needs an opposition press. We damn well have one now.

Taken together—and suspending judgment on which side is right on any particular issue—it is deeply encouraging that the sinews of institutional resistance to a potentially threatening executive remain quite resilient.

Madison's genius was to understand that the best bulwark against tyranny was not virtue—virtue helps, but should never be relied upon—but ambition counteracting ambition, faction counteracting faction.

You see it even in the confirmation process for Neil Gorsuch, Trump's supremely qualified and measured Supreme Court nominee. He's a slam dunk, yet some factions have scraped together a campaign to block him. Their ads are plaintive and pathetic. Yet I find them warmly reassuring. What a country—where even the vacuous have a voice.

The anti-Trump opposition flatters itself as "the resistance." As if this is Vichy France. It's not. It's 21st-century America. And the good news is that the checks and balances are working just fine.

The Washington Post, March 24, 2017

CHAPTER 15

ON LIBERTY

Constitutions, Conservatism and the Genius of the Founders

An Address at the Hillsdale College Constitution Day Celebration

I

Why do we celebrate Constitution Day? Let me start with an incident that happened 30 years ago. When Egyptian president Anwar Sadat was assassinated, the networks ran over to Cairo and began covering the events all day and all night. The only thing I remember of all that coverage was a news anchor bringing in a Middle East expert and saying, "We've just looked at the Egyptian constitution, and our researchers tell us that the next in line for the presidency is the speaker of the parliament." The Middle East expert burst out laughing and said, "Nobody in Egypt has read the constitution in 30 years. No one knows it exists. And no one cares what's in it." He asked, "Who's the leader of the military?" The anchor said, "Hosni Mubarak," and the expert said, "He's your next president."

Two things struck me about that. First, how naïve we are about what constitutions are and what they mean around the world. And the second thing, the reason for the first, is how much reverence we have—in the United States and very few other countries—for this document.

Many things are miraculous about the Constitution. The first is that, somehow, on this edge of the civilized world 250 years ago, there could have been a collection of such political geniuses as to have actually written it.

The second miracle is the actual substance of it, the way that these people, drawing from Locke and Montesquieu and from the Greeks, created an extraordinary political apparatus that a quarter of a millennium later works and has worked with incredible success over these many years.

But the third miracle, and the one that I think we appreciate the least, is the fact of the reverence that we have for it. This is as rare as the other two elements that I mentioned. This reverence is so deeply ingrained that we don't even see it; we just think it's in the air that we breathe. But it is extraordinarily rare. It exists in only a handful of countries. For almost all of the world, it is completely alien.

I remember when the British decolonized Africa, in the late '50s and early '60s, and they had these great ceremonies transferring power to the local new institutions, which were all established in imitation of the British system. You'd see the governor general arrive wearing a wig, and he would invest power in the new prime minister and in the new high court and within six months it had all been swept away because it was artificial, it was not intrinsic and there was no reverence for those institutions. It takes time. In Britain, it's been around for eight centuries, and they manage a constitution that's actually unwritten, which is even more difficult than what we do. But it is ingrained in the consciences of the people.

Consider the oath of office that we take for granted. I remember taking it 30 years ago, and how moved I was by the words and by the idea. Whenever we bestow upon anyone the authority to wield the power of the state over free citizens, we make them swear to protect not the people, not the nation, not the flag, but the Constitution of the United States. A piece of paper. Of course, it stands for the pillars of the American experiment itself: the ideas, the structures, the philosophy that define a limited government with enumerated powers, whose mission is to preserve liberty and individual rights.

This is a gift—that we intrinsically have this sense of reverence for the Constitution. And it's important to remember that it is a gift from the past. It is not something that we can in any way credit to ourselves. If anything, recent generations have allowed that kind of reverence to diminish, to bleed away over the decades, as we try—as it were—to adapt constitutionalism to modernity. This is in particular a liberal specialty: the idea of the living, breathing, ever-changing, ever-whimsical new Constitution that evolves day by day. And that is why a new conservative idea is now focused on a revival of constitutionalism. We can almost say that this new conservatism is, in essence, a constitutionalism in and of itself.

II

First, a bit of history for context. In the 20th century, liberalism outgrew its 19th-century roots—the classical individualism of John Stuart Mill and others—and it fell in thrall to the romantic progressivism of the age. Mill held that truth emerges from an unfettered competition of ideas and that individual character is most improved when allowed to find its own way, unmolested and with government standing to the side. But that vision was insufficient for the ambitions of 20th-century liberalism. It lacked glory and it lacked sweep. Twentieth-century liberalism's newfound perfectionist ambitions—reflected in its current euphemism, *progressivism*—sought to harness the power of government, the mystique of science and the rule of experts to shape society and individual character, and bring them both, willing or not, to a higher state of being.

Contemporary conservatism is a reaction to precisely that kind of overreaching, overarching ambition. It is deeply skeptical of belief in a progressive history or a redemptive politics. It believes that the first duty of government is to conserve what is, and most especially the great gift of the Enlightenment: the autonomy of the individual and the universe of free associations—the essence of civil society that Tocqueville saw was so essential to American democracy, what Edmund Burke called "the little platoons"— that are created beneath, against and apart from the behemoth of government.

Conservatism's choice, among all the great modern revolutions, is always the American Revolution, with its constitutional structures that limit and contain power, that create checks and balances to frustrate tyranny and that view government as subordinate to the individuals from whom it derives its just powers. The conservative instinct is skeptical and individualistic, and, in the American context, constitutional.

What's so remarkable is that constitutions are highly reactionary documents. The very essence of a constitution is to constrain the enthusiasms of a future that one cannot even see. In America, constitutionalism demands that even the most distant progeny swear allegiance to a past embodied in a document written in the late 1780s. If "tradition . . . is the democracy of the dead," as G. K. Chesterton had it, then constitutionalism—which is ancient wisdom rendered into legal code—is the tyranny of the dead, the ultimate reach of the past into the future.

And in America, it succeeded. The propagandist Lincoln Steffens famously said, upon visiting Bolshevik Russia shortly after the revolution: "I have seen the future, and it works." American constitutionalism declares: "We have seen the past, and it works." Paradoxically, for all the forward-looking, blue-sky, futuristic spirit of its people, the astonishing stability, majesty and success of the American experiment owe much to the inherent restraint and conservatism of its original constitutional blueprint. Compare the American Revolution and its prudential institution-building with the near-contemporaneous French Revolution—the apotheosis of political romanticism—with its worship of reason and abstraction. It is no accident that France is on its Fifth Republic, while America is still on its first.

III

But we need not look that far back into history to understand why we celebrate Constitution Day. Consider what has been happening in our contemporary world. Today, Americans are in the midst of a great national debate over the power, scope and reach of the government that was established by that document. The debate was sparked by the Obama administration's bold push for government expansion: a massive fiscal stimulus, Obamacare, financial regulation, various attempts at controlling the energy economy and other attempts to regulate the private and economic life of Americans.

Obama's vision is one that seeks to move America away from its tradition of a constitutionally restrained and individualistic system to a system more like the social democracies of Europe.

I think he has been rather open and honest about that, and for that I give him credit. He unveiled a plan, very openly speaking in those terms—of changing America fundamentally—within a month of his succession to office.

Incidentally, my favorite way to understand this kind of vision is with a story famously told about Winston Churchill, shortly after he lost the election of 1945. Clement Attlee, the socialist, became the prime minister, and Churchill became leader of the opposition. One day Churchill went down to the men's room at the House of Commons—that's as risqué as the story gets—and he sees Attlee standing at one of the urinals. The men's room is empty otherwise, and yet Churchill deliberately walks to the other end of the men's room, 18 stalls away, and Attlee is rather surprised. And so he calls out and says, "Feeling a bit standoffish today, Winston?" To which Churchill replied, "No, my dear Clement. It's just that anytime you see something large, you want to nationalize it." I love that story as much as you do, but I digress.

In America today, the kind of social democratic vision promoted by President Obama has engendered a spontaneous, popular countervailing reaction. This movement has been called the Tea Party, but in reality it is much more widespread. It calls for a more restricted vision of government that is more consistent with the intent and the aim of the Founders.

I would call it constitutionalism, or a return to constitutionalism. And what's interesting is that, in essence, constitutionalism is the intellectual counterpart and the spiritual progeny of the originalism movement that we see in jurisprudence. Judicial originalists (led by Antonin Scalia and other notable conservative jurists) insist that legal interpretation be bound by something—namely, the text of the Constitution as understood by those who wrote it and their contemporaries. Originalism—once scorned as a kind of fringe tendency—has now grown to become the major challenger to the liberal "living constitution" school of thought, under which high courts are channelers of the spirit of the age, free to create new constitutional principles accordingly.

What originalism is to jurisprudence, constitutionalism is to governance: an appeal for restraint rooted in constitutional text. Constitutionalism as a *political* philosophy represents a reformed, self-regulating conservatism that bases its call for minimalist government—for reining in the willfulness of presidents and congresses—in the words and the meaning of the Constitution.

IV

What does this mean in practical terms? Let me give an example and contrast constitutional conservatism with its nearest predecessor, the compassionate variety of George W. Bush. Its heart was in the right place, but compassionate conservatism failed to endure, not just for practical reasons—profligate spending and expansion of government—but because of its philosophical shortcomings.

First, its very name implied that other conservatisms are not compassionate, conceding the central liberal premise that small government and belief in markets is hardhearted, rather than being a philosophy that is better suited to organizing society and, among other things, helping the poor and the disadvantaged to flourish.

The second problem with that variety of conservative thought is that it is arbitrary. It believes in small government except when the president decides there is an overriding imperative to provide a prescription drug benefit or launch a massive African program for AIDS. Now, I have no particular objection to either of these noble initiatives. But here's the problem: Why AIDS and not river blindness? Why Africa and not the scourges of the poor precincts of South America or Asia? Why prescription drugs for seniors, but not for children? It is undisciplined, and that's why it has trouble as a philosophical proposition, as well as having all the practical difficulties of tending to encourage the expansion of government.

The new constitutionalism is a kind of self-enforced discipline—guided by a conscious grounding in constitutional text. Its first symbolic moment occurred this January, when the 112th House of Representatives opened with a reading of the Constitution. Remarkably, this had never been done before in American history, perhaps because it had never been so needed. The reading reflected the feeling, expressed powerfully in the last election, that we have moved far from a government of constitutionally limited and enumerated powers, and in the direction of government constrained only by its perception of social need. The most galvanizing example of this expansive shift was the Democrats' health care reform, which aimed to revolutionize one-sixth of the American economy.

V

The most interesting and encouraging aspect of the pushback against this government power-grab was the form it took. There was, of course, the usual opposition on the usual grounds for objecting to welfare state expansion: that it was ruinously expensive, and therefore unsustainable economically, and that it was introducing massive inefficiencies, complexity and arbitrariness that would degrade the entire medical system itself as well as contributing to our looming national insolvency. That kind of protest and those kinds of arguments would have been the norm in preceding decades and it might have stopped there.

But this time, an additional argument arose and became very powerful: constitutional illegitimacy. This objection manifested itself in two forms: popular opposition and political argument on the one hand, and serious legal challenge on the other. The object of the aversion on the part of conservatives was the individual mandate—the requirement by the federal government that every citizen must buy health insurance from a private entity, under the penalty of a fine from Washington. From town hall to town hall, from campaign debates to arguments on the floor of Congress, people instinctively felt and saw that this was a bridge too far. That on principle, even if Obamacare was economical, beneficent and efficient, it was impermissible to force a citizen to do something against his will—not just to prohibit certain actions, but to compel the positive undertaking of action—simply to promote what the government saw as some social good.

Even more interestingly, it spawned a legal challenge that was at first dismissed by the better thinkers in Washington as just the work of fringe elements. Democrats were extremely dismissive of this constitutional objection at the beginning. Yet within several months the legal challenge was joined by a majority of the 50 states. The basis of the argument was that the government had exceeded its enumerated powers.

I want to make one point about how refreshing that line of argument is. It's a subtle point, but one that I believe is important to understand and to emphasize. The traditional defense against government encroachment over the last decades has not been to argue about enumerated powers, but instead to resort to the Bill of Rights and the claim of an inviolable sphere of freedom and sovereignty for the individual: "You can't do X because it goes against the individual rights of Y as guaranteed in the Bill of

Rights." But that kind of defense tends to concede that outside of that private sphere surrounding the individual, the government is free to roam and to rule.

The new argument does not depend on the Bill of Rights. There is no proposed amendment stating "Congress shall pass no law mandating that you engage in a private contract with a private entity." Rather, the new argument rests on the basis of enumerated powers. It is a stronger attack on big government because it posits that it is government, not the individual, that is constrained by a sphere surrounding it—a sphere whose boundaries are defined by the enumerated powers in the Constitution, beyond which government may not go.

The essence of constitutional power has always lain in the fundamental Madisonian idea of a government of enumerated powers. Indeed, at first it was thought that a newly born United States would not need a Bill of Rights that would enumerate rights against a government. It was assumed that after the tyranny of the British king and parliament, Americans would simply accept a system in which the limited powers of the branches of government, spelled out in the Constitution, would be a sufficient bar to overreaching. And as a fail-safe, the separation of powers and the inherent rivalry among the branches would check the ambitions of any potential tyrants.

There were skeptics, of course, who thought that this was not barrier enough. They insisted on the Bill of Rights, not trusting that the enumeration of powers would be enough to actually prevent tyrannical rule. They ensured that each citizen would explicitly be given a sphere of inviolability in the form of rights against the government—inside of which the citizen remains sovereign and free.

Over the last century, with the ascendancy of the progressive and liberal tradition, with the expansion of government and its regulations, dictations and overall presumptions, the Bill of Rights has gone from being a simple checklist of areas regarding which "Congress shall not" to being a last redoubt of the individual against governmental power which otherwise sees itself as unlimited.

We are now witnessing, quite remarkably, a serious revision of this strategy. For most of the 20th century, protection against big government was to be found in individual rights. Now a more ambitious challenge to big government is emerging: an insistence that the enumerated powers of Congress and the presidency strictly define the limits of their competence, that government's power ends long before it intrudes upon the individual rights in the first 10 amendments.

Government is limited to its sphere, and that means that everything outside of it—which is everything else in life—is the sovereign domain of the individual and of civil society. It's akin to the difference in figure-ground perception. With the focus on enumerated powers, the ultimate objective is to restrain the government and to keep it in a box where it cannot touch anything else, whereas a focus on the individual leads to the traditional defense that draws an impenetrable box around the individual, but everything outside of it is ceded to government.

Which is the better way to define the border between citizen and state: an enumeration of powers within which Congress and the president may act but beyond which they may not reach? Or an enumeration of rights delineating the inviolability of the individual, outside of which the government may do nearly anything?

Both approaches are of course valid and valuable. But the revival of the first—the insistence on the enumeration of powers as the limit of congressional power—is a salutary development. The Bill of Rights is the last resort, the last redoubt of the individual against intrusive, overbearing government. But better to meet big government first on the field of battle, on the grounds of enumerated powers.

In some ways, this is a recapitulation of the argument on the basis of the Tenth Amendment, but it has a larger implication. Because once you talk about enumerated powers, you're going to the heart of the expansion of the state ever since the New Deal. The challenge to the individual mandate is not, at its core, a claim of one or another individual right under the guarantees of the Bill of Rights. The argument is that the use of the Commerce Clause to compel the individual to enter into a private contract in the name of promoting interstate commerce is stretching the clause beyond recognition, beyond reason, and to the point where there would be no conceivable limit to the indefinite and infinite expansion of federal power. If you permit this, then in the future how can you possibly prevent Congress from doing anything it deems necessary to promote some stated policy preference?

This is a frontal judicial attack on big government. The Commerce Clause has been the high road to the expansion of government for 80 years, which is why the framers of Obamacare were so contemptuous and dismissive at the beginning of any constitutional challenge. They knew every administration had been using it ever since the '30s, so they assumed they'd just use it again. Now that it's under challenge, they are dismissive no more. They might be rebuked by the courts, which would be a singular victory. Or even if not, they might be rebuked at the polls in November.

That's why I have hope for the future: What is so extraordinary about the popular and judicial reaction to this federal overreach is the fact that the opposition grounds itself not just in policy but in constitutional principle. This reaction—inchoate, unorganized, undirected—is a wondrous sign of the health of the body politic. The movement has concentrated on exactly the correct constitutional issues and found its strength in constitutionalism itself. It's not just the traditional arguments that Obamacare or these other expansions are inefficient, that they are not economically sound, that they lead to bureaucratic inefficiency. Those would be valid, but they wouldn't be enough, not at this time. The issue is important not just for how it will affect one-sixth of the economy and the most vital part of our social and family life. It is equally important for what it portends for future challenges to government overreaching. The argument now is emphasizing and rooted in an attack on the constitutional illegitimacy of what is being done, and that—in a constitutional republic—is the heart of the matter.

This does not in any way denigrate the other forms of the conservative critique of modern liberalism. But it does serve to reinforce it. In choosing to focus on a majestic document that bears both study and recitation, this kind of reformed conservatism has found not just a symbol but an anchor. Constitutionalism as a guiding tendency will require careful and thoughtful development, just as its counterpart in jurisprudence—originalism—has required careful thought and development. But the very existence and power of this critique—and of the popular and spiritual support it has received—is a reason for hope, if not for change.

VI

In coming to a close, I'd like to leave you with a more personal reflection. I've always had a sense that there is something providential about American history. And this is from somebody who isn't exactly religious. But starting with the Declaration of Independence and the Constitution: Here is a nation founded on the edge of civilization—a tiny colony, living on the outskirts of the civilized world—that at a time when it needed it miraculously produced the greatest generation of political thinkers in the history of the world. Then a century later, when it needed a Lincoln to save the republic, it found a Lincoln. In the first half of the 20th century, when it needed an FDR to get through the Depression and defeat fascism, it found him. In the second half, when it needed a Reagan to revive the country, he was there.

This is not to say that we will always be able to find our way. I don't see or expect or wait for the next great figure. But I do think that what I mentioned earlier—the kind of spontaneous popular reaction we saw against government overreach and in support of constitutional principles, which manifested itself so extraordinarily in these past years—is another sign of hope.

There is something about the American spirit—about the bedrock decency and common sense of the American—that seems to help us find our way, something about American history that redeems itself in a way that inspires all. I would summarize it by quoting my favorite pundit, Otto von Bismarck. Not known for his punditry, but he is famously said to have said: "God looks after children, drunkards, idiots and the United States of America." I think he still does. I hope he still does.

Adapted from the author's address at the Hillsdale College Constitution Day Celebration in Washington, DC, September 18, 2011

The Meaning of Human Rights

We need no lessons from those who try to undermine the American idea of rights.

In Vienna this week representatives of every country on earth are in conference on human rights. The conference's principal aim—as is to be expected of any conclave of 183 governments, the majority of which are despotic—is to destroy the human rights idea.

On Monday, Secretary of State Warren Christopher went to Vienna to hold the fort. The results were mixed.

The destroyers—led by China, Iran, Cuba, Vietnam and other paragons of human rights—are not very subtle. Their strategy is to shred the idea of human rights by having the world deny that they are universal and by insisting that they "must be considered in the context of . . . national and regional particularities and various historical, cultural and religious backgrounds."

That is UN-ese for saying that human rights is a Western invention and that non-Westerners have their own definition of human rights, which—as a cursory look at China, Myanmar, Iran and other signatories of the so-called Bangkok Declaration of April 1993 will tell you—includes the right to repress.

The only right this gang truly believes in is "the right to development," meaning their right to Western aid money. That these thugs and kleptocrats should elevate their claim to a piece of your paycheck to an inalienable human right is a sign of the contempt with which human rights are treated in international forums.

Given what he had to deal with, Christopher delivered a speech offering a fine, hard-line defense of the universality of human rights. He even coined a good line: "We cannot let cultural relativism become the last refuge of repression."

Unfortunately, the attack on universality is only one aggression against the human rights idea, and the easiest to fend off. There is another, more subtle attack that Christopher did not parry. In fact, he caved.

He agreed to embrace the "International Covenant of Economic, Social and Cultural Rights," a document that for 15 years the United States has refused to ratify. Why? Because it undermines what we in America have long understood by the idea of rights.

The enemies of human rights like to pretend that there are two kinds: "political rights" (free speech, worship, etc.) that the West emphasizes, and "economic and social and cultural rights" (the right to social and economic services guaranteed by the state) that non-Western, non-democratic (and especially communist) countries champion.

What's wrong with expanding the list of rights to include such nice things as the right to a guaranteed job, the right to "social insurance," the right "to enjoy the benefits of scientific progress" and the right to "periodic holidays with pay, as well as remuneration for public holidays"?

What's wrong is that these rights undermine—intentionally undermine—the very idea of political rights. A right is something that the individual claims against the state. You have the right to free speech. It is a personal liberty, a sphere of activity protected from state encroachment.

Economic rights are not claims of the individual against the state. They are claims on the state, demands for things to be granted by the state to the individual. As such, they guarantee the individual's dependence on the state for the necessities of life and thus are instruments for increasing state power over the individual.

Now if the government owes you economic and social and cultural well-being by right, it is no wonder that many governments then claim that they cannot possibly be burdened with those restrictive "political rights"—say, having to tolerate an opposition—and still deliver the goods. The Soviets used to say: "We have economic rights—a guaranteed job, free health care, cheap transportation. You have political rights—free speech, free worship, free emigration. To each his own."

Of course, it was all a lie. The Soviet people lived not just in repression, but in abysmal living conditions. They had neither political nor economic well-being. The West had both.

That is because this supposed trade-off between economic and political rights is nonsense. In fact, those societies that cherish political rights also offer their citizens the most economic and social possibilities.

With the fall of the Soviet empire and the exposure for all the world of its Potemkin "rights," the debate on economic vs. political rights is over. We won. Having won the debate, the administration now proceeds to concede it.

Christopher not only promised to submit the economic, social and cultural rights convention for Senate ratification. He praised it and a few other unratified treaties as "far-reaching documents" and "solemn commitments." The *New York Times* quotes State Department officials as saying that they made the concession to avoid "a sterile debate in Vienna."

Sterile? If everything is a human right, then nothing is a human right. That is the obvious reason for this proliferation of "rights": to diminish and dilute the very idea of rights. That is why every thug regime in the world is so committed to these "rights."

That is why the gang at Bangkok "reaffirmed the interdependence and indivisibility of economic, social, cultural, civil and political rights and the need to give equal emphasis to all categories of human rights."

It is true that the original Universal Declaration of Human Rights of 1948 had some economic and social clauses. But that does not justify compounding the error with an entirely new and comprehensively destructive covenant.

"The Universal Declaration of Human Rights," writes historian Arthur Schlesinger Jr., ". . . included both 'civil and political rights' and 'economic, social and cultural rights,' the second category designed to please states that denied their subjects the first."

Why please them again?

The Washington Post, June 18, 1993

PART IV

COMPETING VISIONS

America's Role and the Course of World History

CHAPTER 16

RELUCTANT COLOSSUS

When to Intervene

What's Worth Fighting For

I

A central problem of America's post–World War II foreign policy has been that it finds itself with the responsibilities of empire, but without the self-justifying ideologies of the old imperial powers. Or, as Henry Fairlie put it in a comparison of the fall of Dien Bien Phu and the fall of Saigon, when Americans find themselves dodging the bullets of natives overseas, they cannot say to themselves, as the imperial armies of the Old World could, that they are merely defending what is theirs. Take away the idea of ownership, take away colonialism, and how do you justify foreign intervention?

One would have thought that Woodrow Wilson had solved the problem early in the century, when he transcended the quasi-imperial notion of Manifest Destiny in favor of a crusade for democracy. It was under the banner of democracy that the United

States was brought into World War I and, irrevocably, into balance of power politics. It remains under that banner now.

The idea of self-government does seem a wholly natural underpinning to American interventionism. But there are problems. One is historical. Wilson's choice of conflicts for first invoking the idea tarnished it. Whatever World War I was, it was hardly a war for democracy. Wilson used the democratic idea as the ideological justification for fighting a war where democracy was only remotely the issue. The cynicism that has greeted subsequent invocations of the democratic idea to justify other faraway fights is also often deserved. In other American interventions abroad—for economic, territorial or purely geopolitical reasons—democracy has often been used as a flag of convenience.

The other problem is logical. There seems to be something self-contradictory about intervening on behalf of self-government. It is a lot more straightforward to intervene the old-fashioned way: on behalf of the alleged superiority of the metropolitan civilization. At best, to intervene on behalf of democracy means leaving quickly. Occupation mocks the idea of self-government. As it was with the recent US experience in Grenada, we have to be thinking of going home from the day we land the Marines.

Still, these are not insuperable obstacles to a theory of intervention based on the notion of promoting democracy. First, there is no reason why past sinfulness should paralyze us now. If in 1954 we overthrew the freely elected Jacobo Arbenz in Guatemala, we now support the freely elected Jose Napoleon Duarte in El Salvador, whose land-reform policies are not very different from Arbenz's. Should the sins of 30 years ago in one country discredit our policy today in another? By that logic the Catholic Church's support for Poland's Solidarity and other social democratic movements is equally suspect, given the church's historical record on democracy. To admit that the democratic idea has been abused in the past is to say no more than that democracy, like equality, fraternity and other good causes, has a long history. It is reason for vigilance, not for surrendering the idea.

The second obstacle must be acknowledged directly: Although democracy can be brought at the point of a bayonet, it flourishes best if the bayonets are quickly removed. Yet sometimes they cannot be. Take cases, successful cases, which is where a theory of intervention should begin. Our bayonets, nuclear tipped, are still in Germany and Japan 40 years after the end of the Second World War. And though many Americans object to the cost, and some to the danger, there is no real opposition on principle. There is no real case to be made that it contravenes our values to be stationing troops on German soil. Yet Germany is not ours. We have no colonial claim. Still, we do have a persuasive reason: We are needed to defend a democracy.

II

But justice is not enough. Intervention needs a further justification: strategic necessity. To intervene solely for reasons of democratic morality is to confuse foreign policy with philanthropy. And a philanthropist gives out his own money. A statesman is a trustee. He spends the blood and treasure of others. On the other hand, to act purely for the reasons of strategy—to act imperially—is not only corrupting, but, for a democracy, unsustainable: A people committed to democratic values and exposed to the free flow of information will not long stand for costly intervention for antidemocratic objectives.

It is true that strategic necessity itself has a moral or at least an ideological foundation. American strategy has one overriding objective: to secure the safety of the United States and of the

Western alliance. That alliance, in turn, is not capriciously cobbled together, but based on certain values. Protection of that alliance, and thus those values, from a rival power or bloc of powers inimical to both requires the exercise of realpolitik. Or, to put it another way, the struggle between the democracies and the chief threat to their survival, the Soviet bloc, hinges on many things. One of them is the fate of the unclaimed territory between them. The struggle between the blocs can be won (in the nuclear age, it must be won, because there is no alternative) by indirection: by surrounding the other side, stripping it of its outer defense, and ultimately putting it in a position where it must bend its will to the other. Containment was invented to prevent just that from happening.

Western realpolitik does, therefore, have a moral foundation. But that does not mean that anything goes. There may be extreme circumstances (Hitler, for example) under which one may ally oneself with a monster (Stalin). But a sustainable theory of intervention cannot argue from the extreme. It cannot, for example, address itself only to ends. It must ask not only "What does this intervention do for the alliance?" but also "What does it do to the country where the intervention takes place?" The Kantian injunction to treat individuals as ends must have application to nations as well. An intervention must not only defend the perimeter or sea-lanes or chromium mines of the alliance; it must better the condition of those on whose behalf we intervene.

Two criteria, then: Intervention must be both morally justified and strategically necessary. If these criteria appear too general and all-encompassing, let me point out that they exclude, and are meant to exclude, considerations that tend to dominate American debates over intervention: international law, world public opinion and the public sentiments of our own allies.

I argue instead for a kind of global unilateralism in the moral arena. We should be confident enough of our own values, and of our own ability to discern what actions abroad will promote them, to act accordingly without being bound by the verdict of others—like the World Court, whose composition and ideology is far less democratic than that of the United States Congress; like the UN, according to which the fight against racism should have taken us by now to the beaches of Tel Aviv; or like the Organization of American States, once aptly described by Irving Kristol as "a kind of mini-United Nations where we can be voted down in only three languages, thereby saving translators' fees." We did not need any of these agencies to help us decide on the nature of the Coard regime in Grenada. And we can debate the nature of the Duarte and Ortega regimes in El Salvador and Nicaragua quite adequately without either their advice or consent.

III

What about our allies' views? Some, like Robert Pastor, a Latin American scholar and NSC aide in the Carter administration, argue that it is a contradiction of the democratic idea for the leader of an alliance of democracies to act alone; global unilateralism defeats its own democratic purposes. There are two answers. First, our allies, particularly our smaller allies in the Third World, are not free agents. They are bound by weakness and fear. They are subject to the kinds of threats and blackmail from which the United States, owing to its power, is immune. Which of Nicaragua's neighbors can say in public what it tells our congressional delegations in private?

Moreover, global unilateralism is not really a choice; it is an existing reality. The European democracies, exhausted by two world wars, depleted and turned inward, did decide to place the ultimate responsibility for their safety in the hands of the United States. It is a fact, unpleasant perhaps, but a fact nonetheless. The United States would prefer otherwise. It constantly tries to change that fact by urging the allies to do more for their own defense. The results of these attempts are well known.

An American foreign policy should be confident enough to define international morality in its own, American terms. Is that parochial? I think it is parochial to do otherwise. If we take our own ideas about democracy, rights and self-government seriously, then it is the height of parochialism, and worse, to believe that these values are applicable only to a few largely white Western countries. We used to hear arguments about what a luxury democracy was in India. It took 30 years for Western intellectuals to realize what the Indians knew on day one: It is a boon. One hardly hears the luxury argument made about India these days. That kind of talk has rotated to places like El Salvador. If democracy succeeds there, it will rotate again to other unfortunate places. If we believe democracy is good for us, then we must believe it will be good for others.

Everywhere? The usual charge against moral unilateralism is that it is hypocritical. If, for example, the US is really trying to overthrow the Sandinista government for the reasons it states—i.e., to create a genuinely pluralist democracy—then why has the United States not created a contra force in Haiti? Why not support the ANC in South Africa?

IV

The reply is clear. Moral justification is a necessary condition for intervention. It is not sufficient. Again: Foreign policy is not philanthropy. One doesn't intervene purely for justice. One intervenes for reasons of strategy, and if justice permits. Neither Haiti nor South Africa is about to allow itself to be used for the projection of Soviet power; the same cannot be said of Nicaragua. (It is true that the oppression of the South African and Haitian regimes may ultimately produce successor regimes hostile to the United States; dealing with the long-range threat requires a different strategy, which is discussed below.) We should commit ourselves only in those places where our interests are threatened—with a severe constraint: that any form of intervention should conform to our notions of democratic morality.

But how to define strategic necessity? It depends, of course, on where one locates the perimeter of American interests and on what one thinks is the nature of the threat to those interests. But strategic arguments are not wholly arbitrary. We can start with areas of consensus. Even those dreaded San Francisco Democrats place NATO, Japan, the Persian Gulf, Israel, Central America and the Caribbean within the Western perimeter. Even during the 1984 Democratic presidential primary campaign Gary Hart expressed willingness to use force to defend the Persian Gulf. And Democratic presidential nominee Walter Mondale later declared that a Soviet base in Nicaragua would warrant an American quarantine. At the time of the false MiG alarm in Nicaragua, there was much talk of air strikes and little dissent even from congressional Democrats.

The heart of the argument over strategy is less "What is worth defending?" than "What kind of regime in those agreed places worth defending is compatible with our interests?" In a place like Central America or the Caribbean, where our principal aim is to keep the Soviets and the Cubans out, the question becomes "Who is most likely to keep them out?" A coalition government in

Salvador? A treaty-bound Ortega in Managua? A Coard-Austin junta in Grenada? The strategic question translates ultimately into a political question. It requires a political answer.

The best political answer is that in much of the Third World the most reliable repository of American strategic interests is what is sometimes called the third force—local centrist parties supportive of democracy and opposed to both right-wing strongmen and anti-Western revolutionaries. True, sometimes, as in Iran in 1979, the third force is an illusion and an excuse not to support the lesser of two evils. But our choices are not always so meager. The degree of success we have seen in El Salvador, for example, is all the more remarkable because of the weakness of the Salvadoran political center and the improbability that a viable third force could be found. The United States should desperately be seeking to support and promote the democratic opposition in places like the Philippines, Chile, South Korea and South Africa; the democratic opposition in Nicaragua; and the democratic government in El Salvador. It does not matter whether our thugs or their thugs are in power. We have learned through bitter experience in places like Cuba and Nicaragua, as we may soon learn in Chile, that our thugs are a fragile vessel for American interests, and their tactic of attacking the center to preserve themselves can only smooth the way to ultimate power for the extreme (and anti-American) left.

A third-force strategy is not a prescription, but a guide to thinking about American strategic needs. Even more important, perhaps, it may be a way for ideological adversaries at home to work toward a new consensus on how and to what end the United States should intervene in the affairs of other states.

The New Republic, May 6, 1985

The Arrow of History

How do you distinguish a foreign policy "idealist" from a "realist," an optimist from a pessimist? Ask one question: Do you believe in the arrow of history? Or to put it another way, do you think history is cyclical or directional? Are we condemned to do the same damn thing over and over, generation after generation—or is there hope for some enduring progress in the world order?

For realists, generally conservative, history is an endless cycle of clashing power politics. The same patterns repeat. Only the names and places change. The best we can do in our own time is to defend ourselves, managing instability and avoiding catastrophe. But expect nothing permanent, no essential alteration in the course of human affairs.

The idealists believe otherwise. They believe that the international system can eventually evolve out of its Hobbesian state of nature into something more humane and hopeful. What is usually overlooked is that this hopefulness for achieving a higher plane of global comity comes in two flavors—one liberal, one conservative.

The liberal variety (as practiced, for example, by the Bill Clinton administration) believes that the creation of a dense web of treaties, agreements, transnational institutions and international organizations (such as the UN, NGOs, the World Trade Organization) can give substance to a cohesive community of nations that would, in time, ensure order and stability.

The conservative view (often called neoconservative and dominant in the George W. Bush years) is that the better way to ensure order and stability is not through international institutions, which are flimsy and generally powerless, but through the spread of democracy. Because, in the end, democracies are inherently more inclined to live in peace.

Liberal internationalists count on globalization, neoconservatives on democratization to get us to the sunny uplands of international harmony. But what unites them is the belief that such uplands exist and are achievable. Both believe in the perfectibility, if not of man, then of the international system. Both believe in the arrow of history.

For realists, this is a comforting delusion that gives high purpose to international exertions where none exists. Sovereign nations remain in incessant pursuit of power and self-interest. The pursuit can be carried out more or less wisely. But nothing fundamentally changes.

Barack Obama is a classic case study in foreign policy idealism. Indeed, one of his favorite quotations is about the arrow of history: "The arc of the moral universe is long, but it bends toward justice." He has spent nearly eight years trying to advance that arc of justice. Hence his initial "apology tour," that burst of confessional soul-searching abroad about America and its sins, from slavery to the loss of our moral compass after 9/11. Friday's trip to Hiroshima completes the arc.

Unfortunately, with "justice" did not come peace. The policies that followed—appeasing Vladimir Putin, the Iranian mullahs, the butchers of Tiananmen Square and lately the Castros—have advanced neither justice nor peace. On the contrary. The consequent withdrawal of American power, that agent of injustice or at least arrogant overreach, has yielded nothing but geopolitical chaos and immense human suffering. (See Syria.)

But now an interesting twist. Two terms as president may not have disabused Obama of his arc-of-justice idealism (see above: Hiroshima visit), but they have forced upon him at least one policy of hardheaded, indeed hardhearted, realism. On his Vietnam trip this week, Obama accepted the reality of an abusive dictatorship while announcing a warming of relations and the lifting of the US arms embargo, thereby enlisting Vietnam as a full partner in the containment of China.

This follows the partial return of the US military to the Philippines, another element of the containment strategy. Indeed, the Trans-Pacific Partnership itself is less about economics than geopolitics, creating a Pacific Rim cordon around China.

There's no idealism in containment. It is raw, soulless realpolitik. No moral arc. No uplifting historical arrow. In fact, it is the same damn thing all over again, a recapitulation of Truman's containment of Russia in the late 1940s. Obama is doing the same, now with China.

He thus leaves a double legacy. His arc-of-justice aspirations, whatever their intention, leave behind tragic geopolitical and human wreckage. Yet this belated acquiescence to realpolitik, laying the foundations for a new containment, will be an essential asset in addressing this century's coming central challenge, the rise of China.

I don't know—no one knows—if history has an arrow. Which is why a dose of coldhearted realism is always welcome. Especially from Obama.

The Washington Post, May 27, 2016

Trump's Foreign Policy Revolution

The flurry of bold executive orders and of highly provocative Cabinet nominations (such as a secretary of education who actually believes in school choice) has been encouraging to conservative skeptics of Donald Trump. But it shouldn't erase the troubling memory of one major element of Trump's inaugural address.

The foreign policy section has received far less attention than so revolutionary a declaration deserved. It radically redefined the American national interest as understood since World War II.

Trump outlined a world in which foreign relations are collapsed into a zero-sum game. They gain, we lose. As in: "For many decades, we've enriched foreign industry at the expense of American industry; subsidized the armies of other countries" while depleting our own.

And most provocatively this: "The wealth of our middle class has been ripped from their homes and then redistributed all across the world." Bernie Sanders believes that a corrupt establishment has ripped off the middle class to give to the rich. Trump believes those miscreants have given away our patrimony to undeserving, ungrateful foreigners as well.

JFK's inaugural pledged to support any friend and oppose any foe to assure the success of liberty. Note that Trump makes no distinction between friend and foe (and no reference to liberty). They're all out to use, exploit and surpass us.

No more, declared Trump: "From this day forward, it's going to be only America First."

Imagine how this resonates abroad. "America First" was the

name of the organization led by Charles Lindbergh that bitterly fought FDR before the US entry into World War II—right through the Battle of Britain—to keep America neutral between Churchill's Britain and Hitler's Reich. (Then came Pearl Harbor. Within a week, America First dissolved itself in shame.)

Not that Trump was consciously imitating Lindbergh. I doubt he was even aware of the reference. He just liked the phrase. But I can assure you that in London and in every world capital they are aware of the antecedent and the intimations of a new American isolationism. Trump gave them good reason to think so, going on to note "the right of all nations to put their own interests first." America included.

Some claim that putting America first is a reassertion of American exceptionalism. On the contrary, it is the antithesis. It makes America no different from all the other countries that define themselves by a particularist blood-and-soil nationalism. What made America exceptional, unique in the world, was defining its own national interest beyond its narrow economic and security needs to encompass the safety and prosperity of a vast array of allies. A free world marked by open trade and mutual defense was President Truman's vision, shared by every president since.

Until now.

Some have argued that Trump is just dangling a bargaining chip to negotiate better terms of trade or alliance. Or that Trump's views are so changeable and unstable—telling European newspapers two weeks ago that NATO is obsolete and then saying "NATO is very important to me"—that this is just another unmoored entry on a ledger of confusion.

But both claims are demonstrably wrong. An inaugural address is no off-the-cuff riff. These words are the product of at least three weeks of deliberate crafting for an address that Trump's spokesman said was intended to express his philosophy. Moreover, to remove any ambiguity, Trump prefaced his "America First" proclamation with: "From this day forward, a new vision will govern our land."

Trump's vision misunderstands the logic underlying the far larger, far-reaching view of Truman. The Marshall Plan surely took wealth away from the American middle class and distributed it abroad. But for a reason. Altruism, in part. But mostly to stabilize Western Europe as a bulwark against an existential global enemy.

We carried many free riders throughout the Cold War. The burden was heavy. But this was not a mindless act of charity; it was an exercise in enlightened self-interest. After all, it was indeed better to subsidize foreign armies—German, South Korean, Turkish and dozens of others—and have them stand with us, rather than stationing even more American troops everywhere around the world at greater risk of both blood and treasure.

We are embarking upon insularity and smallness. Nor is this just theory. Trump's long-promised but nonetheless abrupt withdrawal from the Trans-Pacific Partnership is the momentous first fruit of his foreign policy doctrine. Last year the prime minister of Singapore told John McCain that if we pulled out of the TPP "you'll be finished in Asia." He knows the region.

For 70 years, we sustained an international system of open commerce and democratic alliances that has enabled America and the West to grow and thrive. Global leadership is what made America great. We abandon it at our peril.

The Washington Post, January 27, 2017

CHAPTER 17

THE END OF
"THE END OF HISTORY"

After a Mere 25 Years, the
Triumph of the West Is Over

Twenty-five years ago—December 1991—communism died, the Cold War ended and the Soviet Union disappeared. It was the largest breakup of an empire in modern history and not a shot was fired. It was an event of biblical proportions that my generation thought it would never live to see. As Wordsworth famously rhapsodized (about the French Revolution), "Bliss was it in that dawn to be alive/But to be young was very heaven!"

That dawn marked the ultimate triumph of the liberal democratic idea. It promised an era of Western dominance led by a preeminent America, the world's last remaining superpower.

And so it was for a decade as the community of democracies expanded, first into Eastern Europe and former Soviet colonies. The US was so dominant that when, on December 31, 1999, it gave up one of the most prized geostrategic assets on the globe—the Panama Canal—no one even noticed.

That era is over. The autocracies are back and rising; democracy is on the defensive; the US is in retreat. Look no further than Aleppo. A Western-backed resistance to a local tyrant—he backed by a resurgent Russia, an expanding Iran and an array of proxy Shiite militias—is on the brink of annihilation. Russia drops bombs; America issues statements.

What better symbol for the end of that heady liberal-democratic historical moment. The West is turning inward and going home, leaving the field to the rising authoritarians—Russia, China and Iran. In France, the conservative party's newly nominated presidential contender is fashionably conservative and populist and soft on Vladimir Putin. As are several of the newer Eastern Europe democracies—Hungary, Bulgaria, even Poland—themselves showing authoritarian tendencies.

And even as Europe tires of the sanctions imposed on Russia for its rape of Ukraine, President Obama's much-touted "isolation" of Russia has ignominiously dissolved, as our secretary of state repeatedly goes cap in hand to Russia to beg for mercy in Syria.

The European Union, the largest democratic club on earth, could itself soon break up as Brexit-like movements spread across the continent. At the same time, its members dash with unseemly haste to reopen economic ties with a tyrannical and aggressive Iran.

As for China, the other great challenger to the post–Cold War order, the administration's "pivot" has turned into an abject failure. The Philippines openly defected to the Chinese side. Malaysia then followed. And the rest of our Asian allies are beginning to hedge their bets. When the president of China addressed the Pacific Rim countries in Peru last month, he suggested that China was prepared to pick up the pieces of the Trans-Pacific Partnership, now abandoned by both political parties in the United States.

The West's retreat began with Obama, who reacted to (perceived) post-9/11 overreach by abandoning Iraq, offering appeasement ("reset") to Russia and accommodating Iran. In 2009, he refused even rhetorical support to the popular revolt against the rule of the ayatollahs.

Donald Trump wants to continue the pullback, though for entirely different reasons. Obama ordered retreat because he's always felt the US was not good enough for the world, too flawed to have earned the moral right to be the world hegemon. Trump would follow suit, disdaining allies and avoiding conflict, because the world is not good enough for us—undeserving, ungrateful, parasitic foreigners living safely under our protection and off our sacrifices. Time to look after our own American interests.

Trump's is not a new argument. As the Cold War was ending in 1990, Jeane Kirkpatrick, the quintessential neoconservative, argued that we should now become "a normal country in a normal time." It was time to give up the 20th-century burden of maintaining world order and of making superhuman exertions on behalf of universal values. Two generations of fighting fascism and communism were quite enough. Had we not earned a restful retirement?

At the time, I argued that we had earned it indeed, but a cruel history would not allow us to enjoy it. Repose presupposes a fantasy world in which stability is self-sustaining without the United States. It is not. We would incur not respite but chaos.

A quarter-century later, we face the same temptation, but this time under more challenging circumstances. Worldwide jihadism has been added to the fight, and we enjoy nothing like the dominance we exercised over conventional adversaries during our 1990s holiday from history.

We may choose repose, but we won't get it.

The Washington Post, December 2, 2016

The Coming Disillusionment
in Liberated Europe

In the euphoria, it is easy to forget that liberation is often the beginning of human folly, not the end. (The book of Exodus is a useful text on the subject.) Liberty is an invitation to folly. In the zones of Eastern Europe newly liberated from the Soviet Union, the invitation is being accepted.

Bulgarians have been free for about a month. What is the first great cause they have taken up with their newfound freedoms of assembly, petition and speech? Chanting "Bulgaria for Bulgarians," they demand the repression of the Muslim minority. The country is racked with civil disorder protesting the repeal by the new Communist regime of oppressive anti-Turkish decrees.

At the first whiff of glasnost, Armenians and Azerbaijanis, Georgians and Ossetians, Uzbeks and Meskhetians marked the lifting of the yoke of the Soviet imperium by taking to the streets to beat each other bloody. The newest riots in southern Azerbaijan, however, have progressed beyond mere ethnic quarreling. The local citizenry, Shiite Muslims, are near insurrection, attacking authorities and tearing down border posts. Their demand? Reunification with Iran.

To my recollection, Paul Johnson was the first (August 1988) to warn of the coming Balkanization of East Europe and the rekindling of ancient ethnic strife as the Soviet empire broke up. By now everyone is familiar with the fact—though few anticipated the fury—of intolerant nationalism as the great bane and potential ruin of the newly liberated Soviet zone.

Another source of potential ruin is now equally obvious: the economic costs of de-communization. A report from Poland last weekend spoke of people losing patience with Solidarity's program of radical economic reform. Polish capitalism was all of six days old at the time.

There is, however, one other bane facing liberated Europe, less obvious than ethnic and economic disillusionment but equally preordained. It is the coming political disillusionment. Democracy in the abstract is a glory second to none. But liberated Europe is about to experience the first half of Churchill's famous quip that democracy is the worst form of government except for all the others.

Not just that it is messy and corrupt. A friend of mine, an adviser to one of Hungary's new democratic parties, brought a group of aspiring Hungarian politicians over to the United States last fall to imbibe democracy at the wellspring. They were treated to a tour of the New York mayoralty and the Virginia gubernatorial campaigns. During their 40 years of jail and repression, of samizdat and secret police, did they dream, could they have imagined, that at the end of the tunnel lay Jackie Mason?

It is not just that Hungary and the rest are headed for party squabbling and backroom deals, tracking polls and campaign lies. The disillusionment with democracy will involve something far deeper.

First, the realization that real democracy actually establishes limits to popular will. Under constitutionalism, not everything is permitted even if the people will it. In one of the liberation's more remarkable twists, Bulgaria's government last week rejected calls in the street for a referendum. The demonstrators demanded a referendum on ethnic rights—in order to deny them to the 15% Turkish minority. A statement pointing out that fundamental human rights cannot be subject to popular vote was issued jointly by the democratic opposition and—how rich our history—the Communist Party.

The second and more deeply disillusioning truth about democracy is that it is designed at its core to be spiritually empty. As Isaiah Berlin wrote 30 years ago in his essay "John Stuart Mill and the Ends of Life," the defining proposition of liberal democracy is that it mandates means (elections, parliaments, markets) but not ends. Democracy leaves the goals of life entirely up to the individual. Where the totalitarian state decrees life's purposes—Deng's Four Modernizations, Castro's Rectification Campaigns, the generic exhortation to "Build Socialism"—democracy leaves the public square naked.

What a shock for those whose lives have been so infused with purpose by the struggle against totalitarianism. That is why the original East German oppositionists looked with dismay at the post-Wall revelers, those content to see the revolution "drowned in West Berlin chocolate." That is why the victory, the miracle, of 1989 will be as disillusioning as it is now exhilarating. The fruit of that victory is bourgeois democracy—the most free, most humane, most decent political system ever invented by man, and the most banal. Dying for it is far more ennobling than living it. Liberated Europe is just getting to the living part.

The Washington Post, January 12, 1990

The Authoritarian Temptation

A quarter-century ago, the impending death of the Soviet Union occasioned a delirium. I was one of the first to succumb. "Political philosophy is over," I wrote even before the Berlin Wall came down. "Finished. Solved. The perennial question that has preoccupied every political philosopher since Plato—what is the best form of governance—has been answered." History had spoken: "liberal, pluralist, capitalist democracy."

The sequence of events that followed seemed to justify the euphoria. First, the fall of the Berlin Wall—marking the dissolution of the external Soviet empire—as the conquered lands of Eastern Europe, forced for decades into communist rule and the Warsaw Pact, threw off Soviet subjugation one by one.

But the fall of empires is nothing new. The next and truly fantastical world-historical event was the disintegration of the Soviet Union itself. On Christmas Day 1991, the internal empire dissolved as well. The 14 non-Russian constituent "republics" that had been ruled by Moscow were turned into independent nations. It marked the disappearance of the world's leading communist state, the end of communism as an actual form of government and the end of the very idea of communism as a plausible system of social and political organization. And the end of six decades of existential struggle between a democratic West and the totalitarianisms of the left and right that had defined world politics since the rise of fascism in the 1930s.

With a whimper, the enemy vanished. The Cold War wasn't just over; it was won. For a generation that never imagined it would live to see that day, this was an event of biblical proportions. It was possible in that dawn to believe, briefly, that we had reached the peak of mankind's political development. The more extravagant romantics among us called it the end of History—the capital "H" being homage to the triumph of the transcendent, self-conscious History of 19th-century German philosophy. I saw it as the endpoint of 2,500 years of Western political theory. It was the vindication of Churchill's aphorism that democracy is the worst form of government except for all the others. The others having been tried and failed, what was left standing was a political system—the modern capitalist democracy of universal suffrage, the rule of law, guaranteed rights and the peaceful and regular transfer of governmental power—that balanced and satisfied individual, communal and national needs.

II

Twenty-five years later, the landscape has changed radically. The great dawn turns out to have been a mirage; the great hope, an act of self-delusion. The slide back away from liberal democracy is well underway. In retrospect, that was perhaps to be expected. History has been unkind to every stripe of utopian thinking. What's been remarkable, however, is how far in a mere 25 years the pendulum has swung the other way. Not only is it not advancing. It is now in retreat. It's not just that we have failed to achieve the messianic future. It's that even the democratic present is under widespread assault. As Freedom House's "Nations in Transit 2017" report noted dryly, we had assumed "that once a country had achieved democracy, it would stay at that end of the scale. Current conditions present a very different picture."

In the first decade, the signs of a democratic flourishing were everywhere. After all, what were the alternatives? A Russian model? Russia was shrinking physically, disordered socially, bleeding economically and caught in a mass of corruption. China? The Chinese communists had learned from Mikhail Gorbachev's example to yield economic but not political space, thereby fostering rapid economic growth while retaining ironfisted political control. To Third World countries with emerging economies and political choice, Beijing's model was more attractive than Moscow's, but hardly competitive with the Western democratic-capitalist model. Nor was Islamism much of a competitor. In 2001, it made its mark, showing itself capable of much destruction. But as a nihilistic offshoot of one particular religious faith, it garnered a decidedly narrow, if fanatical, following.

A democratic future, gradually expanding throughout the globe, seemed assured. After all, the spread of democracy had already been underway when the Soviet Union collapsed. Throughout the '80s, the number of democracies had been increasing inexorably. In Latin America, the recruits were coming from the right. Argentina's military yielded control to civilians in 1983; Brazil's in 1985. In Chile, General Augusto Pinochet lost first a plebiscite (1988), then a presidential election (1989), setting off a momentous return to democratic government.

In East Asia, the trend had also begun when the military in two of the major economic tigers, South Korea and Taiwan, ceded power in 1987.

The trickle turned into a flood in the 1990s as former Warsaw Pact Soviet satellites and former Soviet republics enlisted in the democratic club. By 2007, most had joined NATO and/or the European Union as emblems of their new status.

It was a rout, on the ground and in the zeitgeist. In the realm of ideas, the international left was reeling, too shocked by the relegation of socialism to the ash heap of history to mount anything more than a halfhearted defense of its political philosophy.

Then came the disappointments. The great rush stalled. History turned yet again.

The most spectacular failure of the leap forward toward democracy was the Arab Spring. Begun in December 2010, it was a generalized revolt against two generations of postcolonial dictatorial rule in the Arab Middle East that had yielded an astonishing harvest of economic, political, social and military disaster (especially vis-à-vis Israel). These were peoples with proud histories and immense latent talent held down and held back by grotesquely dysfunctional politics.

The revolt charmed the West and inspired the young. It ended in tears. In Egypt, it produced little more than an exchange of military dictatorships, sandwiched around a year of Muslim Brotherhood misrule. In Syria, it has led to a merciless multi-sided civil war. And in Iraq, an American invasion that toppled the traditional postcolonial strongman gave way to a brittle, formally democratic regime overwhelmed by bloody sectarian strife and undermined by growing Iranian domination.

There were similar hopes in Africa. Nelson Mandela's South Africa provided the model for a dignified, democratic transition to self-rule. But for most of the continent, the promising starts ended badly—from Zimbabwe, which from independence degenerated rapidly into self-destructive one-man rule, to South Sudan, which collapsed into civil war, to Libya, liberated from Qaddafi only to fall into a countrywide war of all against all.

III

This was one level of democratic failure, the inability to forge stable democratic regimes out of collapsed dictatorships. For all its disappointments, the failure was nonetheless understandable given how difficult and prolonged the transition to democracy has proved even in the West. More dispiriting, therefore, was the second level of democratic failure: regression and rollback where the foundations of democracy had already been laid. These are functioning democracies that have been systematically undone and effectively transformed into dictatorships—most prominently Turkey and Venezuela.

One might have added Russia to that list, if the post-Soviet regime that emerged in the 1990s had not been so unstable and dysfunctional to begin with. Consigned to the tender hands of Vladimir Putin at the turn of the millennium, its democratic superstructure was methodically dismantled, year by year, institution by institution. It's a bitter history. Once again, Russia had a chance at democracy and ended up with yet another repressive dictatorship, this time KGB rule stripped of the ideological pretensions of communism.

Russia qualifies, therefore, as a might-have-been. Venezuela and Turkey actually were—democracies, that is—before embarking on their projects of constitutional demolition. These are the greater blow to the democratic faith. Venezuela had a proud democratic tradition going back half a century, then allowed itself to succumb to a Cuba-inspired caudillo who emasculated every rival center of power. His successor has proven even more incompetent and authoritarian. The result is a dictatorship of unusual malice and spectacular ineptitude.

Meanwhile, in 2003 Turkey elected an Islamist prime minister who was at the time held out as a model of moderation for the rest of the Muslim world. Hardly. Recep Erdogan proceeded to remorselessly tighten his grip on power through systematic intimidation, incarceration and infiltration of rival centers of power, most especially the pillars of the traditional constitutional structures—the courts, the military, the legislature, the press.

Since Mustafa Kemal Ataturk founded modern Turkey as a secular republic a century ago, the military had guaranteed the openness and secularism of its quasi-democratic system. These guarantees are gone. More journalists are in jail in Turkey than in any other country, China included. Tens of thousands are now imprisoned following the shadowy abortive coup of 2016. The April 2017 referendum made it official. It abolished Turkey's parliamentary system, vastly expanded the powers of the presidency and essentially marked the end of Turkish democracy. Erdogan is famously reported to have said that "democracy is a bus ride; once I get to my stop, I'm getting off." The bus has arrived. Turkish democracy is done.

So far we've dealt with two categories of democratic reversal: traditional dictatorships that have failed to transform into democracies, and formerly successful Third World democracies that have regressed. Most dispiriting of all, however, is the third phenomenon beginning to unfold, which more than any other makes a mockery of the democratic hopes of the post–Cold War dawn: an authoritarian temptation now rising in the heart of the West, the world's most established, entrenched, seemingly secure repository of liberal democracy.

IV

In what would have been unimaginable 25 years ago, mature Western democracies are experiencing a surge of ethno-nationalism, a blood-and-soil patriotism tinged with xenophobia, a weariness with parliamentary dysfunction and an attraction—still only an attraction, not yet a commitment—to strongman rule.

Its most conspicuous symptom is a curious and growing affinity for Vladimir Putin, Czar of all the Russias. Remarkably, this tendency is most pronounced on the right. The reversal is head-snapping. Throughout the 20th century and the early 21st, Western conservatives had viewed Russia with revulsion, fear and contempt. This was particularly pronounced during the half-century of Cold War, during which opposition to Russian communist ideology and expansionism was a pillar of conservative faith. Today, some on the right have begun to profess a certain admiration of and attraction to Putinism and his brand of Russian authoritarianism.

The result is jarring. After decades of left-wing apologists for Russia, it is now lifelong conservatives who are asking: What's so bad about Putin anyway? Upholder of traditional values (he is a particular scourge of homosexuality), defender of the faith (Orthodox in his case, but any variant of Christianity will do), restorer of order through ruthlessly centralized power that dispenses with the niceties of checks and balances (federalism, free elections, an independent press), he took a basket case of a country and made Russia great again, has he not?

Sure he emasculated the political opposition, shut down independent media and regularly kills political opponents and journalists. But he's got omelets to make. Moreover, as President

Donald Trump said when asked about the killings, "There are a lot of killers. We've got a lot of killers. What, you think our country is so innocent?"

Moral equivalence so shocking, emanating from the elected leader of the United States, is not to be ignored. And the willingness to overlook authoritarian excesses is accompanied by an open admiration of strongman rule and a barely concealed envy for the willfulness and freedom of action that enables it.

Contrast that with the decline and decay of the West. Paralyzed by process and grown decadent, it cannot rouse itself to defend its values—sacrificing civilizational pride to a thin gruel of multicultural mediocrity; to defend its borders—supinely permitting an invasion of the unwanted and uninvited; and to defend its history—allowing its once-proud nation-states to be constrained by transnational institutions and, in the case of Europe, absorbed into a soulless superstate run from Brussels by cosmopolitan bureaucrats. All this, as the West passively watches the debasement of its foundational institutions of family, church and community.

European fascination with Putin-style authoritarianism is far more developed than the American variety. Marine Le Pen of the National Front, runner-up for the French presidency who garnered 40% of the vote and supplanted the two major establishment parties that had alternated power for half a century, has expressed support and admiration for Putin, promised to drop post-Crimea sanctions and went so far as to pay him the homage of a visit to the Kremlin just weeks before France's presidential election.

Not surprising. The distance between Putin and Le Pen is not all that great. All the characteristics of Putinism—blood-and-soil nationalism, reimposition of traditional values, narrowly redefined national interests, a longing for powerful central government—are to be found in the ideology of the National Front, which called, for example, for repealing same-sex marriage. It's part of a wider trend sweeping Europe, a rising populism attracted to a new model of governance—traditional, reactionary and, above all, unapologetically nationalist.

The victory of the centrist Emmanuel Macron showed that there is nothing inevitable about the rising populism. But his very victory is rightly seen as a singular and therefore crucial challenge for the centrist politics he represents. Should he fail—and his plans to reform French labor and tax law are highly ambitious and therefore problematic—the crisis of the establishment center will become all the more acute, leaving an opening for a radical populism of the right or left.

Note that the far left and arguably communist Jean-Luc Mélenchon ran only two points behind Le Pen in the first round of the 2017 presidential elections. This is almost as dismaying as the showing of Jeremy Corbyn of the British Labour Party in Britain's general election, which occurred only one month later. Here too was an essentially unreconstructed communist who, though not winning the election, was clearly the biggest winner. Corbyn increased his party's representation in Parliament by 32, leaving it not only the principal opposition party but the leading candidate to defeat the Conservatives in the next elections.

Nor is the tug of the populist extremes confined to Western Europe. Indeed, its most alarming manifestation is to be found in two leading post-Soviet democracies, once the herald of the post–Cold War dawn: Hungary and Poland.

In Hungary, the highly nationalist, anti-immigrant government has given the president effective control of the courts while suppressing opposition media. In Poland, the executive has similarly taken over the Constitutional Tribunal and captured the public media. The "spectacular breakdown of democracy" (to quote Freedom House) in these linchpin post-communist states is a reminder of the fragility and the reversibility of democratic gains everywhere.

V

How to account for the retreat? In the immediate post–World War II era, the same question arose in trying to explain that period's totalitarian temptation: the rising, powerful communist parties of the West. At the time, conventional wisdom described it as a flight from freedom. The burdens of freedom were too heavy, the attractions of security too many.

A byproduct was the vogue for a new set of economic and social "rights." Traditional rights—the "negative liberty" of being left alone by others, especially the state—were derided as bourgeois. True human rights were the more concrete and material—the right to sustenance, to work, to shelter, to physical protection. Note that these were not freedoms from the state, but benefits that could only be conferred by the state. The resulting dependency is the very antithesis of freedom.

That new vocabulary of rights generated a linguistic sleight-of-hand that allowed the complete overturning of the very notion of freedom. The most ruthless dictatorships took to calling themselves democracies, as in the "Democratic Republic of" this or that—the German Democratic Republic and the Democratic People's Republic of Korea being the most notorious of these frauds until the rise of Democratic Kampuchea (Cambodia) in the 1970s. Its specialty was genocide.

But the argument found many takers. After all, went the cliché, what was free speech to people with empty stomachs?

The choice was presented as binary. Millions chose security (often, ironically, in free elections). Psychologically, they preferred not to bear the burdens, the responsibilities, the risks of freedom. They preferred a state that gave them their daily bread.

Given the abject destitution and privation that Europe was suffering amid the rubble of World War II, that may be an adequate explanation for the attraction of the totalitarian parties in the '40s and '50s. It is not, however, an adequate explanation for the flight from freedom today. After all, it's been well and widely demonstrated that liberal democracy is infinitely superior in producing not just freedom but prosperity as well. The economic security promised by socialism and the various collectivisms has turned out to be a fraud. The wreckage wrought by socialism on a wealthy country with the largest oil reserves in the Western Hemisphere—Venezuela—is only the latest empirical evidence. This follows three Cold War social experiments that demonstrated unequivocally the superiority of democratic capitalism in providing for physical wants: North vs. South Korea, East vs. West Germany, China (pre-Deng Xiaoping) vs. Taiwan.

No. What drives people away today from the classic liberal democratic model are considerations not economic but cultural. The hunger is not for bread but for ethnic and nationalist validation. For strength, respect, recognition.

VI

The most dramatic manifestation of this nationalist revival is growing resistance to the European idea and, most especially, the European Union. And no wonder. It was founded with the very aim to dilute the nationalism that was seen as the toxic fuel that led to the two great wars. The whole purpose of the European Coal and Steel Community (that ultimately evolved into the European Union) was to create a structure—at the beginning merely economic but with political aspirations—to attenuate national sentiments in order to render unthinkable the very idea of war between European peoples.

And it worked. Half a millennium of near-continuous intra-European war gave way to a 70-year interlude of intra-European peace. Unfortunately, one of the side effects was a distasteful hubris among the cosmopolitan elites that helped engineer the entire project. They came to ignore repeated popular expressions—often by referendum—of resistance to the remorseless integration that submerged and suppressed national habits and feelings. Britons, for example, did not like being told by Brussels the proper size of pomegranates. They especially resented being deprived of full say over immigration from the 27 other EU countries, the most powerful issue in propelling the Brexit victory of 2016. Turns out that a flag flying no symbols, an anthem stirring no memory, a ruling body commanding no allegiance leaves a void—and, amid the void, a renewed longing for the symbols, memories and allegiances of tribe and nation.

Like the Marxists before them, the Europeanists grossly underestimated the enduring power of ethnic nationalism. Add to that the sudden influx of a mass migration of culturally alien Muslims—and the apparent indifference of the ruling elites to the social and economic upheavals that followed—and you have the ingredients for a revolt against the ultimate expression of the post–Cold War liberal ideal: a European Union increasingly integrated into a transnational superstate.

To be sure, we should be careful not to identify anti-EU

feelings necessarily with authoritarianism or with a kind of hyper-nationalism that prefers non-democratic norms. In fact, those who oppose the European project often paint themselves as the real democrats. Brexit proponents presented themselves as champions of a return to traditional British democracy where British subjects get to decide their own fate. They made a cogent case that they were resisting an increasingly antidemocratic regime under which half of Britain's laws and regulations are issued from Brussels, not Westminster.

Nonetheless, it is certainly true that there is often an affinity between anti-EU and antidemocratic tendencies. It's no accident that Nigel Farage embraces Julian Assange (at the Embassy of Ecuador, no less, leftist stepchild of Chavez's Bolivarian revolution); that Marine Le Pen, aside from paying homage to Putin, advocates withdrawal from the EU and escape from the grip of the "globalists," accusing her Europeanist challenger, Emmanuel Macron, of treason; and that the most vociferous enemies of globalization—on both sides of the Atlantic—are the greatest advocates of national "strength" and self-assertion with the most minimal regard for constitutional restraint.

Strength is the operative word. National, ethnic, tribal. Betrayed by globalist elites, pettifogging democrats, politically correct politicians, what attracts Westerners to authority is this image of strength. It's an appeal that more than anything carried Trump to the White House.

Trump's admiration for strength is not limited to his one-time bromance with Putin. It extends, amazingly, to the butchers of Tiananmen Square. In Trump's reading, the Chinese leadership flinched until it was almost too late: "When the students poured into Tiananmen Square, the Chinese government almost blew it. Then they were vicious, they were horrible, but they put it down with strength. That shows you the power of strength."

In contrast, "our country is right now perceived as weak . . . as being spit on by the rest of the world." He said all that 30 years ago—and has never wavered since. Indeed, he conducted a 17-month presidential campaign on the promise to return us to a time of national strength, when America was—but presumably is no longer—great.

The good news of the early Trump presidency is that America's political institutions, so decried as weak and pliant, have proved a resilient and powerful check on antidemocratic tendencies in the executive. The courts, the states, the Congress, and the media have provided a resistance few would have predicted to Trump's appeal to ethnonationalism, authoritarianism, protectionism (which is state control of trade). Moreover, the exigencies of American interests—interests are permanent, ideologies come and go—have, by and large, bent even the Trump foreign policy from insurgency to postwar normalcy.

The ringing promises of "America First," the call for a more insular and inward, more narrow and self-interested, more ethnic and nationalist America that permeated the inaugural address, remain for the most part merely rhetorical. As the imperatives of national interest and geopolitical reality inexorably assert themselves, Trump's presidency appears to have been, at least for now, effectively "normalized."

And Le Pen lost. As did Geert Wilders in Holland. As will the extreme right in Germany. The EU still survives. And in the United States, the tentpole of the democratic world, the forebodings about an assault on democracy itself that so permeated the 2016 campaign have largely abated.

And Macron won. To be slightly perverse about it, one could say that you know the West is in trouble when its greatest hope lies in France. Macron will indeed be a test of whether the traditional democratic center can maintain itself against the populist authoritarian challenge.

It's far too soon to declare the populist wave crested. The demagoguery of 2016 did carry the day. We may be in a period of equilibrium, but equilibria are inherently unstable. The danger remains. That the traditional left-right political divide of the last two centuries is increasingly being surpassed by the nationalist-globalist and authoritarian-democratic divide is disturbing and potentially ominous.

Left vs. right we learned how to manage, if after a century and a half. Authoritarian vs. democratic may be more difficult. It's not just new; it's coming at a time of profound civilizational self-doubt. In such circumstances, the unimaginable often becomes imaginable.

We have traveled far in the last 25 years. In precisely the wrong direction. Wrote Wordsworth in the romantic rapture that was the promise of 1789: "Bliss was it in that dawn to be alive,/But to be young was very heaven!" We know how that ended. How does the End of History end?

Washington, DC, July 3, 2017

PART V

SPEAKING IN THE
FIRST PERSON

CHAPTER 18

A LIFE WITHOUT REGRETS

An Anniversary of Sorts

Reflections on a Career in
Column Writing

Twenty-five years ago this week, I wrote my first column. I'm not much given to self-reflection—why do you think I quit psychiatry?—but I figure once every quarter-century is not excessive.

When Editorial Page Editor Meg Greenfield approached me to do a column for the *Washington Post*, I was somewhat daunted. The norm in those days was to write two or three a week, hence the old joke that being a columnist is like being married to a nymphomaniac—as soon as you're done, you've got to do it again.

So I proposed once a week. First, I explained, because I was enjoying the leisurely life of a magazine writer and, with a child on the way, I was looking forward to fatherhood. Second, because I don't have two ideas a week; I barely have one (as many of my critics no doubt agree).

The first objection she dismissed as mere sloth (Meg was

always a good judge of character). The second reason she bought. On December 14, 1984, my first column appeared.

Longevity for a columnist is a simple proposition: Once you start, you don't stop. You do it until you die or can no longer put a sentence together. It has always been my intention to die at my desk, although my most cherished ambition is to outlive the estate tax.

Looking back on the quarter-century, the most remarkable period, strangely enough, was the '90s. That decade began on December 26, 1991 (just as the '60s, as many have observed, ended with Nixon's resignation on August 9, 1974), with a deliverance of biblical proportions—the disappearance of the Soviet Union. It marked the end of 60 years of existential conflict, the collapse of a deeply evil empire and the death of one of the most perverse political ideas in history. This miracle, in major part wrought by Ronald Reagan, bequeathed the ultimate peace dividend: a golden age of the most profound peace and prosperity.

"I recently told an assembly at my son's high school," I wrote in 1997, "that they were living through a time so blessed they would tell their grandchildren about it. They looked at me uncomprehendingly . . . because it is hard for anyone to apprehend the sheer felicity of one's own time until it is gone."

I concluded with "golden ages never last." Throughout the decade, and most especially as it began to wane, I returned to this theme of the wondrous oddity, the sheer impossibility of an age of such post-historical tranquility.

And inevitable ennui. So profound was that tranquility, so trivial the history of that time, that my colleague George Will and I would muse that if this kept up—an era whose dominant issue was a president's zipper problem—he might as well go back to the academy and I to psychiatry.

Of course, it didn't keep up. It never does. History is tragic, not redemptive. Our holiday from history ended in fire, giving birth to a post-9/11 decade of turbulence and disorientation as we were faced with the unexpected resurgence of radical eschatological evil.

Which brings us to the age of Obama, perhaps—*mirabile dictu*—the most exhilarating time of all. There is nothing as bracing for democracy as the alternation of power, particularly when it yields as serious, determined and challenging an ideological agenda as Barack Obama's. This third wave of transformative liberalism—FDR, then LBJ, now Obama—is no time for triangulation. This is not incrementalism. We're not debating school uniforms. When Obama once declared Ronald Reagan historically consequential and Bill Clinton not, he meant it. Obama intends to be the Reagan of the new liberalism.

It's no secret that I oppose nearly everything Obama has proposed. But after the enervating 1990s and the tragic 2000s, the prospect of combative and clarifying 2010s, of sharply defined and radically opposed visions, is both politically and intellectually invigorating.

For which I'm tanned, rested and ready. And grateful. To be doing every day what you enjoy doing is rare. Rarer still is to be doing what you were meant to do, particularly if you got there by sheer serendipity. Until I was almost 30, I'd fully expected to spend my life as a doctor. My present life was never planned or even imagined. Near the beginning of these 25 years, an intern at *The New Republic* asked me how to become a nationally syndicated columnist. "Well," I replied, "first you go to medical school . . ."

The Washington Post, December 18, 2009

Choosing a Life

An Award Acceptance Speech to the
American Academy of Achievement

Thank you for the great honor, and particularly for the honor of being recognized in such august and distinguished company. As you heard, the achievement for which I'm being recognized, indeed my entire career as a writer and editor and columnist, is a second career.

I never wrote a word, I never published a word before I was 30. And the reason I bring this up is because I want to speak to the young students here tonight about choice, about choosing a life.

When you are at this stage you are at right now all of life is open to you. But soon you are going to suffer the agony of excellence. With so many talents and so much excellence, at one point in your life soon you're going to have to choose. And every choice means an exclusion; every time you open a door, you're closing a door.

If you decide to be a nuclear scientist and you think you won't ever be able to be a Shakespearean scholar, well, I'm here to tell you that that's false. I started my life out as a doctor, I spent seven years as a doctor and a psychiatrist. And then one day at the end of those seven years I realized that this was not what I was born to do and to be. So I said goodbye to my last patient, I turned in my beeper and I quit.

At the same time, my wife, who was a lawyer, decided that she didn't love the law and she quit as well. We left our home and we came to Washington to seek our fortune. She became an artist and a sculptor, and I became a writer and a columnist. And things have turned out rather well.

The moral of the story is: Don't be afraid to choose, and don't be afraid to start all over if you have to. T. E. Lawrence once said, at least in the version of his life by David Lean, "Nothing is written."

And by that he meant: Life is open, everything is choice, nothing is inevitable. So the message I have to you young people is: Don't be afraid to choose. Choose what you love. And if you don't love what you've chosen, choose again.

Adapted from the author's speech accepting the Golden Plate Award from the American Academy of Achievement in Washington, DC, June 19, 1999

A Statement of Principle

From 2001 to 2006, my father sat on the President's Council on Bioethics. During a session debating the creation of cloned human embryos for research, he made a statement that Dr. Leon Kass, the chairman of the council at the time, described as "the single most profound thing ever said in that room."

This statement is included here not for its specific point about embryonic research guidelines (my father believed reasonable people of good will could disagree on the exact legal boundaries of such research), but rather for the moral injunction it made to always treat every human life as an end in and of itself, never as a means to be used by others. And for how it showed my father's commitment—even above his own life's interests—to preserving the principles he believed in for the world that would outlive him.

—Daniel Krauthammer

The Subject: Ethical issues regarding the creation of cloned human embryos for research purposes, in hope of developing transplantable tissues that could alleviate various chronic diseases and disabilities.

The Question: What do we owe the patients with these diseases and disabilities? What should people who oppose creation of embryos for research purposes say to such patients?

Charles Krauthammer: Well, as it happens, I am one of those patients. Mary Ann Glendon has talked about all of us being patients or having relatives who are patients. I have a very obvious

322

connection with this issue. I am one of those in whose name people have spoken and said this research has to be permitted so that I can walk or people like me can walk. Spinal cord injuries are always on the list, so I am acutely aware of this issue. But I am not only a patient.

I am also a father. And what I would say to myself, and I have said to myself about this issue, and I think we ought to say to other people who suffer from similar problems and disabilities, is that we have children. And we want to raise them in a world—we want to bequeath to them a world, a moral universe, in which we think they ought to live. And that we may be jeopardizing the moral quality of that universe, the humanity of that universe, by cavalierly breaking moral rules that we have observed for generations in order that people like me can walk.

So I think there is a serious moral issue here. And I think the assumption that all that people who suffer from disabilities want is a cure at all costs is a misreading of their own humanity.

Transcript: The President's Council on Bioethics, Meeting No. 2, Second Session, Washington, DC, February 14, 2002

Beauty and Soul

An Award Acceptance Speech to
the Bradley Foundation

A n occasion like this is not a time for pronouncements. Those
are for print (and television), and I certainly make enough
of them every week. This is a time for speaking as one would with
friends, and I am here among many friends. So forgive me for
being autobiographical, but some of my checkered past requires
explanation.

I started life out as a doctor. I am not sure whether I am still
a doctor, an ex-physician or a retired psychiatrist—I have decided
that I am a psychiatrist in remission. Doing very well, thank you.
Have not had a relapse in 25 years. Sometimes I am asked to
compare what I do today as a political essayist in Washington
with what I did 25 years ago as a psychiatrist in Boston. There
is not very much difference: In both lines of work I spend my
days studying people who suffer from paranoia and delusions of
grandeur—except that in Washington they have access to nuclear
weapons. Which makes the stakes higher, and the work a little
more interesting.

This is only a half tongue-in-cheek accounting of the reason
I am here. When I left psychiatry to start writing—a movement
that my late father wryly noted was not very well calculated for
upward mobility—I did so not out of any regret for the seven
years I had spent in medicine, years that I treasure for deepening
and broadening my sensibilities, but because I felt history happening outside the examining-room door. That history was being

shaped by a war of ideas and I wanted to be in the arena. Not for its own sake. I enjoy intellectual combat, but I do not live for it. I wanted to be in the arena because some things matter, some things need to be said, some things need defending. That has been my vocation for the last 20 years.

That is *the why* I'm here. But it does not tell you *the how*. The how is very simple. My award, my achievement, my entire career as a writer is owed to one person.

When I was in medicine, restless and unfulfilled, there was one person urging me to take the risk to do what I really wanted to do, to do what I was meant to do. One person who was not just ready, but urging that we give up all the certainties of our life together, our professions—hers as a lawyer, mine as a doctor—our friends, our community, our home, and that we come to Washington, a place we had never been and where we knew no one. It was not "wither thou goest, I go." It was at *her* urging, with *her* encouragement and with *her* support that we set off on the road that brought us here. And when here, I began writing and she left behind her training in the law to do what moved her—produce paintings and sculptures of remarkable beauty and soul.

Her own beauty and soul have sustained me these many years. I was merely the scribe. This prize rightly belongs to my dear wife, Robyn.

Adapted from the author's speech accepting the inaugural Bradley Prize from the Bradley Foundation at the Library of Congress in Washington, DC, October 7, 2003

A Note to Readers

The Last Published Words of
Charles Krauthammer

I have been uncharacteristically silent these past ten months. I had thought that silence would soon be coming to an end, but I'm afraid I must tell you now that fate has decided on a different course for me.

In August of last year, I underwent surgery to remove a cancerous tumor in my abdomen. That operation was thought to have been a success, but it caused a cascade of secondary complications—which I have been fighting in hospital ever since. It was a long and hard fight with many setbacks, but I was steadily, if slowly, overcoming each obstacle along the way and gradually making my way back to health.

However, recent tests have revealed that the cancer has returned. There was no sign of it as recently as a month ago, which means it is aggressive and spreading rapidly. My doctors tell me their best estimate is that I have only a few weeks left to live. This is the final verdict. My fight is over.

I wish to thank my doctors and caregivers, whose efforts have been magnificent. My dear friends, who have given me a lifetime of memories and whose support has sustained me through these difficult months. And all of my partners at the *Washington Post*, Fox News and Crown Publishing.

Lastly, I thank my colleagues, my readers and my viewers, who have made my career possible and given consequence to my life's work. I believe that the pursuit of truth and right ideas through honest debate and rigorous argument is a noble undertaking. I am grateful to have played a small role in the conversations that have helped guide this extraordinary nation's destiny.

I leave this life with no regrets. It was a wonderful life—full and complete with the great loves and great endeavors that make it worth living. I am sad to leave, but I leave with the knowledge that I lived the life that I intended.

The Washington Post, June 8, 2018

Eulogy for Charles Krauthammer

By Daniel Krauthammer

Before my father underwent surgery last August, he wrote a set of final directives to be followed in the event that the operation was not successful. His instructions for this funeral were spare and simple. He wrote the following:

> I would be shrouded and ritually bathed at our synagogue, as is the custom. I would be in a plain pine coffin. The ceremony would be presided over by Rabbi Fishman. The only speaker that I designate is my son Daniel. . . . I would like the ceremony to be very simple with just three liturgical features. . . . I leave everything else up to my wife and son to decide. They will be guided by Dr. Fishman as to what is the usual Jewish practice.

This simple document is emblematic of the man my father was. The grace, dignity, equanimity, understatedness and clear-mindedness with which my father faced the possibility and the eventuality of death—in this document, in the last ten months he spent in hospital and in the 46 years since his accident—are the same attributes with which he lived his extraordinary life.

We live in an age that often promotes and idealizes introspection, self-reflection and catharsis. The opening up of one's emotions and declaring of one's deepest feelings to the world. Taken to excess, as is all too often the case, these can amount to self-indulgence. My father did not subscribe to this mindset.

If there was one thing that he was the complete opposite of, it was self-indulgent: intellectually, emotionally, spiritually, in every sense that I can think of.

He did not disregard the self. Actually, I think it's safe to say he had quite a high self-regard, as I'm sure many of you can recount—especially my mother. But to him, the self just wasn't all that important. Not because of any inherent sin or moral failing of being self-interested. But quite simply because, ultimately, it is not very interesting. Why focus endlessly inward when there is so much more to explore and understand and experience on the outside: the universe, our world, all the fascinating people in it, the complex activities we busy ourselves with, and the transcendent bonds of love and family and friendship we are able to forge with one another. And so he chose to focus all his gifts, all his exquisite qualities outward to the world beyond himself. We who knew him are all the recipients and beneficiaries of the strength, the warmth, the generosity and the wisdom that he radiated.

Everyone who came into contact with him—whether it was through a close friendship or just reading and watching his thoughts from afar—felt the force and power of his personality. In almost any room he entered, at any dinner table where he ate or any TV news panel where he sat, it seemed he would almost immediately become the central hub of the conversation and of everyone's attention. Not because he made it all about himself, but in fact because he did precisely the opposite. He would ask you what *you* enjoyed, what *you* were fascinated by, what *you* were pondering and what *you* were doing with your life. He would connect with you on exactly that topic and then beat a trail with you to a deeper insight that you didn't even know was there.

And he did it with such fun and verve and acerbic wit and deadpan hilarity. He was, to put it simply, a cool guy. People just wanted to be around him. And it was because he wasn't putting on a show for anyone. He wasn't trying to look smart or to impress you. And he didn't take himself too seriously. He simply said what he believed, and he did what he loved because he genuinely enjoyed it. He brought that joy to most everything he did in life and he shared it generously. Whether he was talking with a young intern about how to launch her career, trading baseball statistics at the ballpark while scarfing down hot dogs, or debating political philosophy on national television. He did it effortlessly, with grace and—very often—with a mischievous twinkle in his eye.

And that twinkle would also appear—more often than not—whenever he beat the odds or got around an obstacle he didn't think should stand in his way. Such an event, of course, was not uncommon in his life. If there's one thing my dad did with astounding consistency, it was beat the odds. He was able to do that because he was armed with immense courage and self-possession. He quite simply willed himself to accomplish things that most people would assume to be impossible.

That was the great lesson of his example: to build the life that you want, that you intend. Don't be defined by what life throws at you and you cannot control. Accept the hand you are dealt with grace, and then go on to play that hand as joyously and industriously and vigorously as you can. What gives life meaning isn't how the outside world defines you. It's what you make of yourself, what you give to the world and what you build with the ones you love. You can make your life extraordinary. It is possible.

Even more remarkably and uniquely, my father lived this exemplary life with great sweetness and gentleness. It was in his very bones, fundamental to his nature. He was just innately kind and caring. And not in a showy or ostentatious way. Just in his own, quiet, subtle, but deeply moving way. And he bestowed this kindness without discrimination to anyone worthy of it, whether it was a prime minister or a 10-year-old schoolmate of his son's still in short pants.

As many of you are no doubt aware, my father was a huge movie buff. It was a shared passion of ours, something the two of us bonded over from my earliest childhood right up until his final days. He had an encyclopedic knowledge and recall of his favorites. Above all, perhaps, *Lawrence of Arabia*, which—along with *Casablanca* and *North by Northwest*—he could recite line for line. One of his favorite lines comes early in the movie, when Lawrence meets Omar Sharif's character for the first time. Sharif has just come upon Lawrence and his guide trespassing at a well in the middle of the desert. Sharif shoots and kills Lawrence's guide, then confronts Lawrence and asks him what his name is. "My name," Lawrence replies, "is for my friends." "My name is for my friends."

To be honest I never quite understood the line or why my dad liked it so much. But in the final weeks of his illness, we watched the movie again together in his room. And the line suddenly filled with new meaning for me in the light of my father's approach to life. The line, first of all, is a courageous stand *for* truth and *against* tyranny. "My name is for my friends." Those who were not worthy, those who wielded power without just authority or with impure intention, were never able to pressure my father to bow to them, to betray his principles or those he loved. But the line also has a more subtle meaning. It is an affirmation of a certain philosophy of love and friendship. "My name is for my friends." My father didn't feel the need to broadcast his identity, didn't have to tell people who he was or declare his friendships out loud. He let his actions speak for themselves. Those who were his friends—knew it. Those whom he loved—knew it. That was what mattered. Not some supposed inner truth that you held cooped up on the inside, or some empty declaration you made to the outside. But what you did for others, the actions you took in the world.

At more points in my life than I can count, I have been told a story by a friend or acquaintance or stranger about some way in which my father acted with extraordinary generosity toward them and literally changed the course of their lives. It was always done quietly, either anonymously or in a manner that almost no one else would ever know about. And it was always to help them do something major in their lives: to get an education, to switch careers and get a new job, to sustain a faltering livelihood or to survive a serious illness.

The few times my father did do something that was publicly visible, it was in order to use his own celebrity to further the causes that he cared about. Particularly so when it came to charities and institutions that furthered Jewish learning and culture, which were central to his identity.

I'm sure there are many people in this room today who were recipients of his acts of generosity. Most of which neither I nor anyone else will ever even know about.

But I feel that I am surely the luckiest recipient of all in this room. The list of things for which I am grateful to my father is far too long, and runs far too deep within me, to even attempt a summation in this speech. As with so many of his greatest qualities, it was the purity and simplicity of his love for me that was his greatest gift. His love was full, unadulterated, unconditional and all-encompassing.

A few weeks before his passing, I was recounting memories with my dad in his room. He asked if I remembered the first time I saw the Statue of Liberty. He proceeded to tell me the story: When I was about six years old, he was taking me on a long drive from Washington, DC, to Long Island, New York, to visit my grandmother, crossing the Verrazano-Narrows Bridge en route.

As we crossed, my dad told me to look out the window so that I could get a glimpse of the Statue of Liberty, which I had never seen before. But I just couldn't manage to see it over the bridge guardrail. So, he told me to take the pillows I had been using to nap on during the long drive, to prop myself up on them, to make sure my seatbelt was firmly tightened and then to sit up as straight and tall as I could. At that moment, he started to brake the car, slowing us down so much that we had half a bridge's worth of almost-stopped traffic piling up behind us. Everyone was honking and yelling and trying to pass us. But my dad didn't care. He was making sure I had the longest, clearest possible view of the Statue of Liberty across the whole crest of the highest point of the bridge.

As he told the story, the memory came flooding back to me. And not only that memory, but so many others just like it. Dozens, hundreds, thousands if I truly wanted to count. It was perfectly indicative of the father he was. He would literally do anything if he thought it would make my life just a little bit better.

And the most precious thing he shared with me was his knowledge. He was the greatest teacher I ever had. He never dictated answers. He opened my mind to the most important questions and helped me find pathways to deeper understandings. Everyone in this room is wiser for having listened to him, as is the whole country, perhaps even the world. But I count myself luckiest of all to have been able to learn from him. He did so generously, openly, lovingly, always sensitive to helping me along my own path, but never directing which road I should take. It was through these pathways he opened up for me that I found my own core bedrock beliefs.

I hope that one day I will be as good a father as he was. And as good a husband. Along with me, my mother was the luckiest recipient of his love and generosity. But he was just as lucky to have her. Perhaps luckier. My father once said in an interview that my mother was "the co-author of [his] life." I cannot think of a truer or more beautiful description. They built their life *together*. As one. Intertwined and inseparable. His accomplishments are hers. And her accomplishments are his. Neither of their lives could have or would have been remotely the same without the other. It was a life built, shared and enjoyed as a loving partnership.

My father once told me a few years ago that he was getting more and more complaints from friends about how he and my mother didn't go out as much anymore and weren't seen around town as often. With a boyish smile, he said to me, "They all think we're kinda turning into hermits. What I think that they don't get is. . . . we just enjoy each other's company. We'd kinda just rather hang out with each other."

They were married for 44 years. Their last anniversary was this past Wednesday. My father passed away on Thursday. It was as full and complete and loving a partnership as I could ever imagine. No language I know possesses words of sufficient depth or power to express my gratitude for having had as parents two people capable of such profound love and generosity.

Just as my father's emotional energies seemed always focused outward, so too was his mind. His raw intellectual horsepower, which as we all know was impressive almost beyond measure, was guided by a spirit of inquiry, of openness, of thoughtfulness. He was incredibly intelligent, yes. But even more importantly, he was wise. Unlike many who are described, or self-described, as "intellectuals," he was exceedingly aware of just how little he—or anyone—actually knew, in the grand scheme of things.

His passion for deep understanding led him to what may have been his most firmly held belief: that the very nature of human understanding is limited, that we must have not only humility, but also reverence in the face of the great unknowns that lie before us and that we will never know.

When I first read his book *Things That Matter*, I wrote my dad a very long letter explaining to him exactly why I thought his book was so extraordinary. He responded to me in kind, and I will now read for you an excerpt from his letter:

> Even more stunningly discerning—and here's where I didn't even see it myself—was [your] rather stunning phrase, describing the underlying philosophical core of my writing as being an "appreciation, even a love of the unknowable." Exactly. Precisely. And it unifies everything. It really is like a grand unified theory that I would never see myself. And then of course it is in accordance with the single piece of literature that had the most profound effect of my entire life, *The Library of Babel* by Jorge Luis Borges. Which is precisely about the appreciation of, the love of and the terror of the unknowable—in the hope that, as he puts it so poignantly in one passage, just some person somewhere anytime in history should have had the knowledge, the revelation, that has been denied to me and always will be.

My father's outlook on the nature of human knowledge shaped many of his remarkable intellectual pursuits. He was drawn to subjects that pushed the human brain to the limits of complexity and perfection—a new unified theory of quantum-relativity, an elegant checkmate in five moves, a perfect double play—and it was at these limits, at the very cusp where human comprehension slips into the realm of the unknowable, that he found beauty, profundity and transcendence.

This humility gave him an intellectual lightness and playfulness that was magnetic to be around. He had an aesthetic, almost romantic appreciation for good ideas and their artful expression.

But this outlook, this appreciation for the inherent limitations of human knowledge, also informed his most deeply and seriously held beliefs.

In politics, it led him to a profound championing of democratic pluralism, of the liberty of the individual, of the right of each mind to find its own way, free of the pretended singular truths of any imagined perfect society.

In religion, it led him to a suspicion of anyone claiming absolute certainty and a monopoly on ultimate truth—both from the religious purist and from the adamant atheist. And it led him toward a deep respect and appreciation for the accumulated wisdom of mankind, for the millennia-worth of religious evolution and philosophical debate we inherit from history and upon which we build our own ideas, and particularly for the sages and traditions of his own beloved Jewish heritage.

It is into the embracing arms of that accumulated wisdom that he wished to consign himself when he knew the end was close at hand. To what we do here to honor him today: to this simple ceremony, these ancient practices, which have been crafted and honed and debated and repeated by generation upon generation of his ancestors for thousands of years.

My father has now made the step into the greatest unknown of them all. He did not know what lay ahead for him, nor did he pretend to know. And neither do I.

I do not know if I will ever see my father again. But I do know that he will always be with me. In my heart, in my mind, and in my soul, until the day I draw my final breath. I love him, and I will miss him.

Adapted from the speech given by Daniel Krauthammer at the funeral of Charles Krauthammer, Chevy Chase, MD, June 24, 2018

ACKNOWLEDGMENTS

By Daniel Krauthammer

A full and proper list of the thanks and appreciations that this book ought to list would stretch back to a time before I was even born. This book, after all, is a culmination of work my father composed over a career that spanned four decades, throughout a life influenced and enriched by so many dear friends and close colleagues along the way.

As my father's son and his appointed shepherd for this book, there were many functions and responsibilities I believed I could perform well on his behalf after his death. But knowing whom to thank and how—for all the wonderful years and rewarding works of his life—is, I'm afraid, not something I'm quite equipped to do. For that I would direct readers to the acknowledgments my father wrote in *Things That Matter*. And I ask all those whose acts of loyalty and friendship meant so much to my father in his life to please know the gratitude that he felt.

For my own part, I wish to thank everyone whose contributions made this book possible, starting from the day I first became involved with the project a year ago. This book was the work of many hands. My heartfelt thanks go to the entire team at Crown Forum, for whom this book was more than just a job, and without whom I would have been lost in this endeavor. In particular, Mary Reynics' and Tina Constable's wisdom, guidance and dedication made this book possible, as did the hard work of their colleagues Derek Reed, Ashley Hong and the entire extended team. My father had many research assistants throughout his career, and two of them—Hillel Ofek and Mike Watson—played important roles in helping to compile and edit the materials for this book. Special thanks go to Steve Hayes, Dana Perino and Pete Wehner, close friends all, who were not only incredible supports to our family, but also generously gave their time to read early drafts of the manuscript and provided their always insightful comments and guidance. Jean Junta, my father's personal assistant, held down the fort and managed a wide array of complex logistics at the office during a most difficult time. And my father's longtime assistants Jason Smith and Bill Mena provided vital help to him and to our family all throughout the same period.

Bob Barnett, my father's longtime attorney and dear friend, made sure this book would live on and help preserve my father's legacy. And even more importantly, he protected and guided my father and my family through the most harrowing of trials. On this count as well, my family's deepest gratitude extends to Bret Baier, whose friendship and loyalty to my father knew no bounds, and who did everything in his power to help return my father to his life. Our sincere thanks go to Fred Hiatt and Don Graham, who were there at every turn for us. The support of all my father's partners and colleagues and friends at Fox News and the *Washington Post*—Rupert Murdoch, Suzanne Scott, Jay Wallace, Richard Aldacushion and Alan Shearer, to name just a few—gave us safe harbor while we were bearing a terrible storm. We will never forget it.

A thanks that can never be adequately expressed, due to its magnitude, goes to the exceptional doctors, nurses, therapists, technicians, assistants, staff and leadership of the Shepherd Center and of Piedmont Hospital in Atlanta, Georgia. In particular, to the entire Shepherd family and to my father's lead physician, Dr. Anna Elmers, whose astounding medical skills were matched equally by her personal dedication and profound caring. To John

Morawski, Dr. David DeRuyter, Dr. Andrew Zadoff, Dr. Roderic Woodson, Dr. Jesse Couk and Dr. Ha Tran. And to Dr. William Davis, my father's dear friend and doctor of many decades, who guarded and oversaw every development from near and far. Our debt to him for his personal and medical care is immeasurable. These doctors exemplify the gold standard of what it means to practice medicine with full excellence, integrity, kindness and imaginative tenacity.

My family's deep thanks go to the friends who helped us navigate all the complexities and challenges we faced in this past year, the hardest of our lives. To Dr. Leon Kass, Dr. David Bluemke and Bonnie Beavan, Dr. Thomas Winkler, Dr. David Green, Karen Whitesell, Irwin and Cita Stelzer, Len and Fleur Harlan, Tovi Glasner, Rochelle Aschheim, Howard Stanislawski, Ambassador Ron and Rhoda Dermer, Bruce and Madeline Ramer, Lionel Chetwynd and Gloria Carlin, Pepe and Dianora Zalaquett, April Lee and the Lee family, Ted and Annette Lerner and the Lerner family. To Rabbi Fishman and Rabbi Sugarman. To Win and Sarah Brown—and Alice, Helen and Polly—whose bonds of friendship pulled us up from the darkest of places and helped us carry the burdens we could not bear on our own. To our family: to Lady Annabelle Weidenfeld and to my father's niece Aviva, whose compassion sustained us, and to Clara, Brett, Jered, Michael, Gillian, Lucy, Shelly, Pippa and Riccardo. To our close friends who supported me and my mother and my father throughout the long night and never let us feel alone—so long as I live, I will remember and honor the extraordinary kindness and loyalty they showed us. To Michael, Christian, Jeremy and Stewart, who were there in my hour of greatest need. And to my dear friends who suffered their own family tragedies and shared so deeply in the heartbreak we all so desperately wished would never come: to Arla, Britt, Bryce, Chris, Jon, Meghan, Mikey, Taylor, Theo and

Vasi. And above all to my girlfriend Klaudia. I could not have endured this trial without her constancy, her strength and her love.

That this book exists is a tribute to the dedication and friendship and support of these extraordinary people and many more. My family and I will be forever grateful. I know with all my heart that my father would have been too.

INDEX

abolitionism, 113
abortion:
  and fetal parts, 116–18
  late-term, 143–44
  words used in debate over,
    112–15
affirmative action, 167–68,
  241–43
Afghanistan, 19, 161
  US invasion of, 216–17
Africa, 260
  AIDS program in, 265–66
African Americans, 167
AIDS/HIV, 138, 265–66
Air Force, US, 82
Alabama, 177
Albania, 35
Aleppo, Syria, 294
Alexis, Aaron, 102–3
Ali, Muhammad, 64
Allen, Scott, 65
Allen, Woody, 53, 136, 138, 197
al-Qaeda:
  decimating of, 216
  defeated in Iraq surge, 218
  as Sunni, 214
Alzheimer's, 107
Amazon, 177
"America First" slogan, 290–92,
  312
American Academy of
  Achievement, 320–21
American Catholic Bishops, 34
American Civil Religion, 181
American exceptionalism, 291

*American Journal of Emergency
  Medicine,* 94
American League playoffs (2003),
  49
American Revolution, 179, 262,
  263
American Samoa, 42
American Studies Association
  (ASA), 200–201
Americans with Disabilities
  Act, 30
Amin, Idi, 207, 208, 209
amnesty, 162
Anbar, Iraq, 220
ancien régime, 180
Andalusia, 56
anencephaly, 105–7
angiogenesis inhibitors, 138
animal liberation, 234–35
antibiotics, 137
anti-Semitism:
  and Israeli boycott, 200–2
  revival of, 203–4
Apollo 8, 70
Apollo program, 85
AR-15, 102
Arab Spring, 302
Arbenz, Jacobo, 280
Argentina, 301
Aristotle, xxi
Arizona, bilingual education in,
  163
Arlington National Cemetery, 178
Armenians, 296
ARPA, 75

About the Author

CHARLES KRAUTHAMMER, winner of the Pulitzer Prize, was a syndicated columnist, political commentator, physician and bestselling author. His *Washington Post* column was syndicated in over 400 newspapers worldwide. He was a Fox News contributor, and for over a decade he appeared nightly on its flagship evening-news broadcast *Special Report.* He was also a weekly panelist on PBS' *Inside Washington* for 23 years. As for doctoring, as a retired but still board-certified psychiatrist, he liked to consider himself a "psychiatrist in remission."

Krauthammer was born in New York City but moved at age five with his family to Montreal, where he lived until graduating college. His summers, however, were always spent at the family cottage in Long Beach, New York, where he enjoyed what he described as "a paradisiacal childhood." He graduated McGill University with First Class Honors in political science and economics, was a Commonwealth Scholar in politics at Balliol College, Oxford, and received his M.D. from Harvard Medical School in 1975.

He served as a resident and then chief resident in psychiatry at the Massachusetts General Hospital from 1975–78. During his residency, he discovered an unusual form of manic-depressive disease ("Secondary Mania," *Archives of General Psychiatry*, November 1978) that continues to be cited in the medical literature. In 1978, he quit the practice of psychiatry and moved to Washington, DC, to work in the Carter administration on planning psychiatric research. During that time, he began contributing articles to *The New Republic*. In 1980, he served as a speechwriter for Vice President Walter Mondale.

In 1981, he joined *The New Republic* as a writer and an editor. Three years later, he won the National Magazine Award for essays and criticism. In 1983, he started writing a monthly back-page essay for *Time*. In 1985, he began his syndicated column for the *Washington Post*, which won the Pulitzer Prize two years later. Throughout his career he published articles in many other periodicals, among them *The Weekly Standard*, *Commentary*, *The National Interest*, *The Public Interest* and *Foreign Affairs*. He received many awards and honors over the years, including the American Enterprise Institute's Irving Kristol Award, the Bradley Prize and the William F. Buckley Jr. Prize for Leadership in Political Thought. In 2006, the *Financial Times* named him the most influential commentator in America.

Krauthammer was a member of the President's Council on Bioethics from 2001 to 2006. He was an avid chess player and a member of Chess Journalists of America. He was also chairman and cofounder, with his wife Robyn, of Pro Musica Hebraica, a nonprofit organization dedicated to the recovery and performance of classical Jewish music. He and Robyn lived in Chevy Chase, Maryland. An Australian lawyer, she happily pursued a career as an artist and sculptor after moving to the United States.

Charles Krauthammer died on June 21, 2018.

About the Editor

DANIEL KRAUTHAMMER's writing has appeared in *The Weekly Standard*, *National Review* and *The New Republic*, where his commentary has spanned topics on politics, economics, technology and film. He grew up in Chevy Chase, Maryland, but had for the last decade, as his father used to put it, "Gone West to seek his fortune" in California. He graduated *summa cum laude* from Harvard University and earned degrees from the University of Oxford and Stanford University in financial economics and business administration. He has worked in government and NGOs, where he focused on economic policymaking, and in recent years pursued projects and start-up ventures in the entertainment and technology sectors. He left California to spend the last year of his father's life close by his side in the hospital, where together they worked on the plans to complete this book.